OLD MAN LOGAN

PAST LIVES

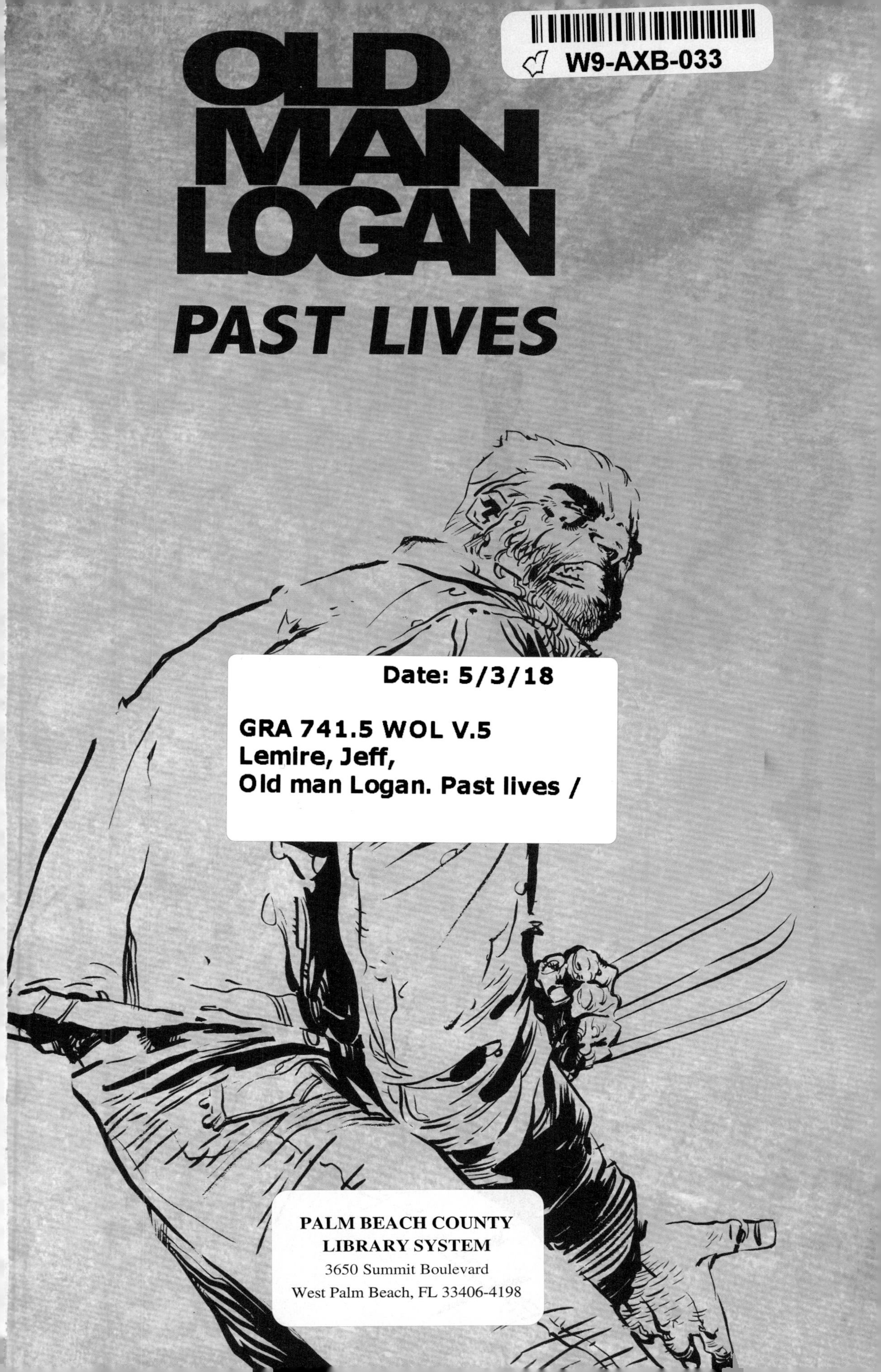

OLD MAN LOGAN
PAST LIVES

WRITER **JEFF LEMIRE**

"GONE REAL BAD"
ARTIST **FILIPE ANDRADE**
COLORIST **JORDAN BOYD**
COVER ARTIST **ANDREA SORRENTINO**

"PAST LIVES"
ARTIST **ERIC NGUYEN**
COLORIST **ANDRES MOSSA**
COVER ARTISTS **ANDREA SORRENTINO & MARCELO MAIOLO**

LETTERER **VC'S CORY PETIT**
ASSISTANT EDITOR **CHRISTINA HARRINGTON**
EDITOR **MARK PANICCIA**

COLLECTION EDITOR **MARK D. BEAZLEY**
ASSISTANT EDITOR **CAITLIN O'CONNELL**
ASSOCIATE MANAGING EDITOR **KATERI WOODY**
ASSOCIATE MANAGER, DIGITAL ASSETS **JOE HOCHSTEIN**
SENIOR EDITOR, SPECIAL PROJECTS **JENNIFER GRÜNWALD**
VP PRODUCTION & SPECIAL PROJECTS **JEFF YOUNGQUIST**
SVP PRINT, SALES & MARKETING **DAVID GABRIEL**
BOOK DESIGNER **ADAM DEL RE**

EDITOR IN CHIEF **AXEL ALONSO**
CHIEF CREATIVE OFFICER **JOE QUESADA**
PRESIDENT **DAN BUCKLEY**
EXECUTIVE PRODUCER **ALAN FINE**

WOLVERINE: OLD MAN LOGAN VOL. 5 — PAST LIVES. Contains material originally published in magazine form as OLD MAN LOGAN #19-24. First printing 2017. ISBN# 978-1-302-90574-3. Published by MARVEL WORLDWIDE, INC.; a subsidiary of MARVEL ENTERTAINMENT, LLC. OFFICE OF PUBLICATION: 135 West 50th Street, New York, NY 10020. Copyright © 2017 MARVEL No similarity between any of the names, characters, persons, and/or institutions in this magazine with those of any living or dead person or institution is intended, and any such similarity which may exist is purely coincidental. **Printed in Canada.** DAN BUCKLEY, President, Marvel Entertainment; JOE QUESADA, Chief Creative Officer; TOM BREVOORT, SVP of Publishing; DAVID BOGART, SVP of Business Affairs & Operations, Publishing & Partnership; C.B. CEBULSKI, VP of Brand Management & Development, Asia; DAVID GABRIEL, SVP of Sales & Marketing, Publishing; JEFF YOUNGQUIST, VP of Production & Special Projects; DAN CARR, Executive Director of Publishing Technology; ALEX MORALES, Director of Publishing Operations; SUSAN CRESPI, Production Manager; STAN LEE, Chairman Emeritus. For information regarding advertising in Marvel Comics or on Marvel.com, please contact Vit DeBellis, Integrated Sales Manager, at vdebellis@marvel.com. For Marvel subscription inquiries, please call 888-511-5480. **Manufactured between 8/4/2017 and 9/5/2017 by SOLISCO PRINTERS, SCOTT, QC, CANADA.**
10 9 8 7 6 5 4 3 2 1

After surviving a future known as the Wastelands where everything good in the world was destroyed, Old Man Logan awoke in the present, determined to prevent the death of his wife and children. Even after accepting this second chance, he is haunted by the loss of his family.

Even beyond familial ties, there are other memories--and obligations--from the Wastelands that Logan cannot forget...

OLD MAN LOGAN

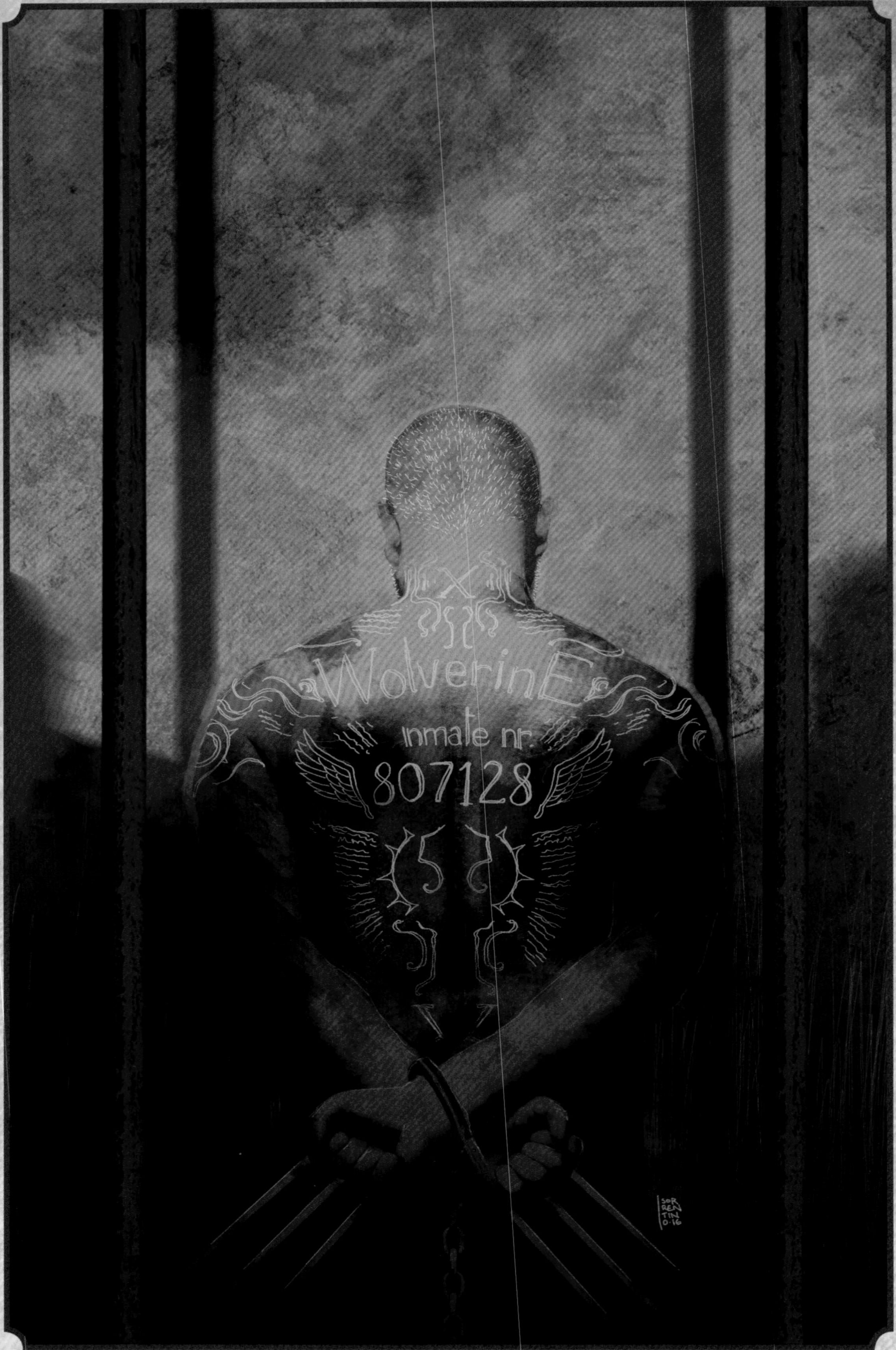
WolverinE
inmate nr.
807128
SOR
REN
TINO·16

19

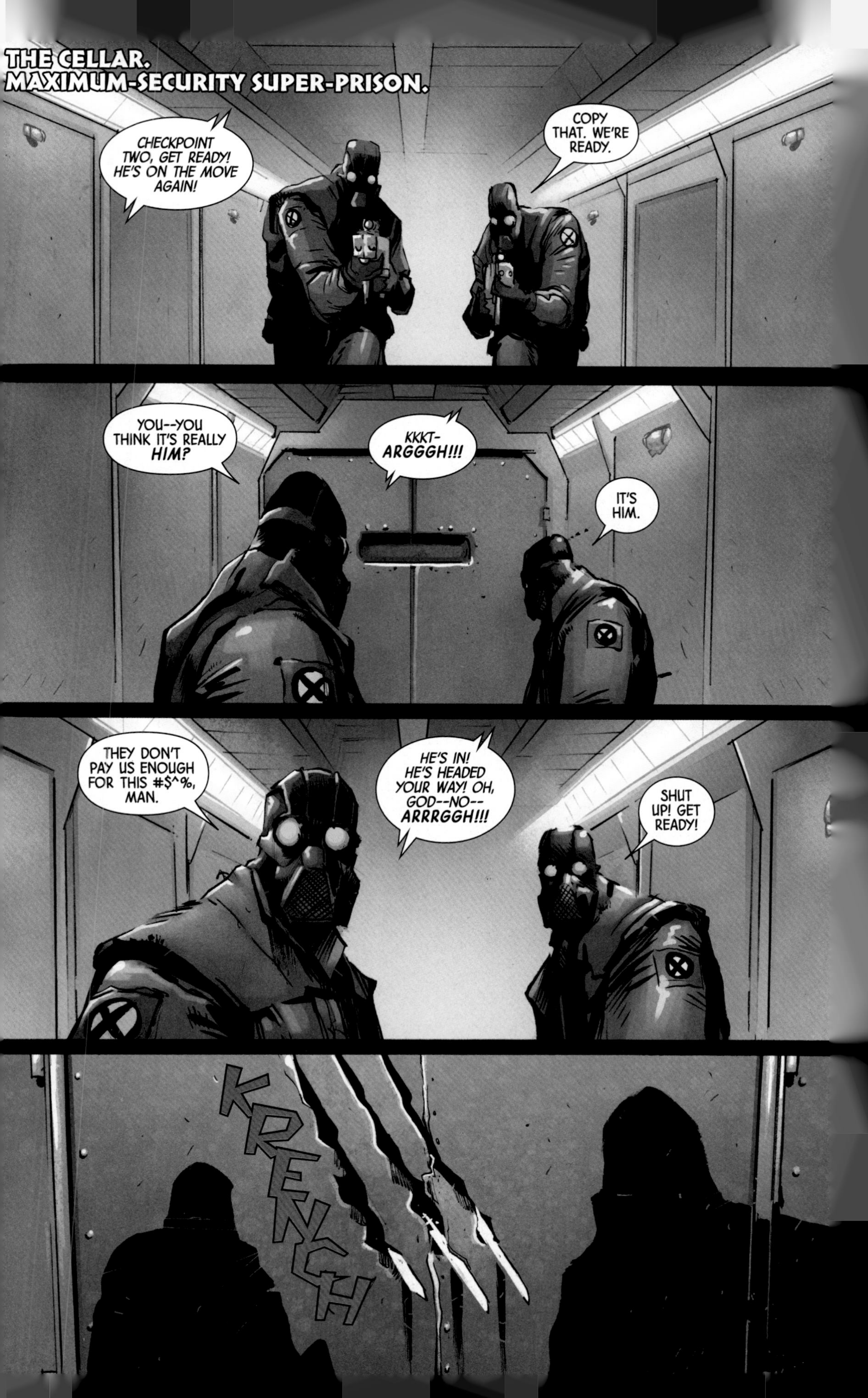
THE CELLAR. MAXIMUM-SECURITY SUPER-PRISON.
CHECKPOINT TWO, GET READY! HE'S ON THE MOVE AGAIN!
COPY THAT. WE'RE READY.
YOU--YOU THINK IT'S REALLY HIM?
KKKT-ARGGGH!!!
IT'S HIM.
THEY DON'T PAY US ENOUGH FOR THIS #$^%, MAN.
HE'S IN! HE'S HEADED YOUR WAY! OH, GOD--NO--ARRRGGH!!!
SHUT UP! GET READY!
KRENCH

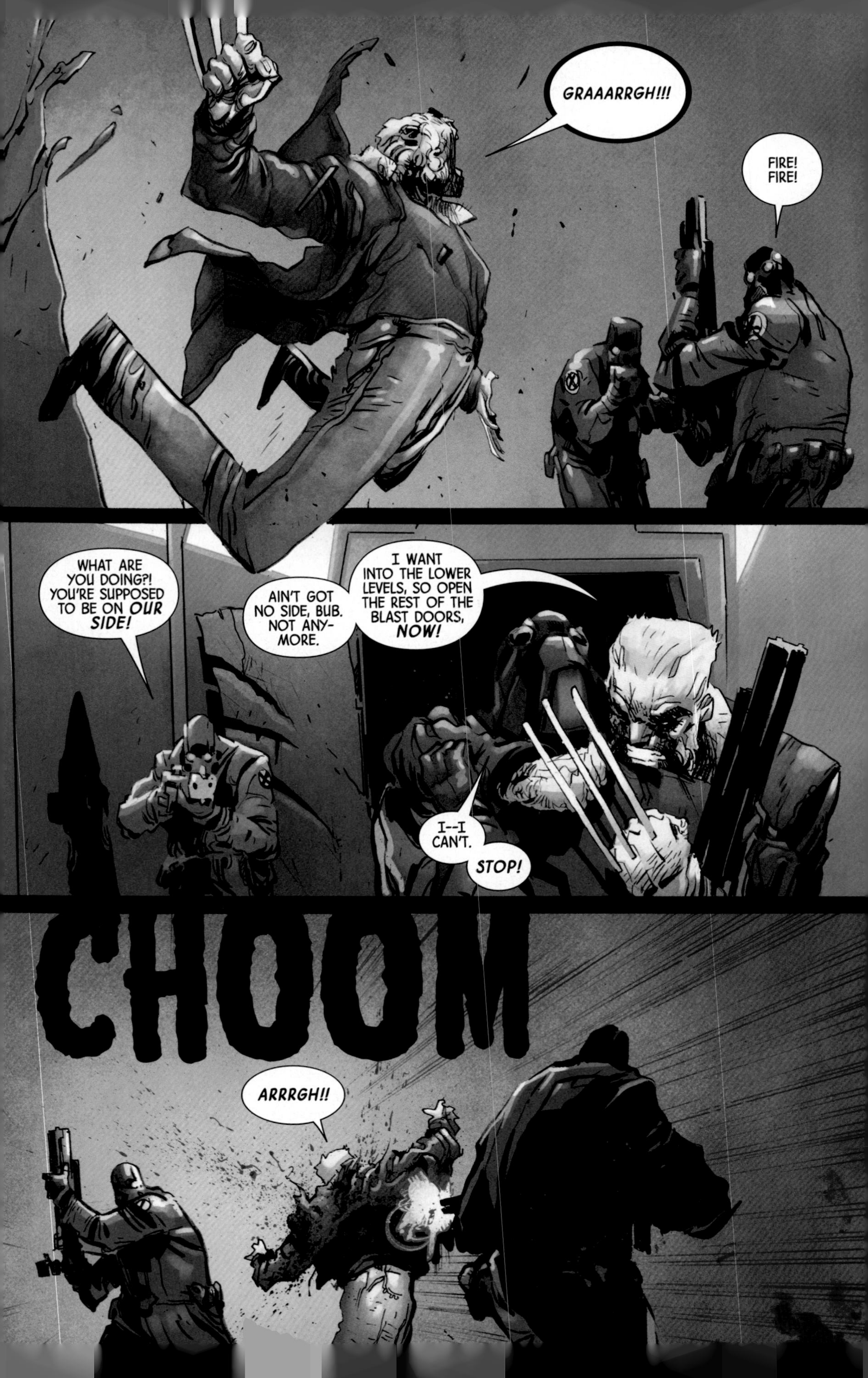
GRAAARRGH!!!
FIRE! FIRE!
WHAT ARE YOU DOING?! YOU'RE SUPPOSED TO BE ON OUR SIDE!
AIN'T GOT NO SIDE, BUB. NOT ANY-MORE.
I WANT INTO THE LOWER LEVELS, SO OPEN THE REST OF THE BLAST DOORS, NOW!
I--I CAN'T.
STOP!
CHOOM
ARRRGH!!

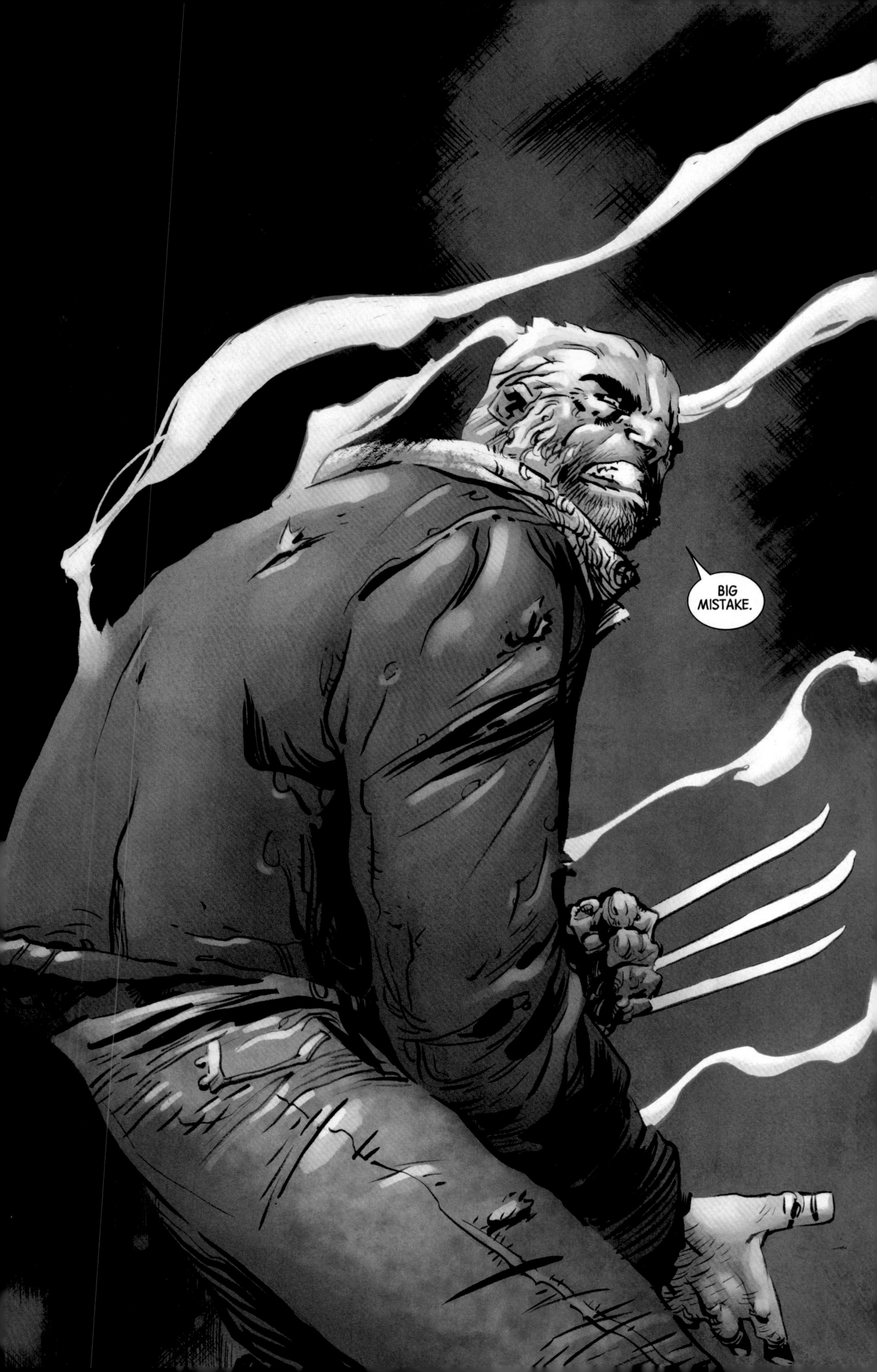
BIG MISTAKE.

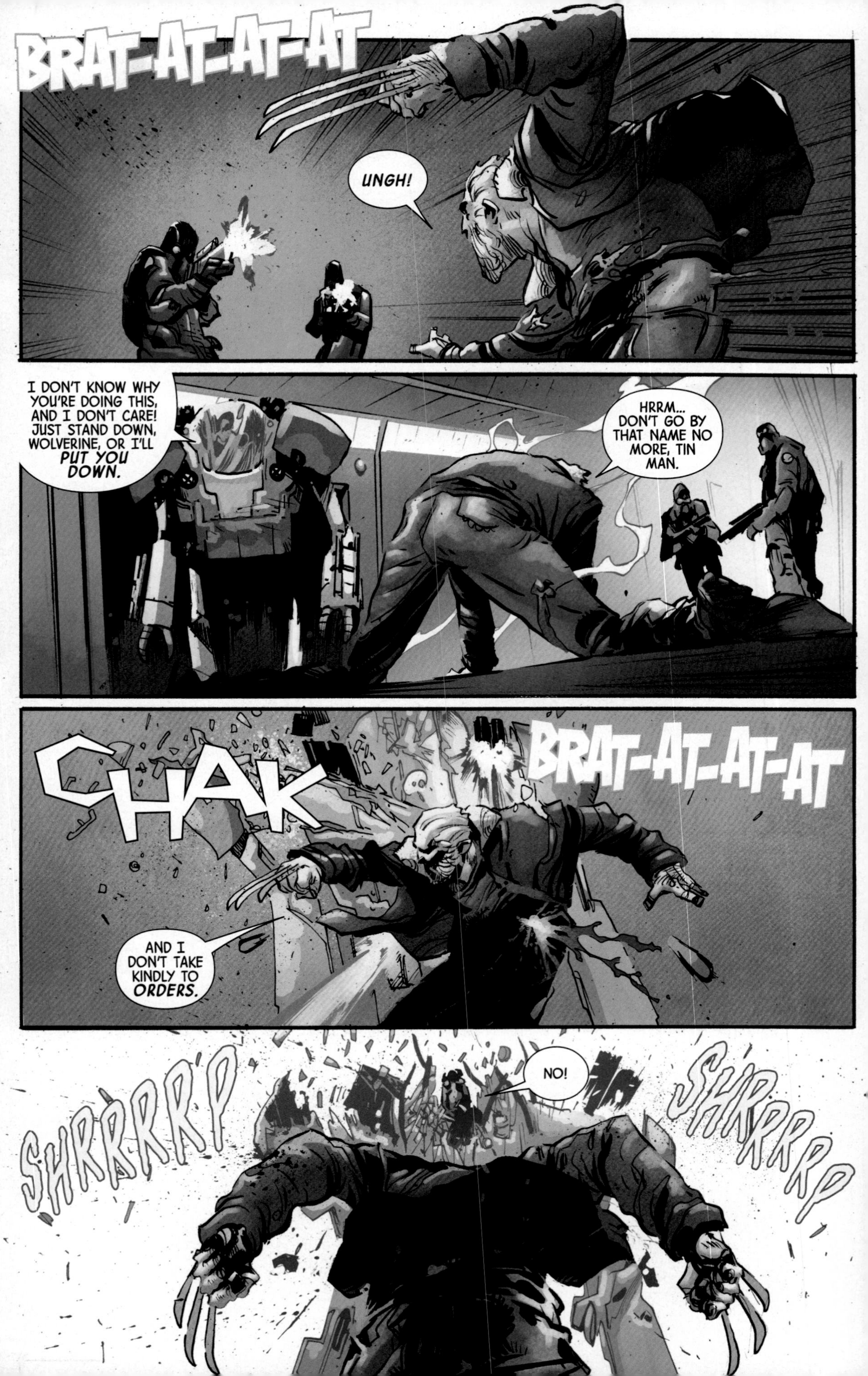
BRAT-AT-AT-AT
UNGH!
I DON'T KNOW WHY YOU'RE DOING THIS, AND I DON'T CARE! JUST STAND DOWN, WOLVERINE, OR I'LL *PUT YOU DOWN.*
HRRM... DON'T GO BY THAT NAME NO MORE, TIN MAN.
CHAK
BRAT-AT-AT-AT
AND I DON'T TAKE KINDLY TO *ORDERS.*
SHRRRRP
NO!
SHRRRRP

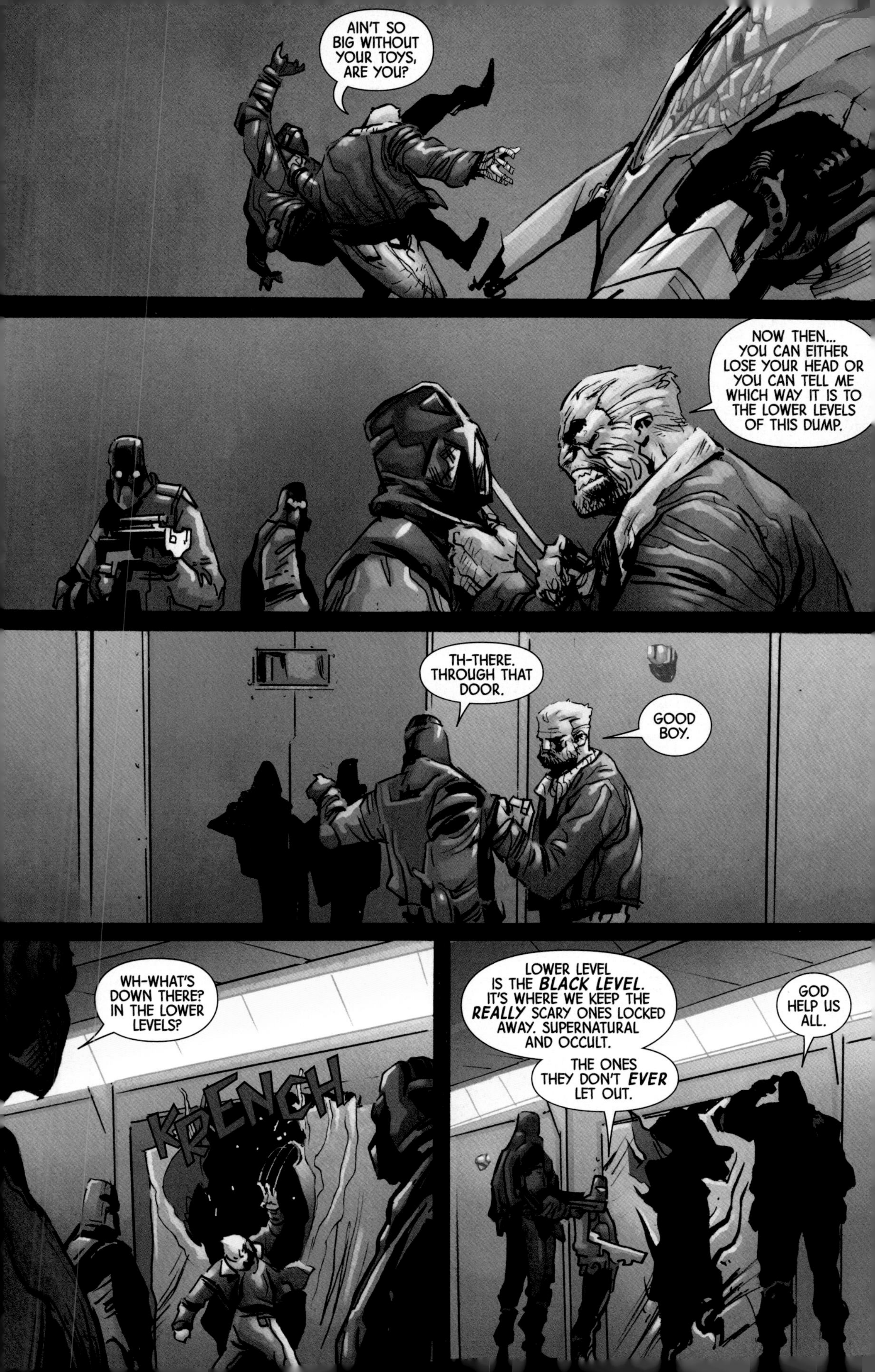
AIN'T SO BIG WITHOUT YOUR TOYS, ARE YOU?
NOW THEN... YOU CAN EITHER LOSE YOUR HEAD OR YOU CAN TELL ME WHICH WAY IT IS TO THE LOWER LEVELS OF THIS DUMP.
TH-THERE. THROUGH THAT DOOR.
GOOD BOY.
WH-WHAT'S DOWN THERE? IN THE LOWER LEVELS?
KRENCH
LOWER LEVEL IS THE BLACK LEVEL. IT'S WHERE WE KEEP THE REALLY SCARY ONES LOCKED AWAY. SUPERNATURAL AND OCCULT.
THE ONES THEY DON'T EVER LET OUT.
GOD HELP US ALL.

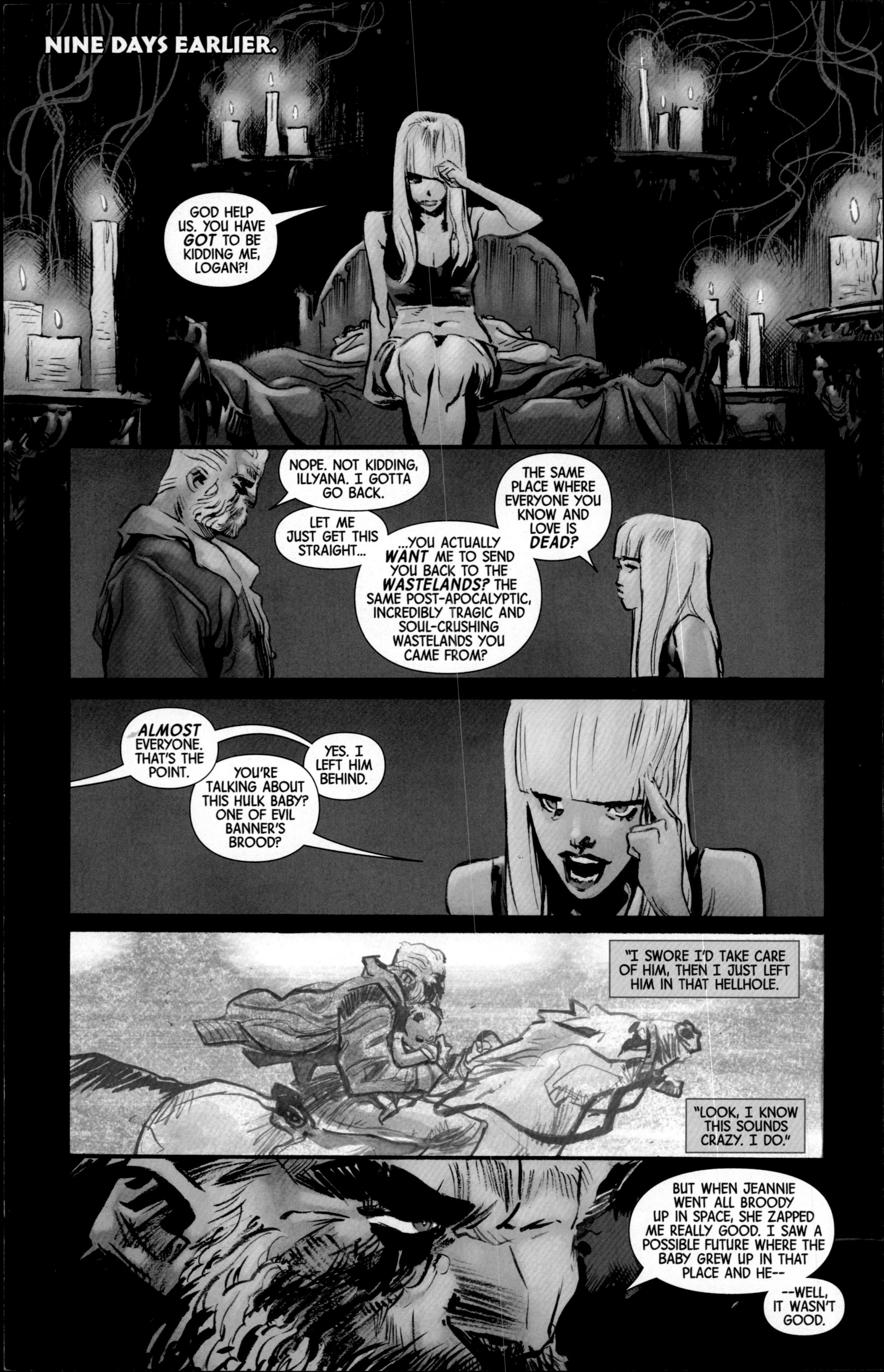
NINE DAYS EARLIER.
GOD HELP US. YOU HAVE GOT TO BE KIDDING ME, LOGAN?!
NOPE. NOT KIDDING, ILLYANA. I GOTTA GO BACK.
LET ME JUST GET THIS STRAIGHT...
...YOU ACTUALLY WANT ME TO SEND YOU BACK TO THE WASTELANDS? THE SAME POST-APOCALYPTIC, INCREDIBLY TRAGIC AND SOUL-CRUSHING WASTELANDS YOU CAME FROM?
THE SAME PLACE WHERE EVERYONE YOU KNOW AND LOVE IS DEAD?
ALMOST EVERYONE. THAT'S THE POINT.
YOU'RE TALKING ABOUT THIS HULK BABY? ONE OF EVIL BANNER'S BROOD?
YES. I LEFT HIM BEHIND.
"I SWORE I'D TAKE CARE OF HIM, THEN I JUST LEFT HIM IN THAT HELLHOLE.
"LOOK, I KNOW THIS SOUNDS CRAZY. I DO."
BUT WHEN JEANNIE WENT ALL BROODY UP IN SPACE, SHE ZAPPED ME REALLY GOOD. I SAW A POSSIBLE FUTURE WHERE THE BABY GREW UP IN THAT PLACE AND HE--
--WELL, IT WASN'T GOOD.

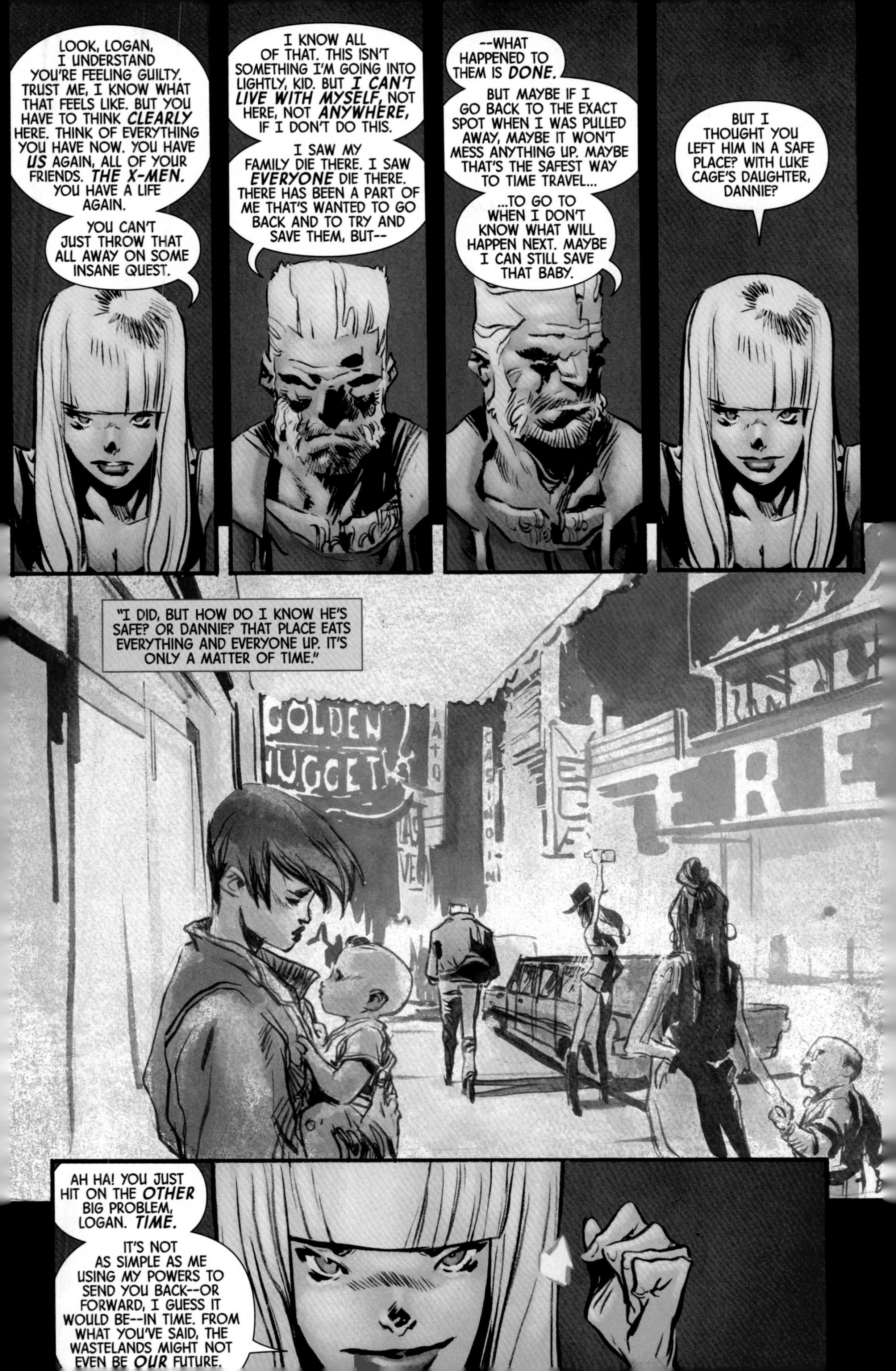
LOOK, LOGAN, I UNDERSTAND YOU'RE FEELING GUILTY. TRUST ME, I KNOW WHAT THAT FEELS LIKE. BUT YOU HAVE TO THINK CLEARLY HERE. THINK OF EVERYTHING YOU HAVE NOW. YOU HAVE US AGAIN, ALL OF YOUR FRIENDS. THE X-MEN. YOU HAVE A LIFE AGAIN.
YOU CAN'T JUST THROW THAT ALL AWAY ON SOME INSANE QUEST.
I KNOW ALL OF THAT. THIS ISN'T SOMETHING I'M GOING INTO LIGHTLY, KID. BUT I CAN'T LIVE WITH MYSELF, NOT HERE, NOT ANYWHERE, IF I DON'T DO THIS.
I SAW MY FAMILY DIE THERE. I SAW EVERYONE DIE THERE. THERE HAS BEEN A PART OF ME THAT'S WANTED TO GO BACK AND TO TRY AND SAVE THEM, BUT--
--WHAT HAPPENED TO THEM IS DONE.
BUT MAYBE IF I GO BACK TO THE EXACT SPOT WHEN I WAS PULLED AWAY, MAYBE IT WON'T MESS ANYTHING UP. MAYBE THAT'S THE SAFEST WAY TO TIME TRAVEL...
...TO GO TO WHEN I DON'T KNOW WHAT WILL HAPPEN NEXT. MAYBE I CAN STILL SAVE THAT BABY.
BUT I THOUGHT YOU LEFT HIM IN A SAFE PLACE? WITH LUKE CAGE'S DAUGHTER, DANNIE?
"I DID, BUT HOW DO I KNOW HE'S SAFE? OR DANNIE? THAT PLACE EATS EVERYTHING AND EVERYONE UP. IT'S ONLY A MATTER OF TIME."
GOLDEN NUGGET
CASINO
AH HA! YOU JUST HIT ON THE OTHER BIG PROBLEM, LOGAN. TIME.
IT'S NOT AS SIMPLE AS ME USING MY POWERS TO SEND YOU BACK--OR FORWARD, I GUESS IT WOULD BE--IN TIME. FROM WHAT YOU'VE SAID, THE WASTELANDS MIGHT NOT EVEN BE OUR FUTURE.

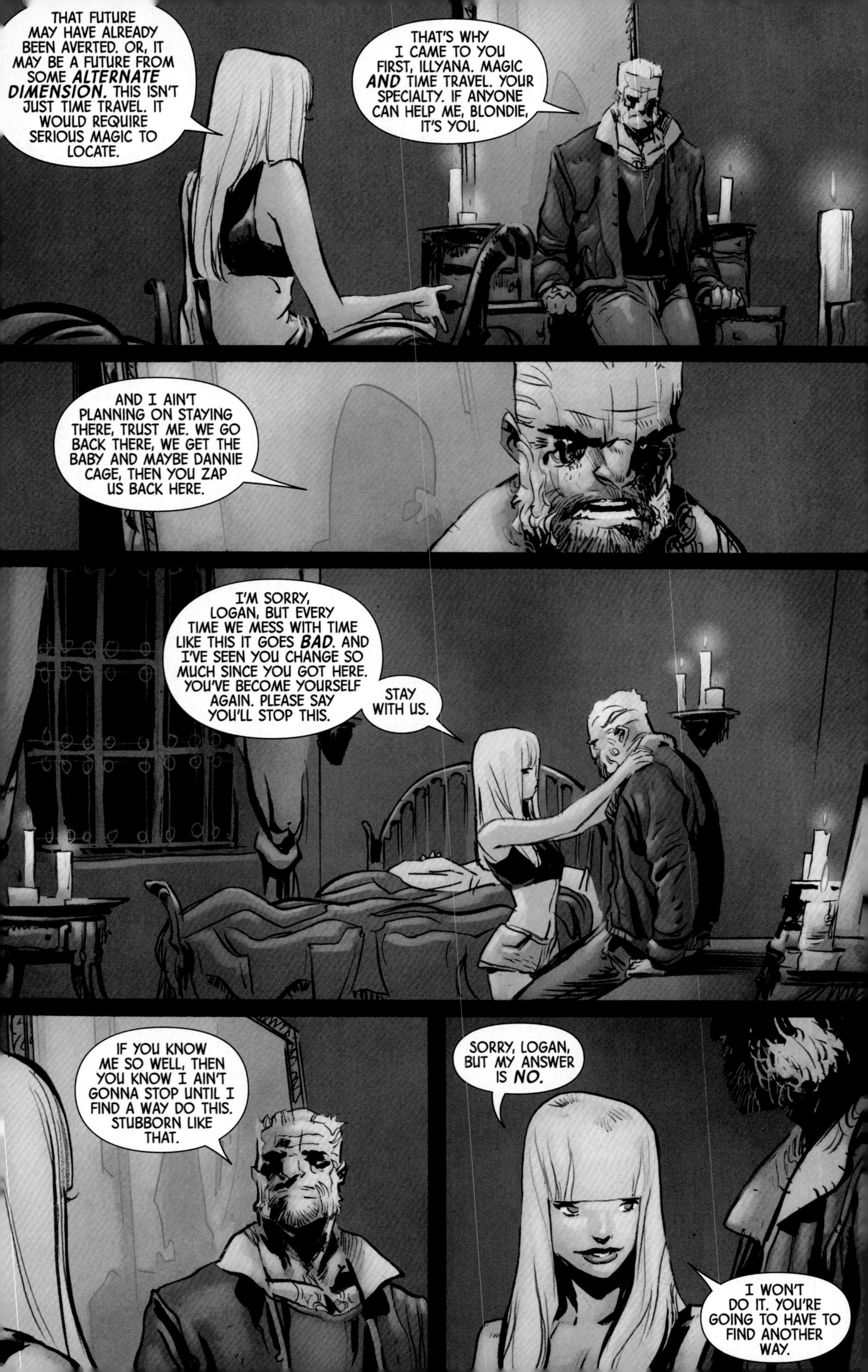
THAT FUTURE MAY HAVE ALREADY BEEN AVERTED. OR, IT MAY BE A FUTURE FROM SOME ALTERNATE DIMENSION. THIS ISN'T JUST TIME TRAVEL. IT WOULD REQUIRE SERIOUS MAGIC TO LOCATE.
THAT'S WHY I CAME TO YOU FIRST, ILLYANA. MAGIC AND TIME TRAVEL. YOUR SPECIALTY. IF ANYONE CAN HELP ME, BLONDIE, IT'S YOU.
AND I AIN'T PLANNING ON STAYING THERE, TRUST ME. WE GO BACK THERE, WE GET THE BABY AND MAYBE DANNIE CAGE, THEN YOU ZAP US BACK HERE.
I'M SORRY, LOGAN, BUT EVERY TIME WE MESS WITH TIME LIKE THIS IT GOES BAD. AND I'VE SEEN YOU CHANGE SO MUCH SINCE YOU GOT HERE. YOU'VE BECOME YOURSELF AGAIN. PLEASE SAY YOU'LL STOP THIS.
STAY WITH US.
IF YOU KNOW ME SO WELL, THEN YOU KNOW I AIN'T GONNA STOP UNTIL I FIND A WAY DO THIS. STUBBORN LIKE THAT.
SORRY, LOGAN, BUT MY ANSWER IS NO.
I WON'T DO IT. YOU'RE GOING TO HAVE TO FIND ANOTHER WAY.

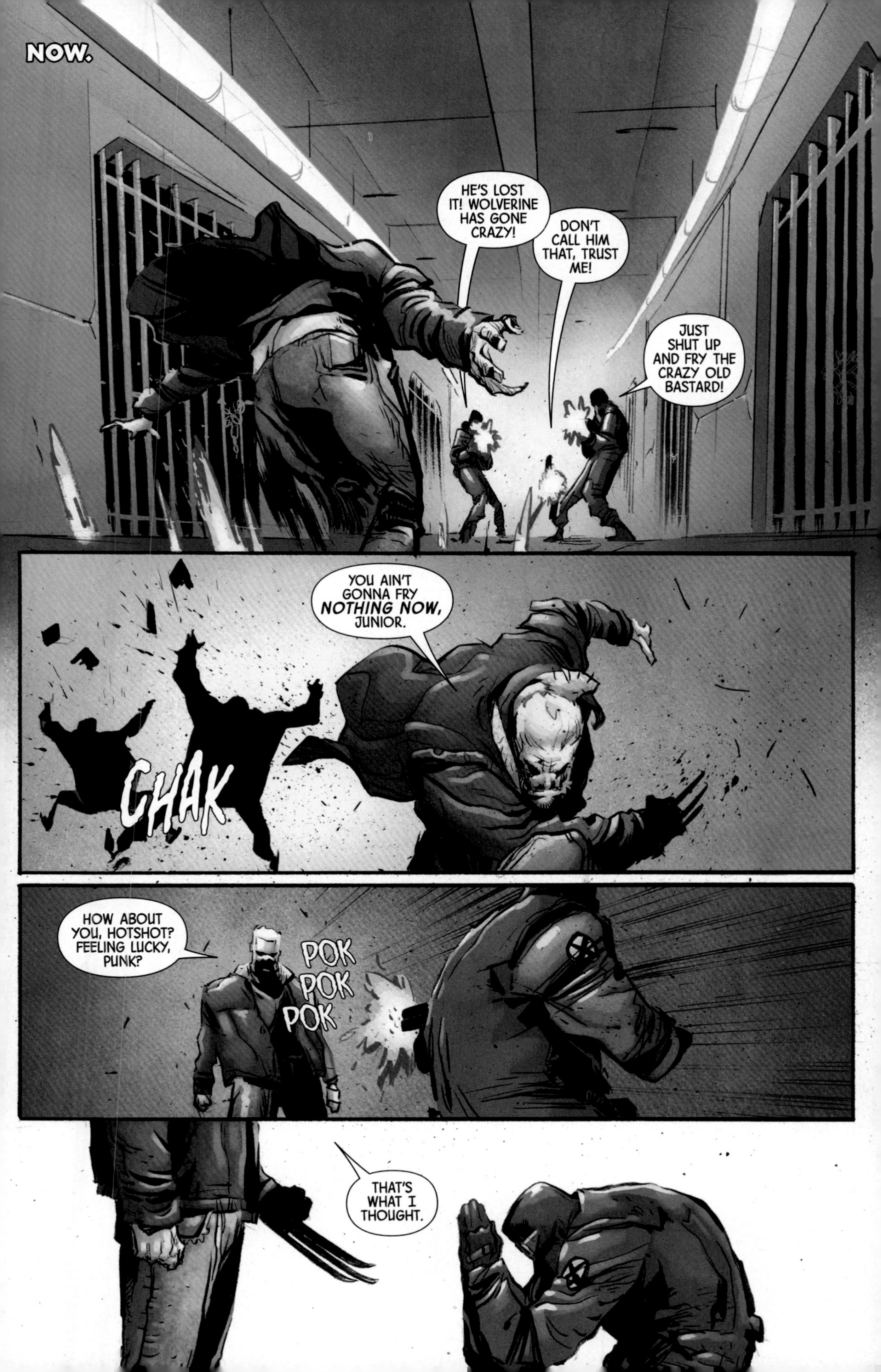
NOW.
HE'S LOST IT! WOLVERINE HAS GONE CRAZY!
DON'T CALL HIM THAT, TRUST ME!
JUST SHUT UP AND FRY THE CRAZY OLD BASTARD!
YOU AIN'T GONNA FRY NOTHING NOW, JUNIOR.
CHAK
HOW ABOUT YOU, HOTSHOT? FEELING LUCKY, PUNK?
POK POK POK
THAT'S WHAT I THOUGHT.

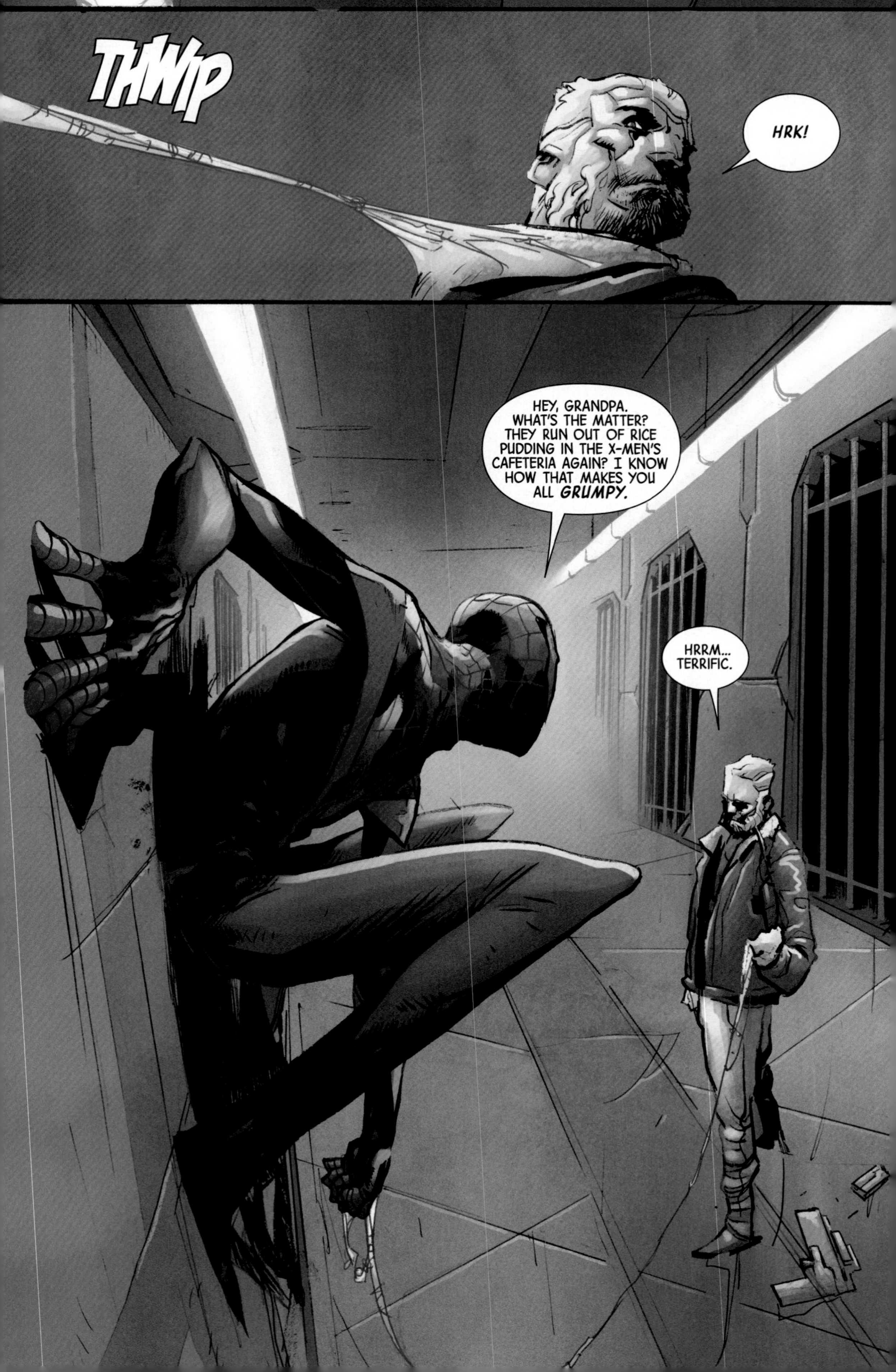
THWIP
HRK!
HEY, GRANDPA. WHAT'S THE MATTER? THEY RUN OUT OF RICE PUDDING IN THE X-MEN'S CAFETERIA AGAIN? I KNOW HOW THAT MAKES YOU ALL GRUMPY.
HRRM... TERRIFIC.

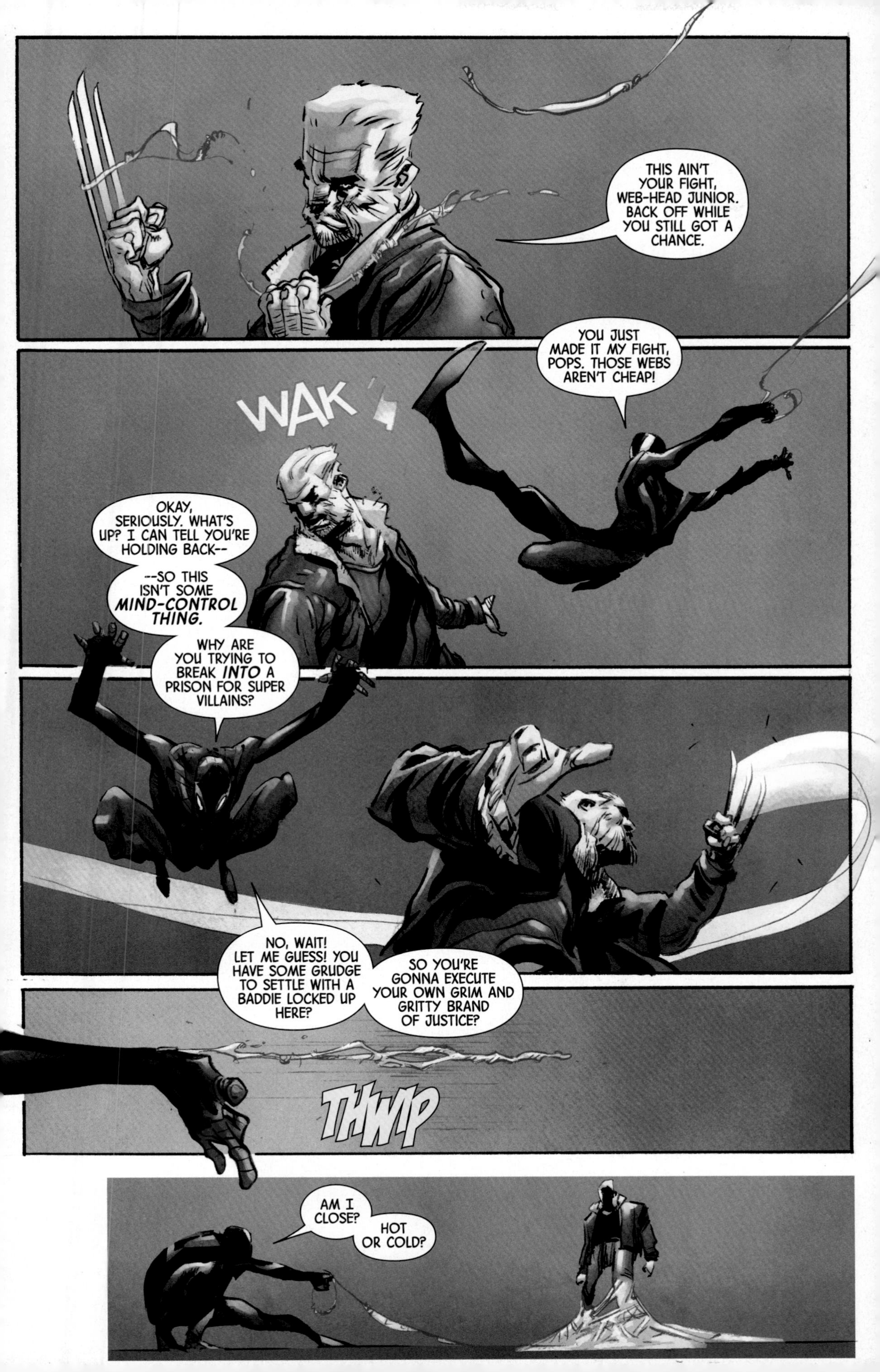

THIS AIN'T YOUR FIGHT, WEB-HEAD JUNIOR. BACK OFF WHILE YOU STILL GOT A CHANCE.
YOU JUST MADE IT MY FIGHT, POPS. THOSE WEBS AREN'T CHEAP!
WAK
OKAY, SERIOUSLY. WHAT'S UP? I CAN TELL YOU'RE HOLDING BACK--
--SO THIS ISN'T SOME *MIND-CONTROL THING.*
WHY ARE YOU TRYING TO BREAK *INTO* A PRISON FOR SUPER VILLAINS?
NO, WAIT! LET ME GUESS! YOU HAVE SOME GRUDGE TO SETTLE WITH A BADDIE LOCKED UP HERE?
SO YOU'RE GONNA EXECUTE YOUR OWN GRIM AND GRITTY BRAND OF JUSTICE?
THWIP
AM I CLOSE?
HOT OR COLD?

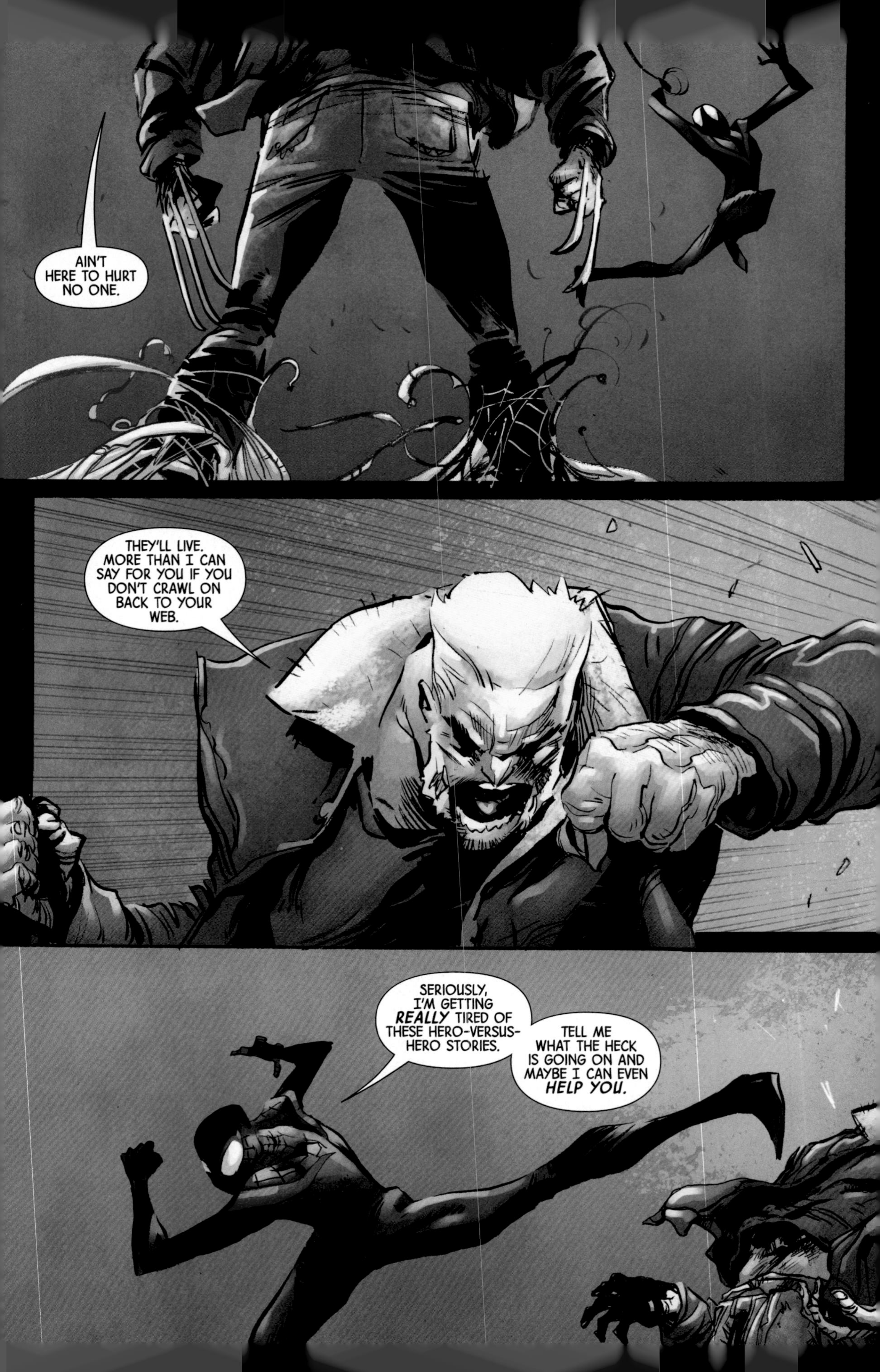
AIN'T HERE TO HURT NO ONE.
THEY'LL LIVE. MORE THAN I CAN SAY FOR YOU IF YOU DON'T CRAWL ON BACK TO YOUR WEB.
SERIOUSLY, I'M GETTING *REALLY* TIRED OF THESE HERO-VERSUS-HERO STORIES.
TELL ME WHAT THE HECK IS GOING ON AND MAYBE I CAN EVEN *HELP YOU.*

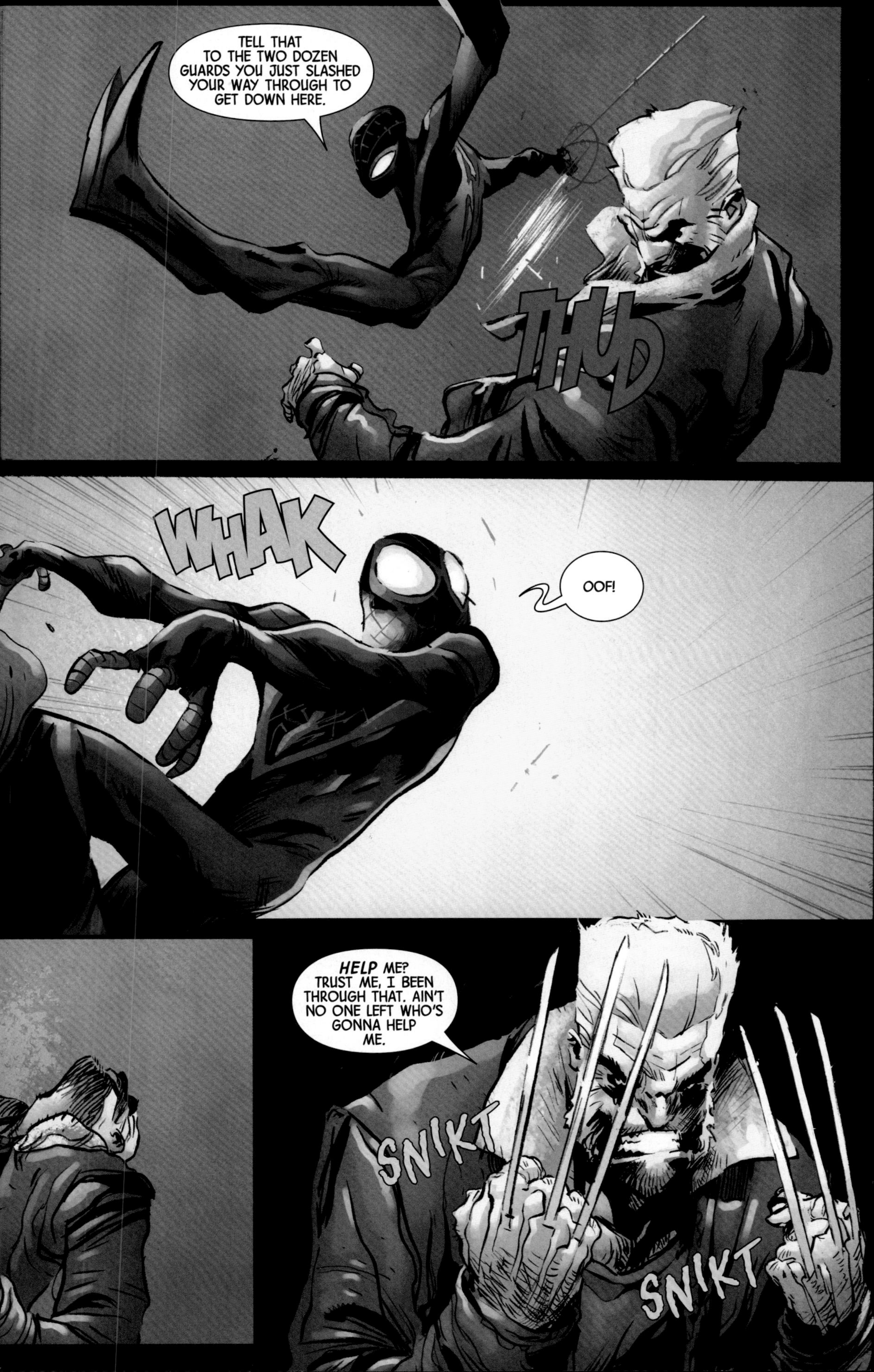
TELL THAT TO THE TWO DOZEN GUARDS YOU JUST SLASHED YOUR WAY THROUGH TO GET DOWN HERE.
THUD
WHAK
OOF!
HELP ME? TRUST ME, I BEEN THROUGH THAT. AIN'T NO ONE LEFT WHO'S GONNA HELP ME.
SNIKT
SNIKT

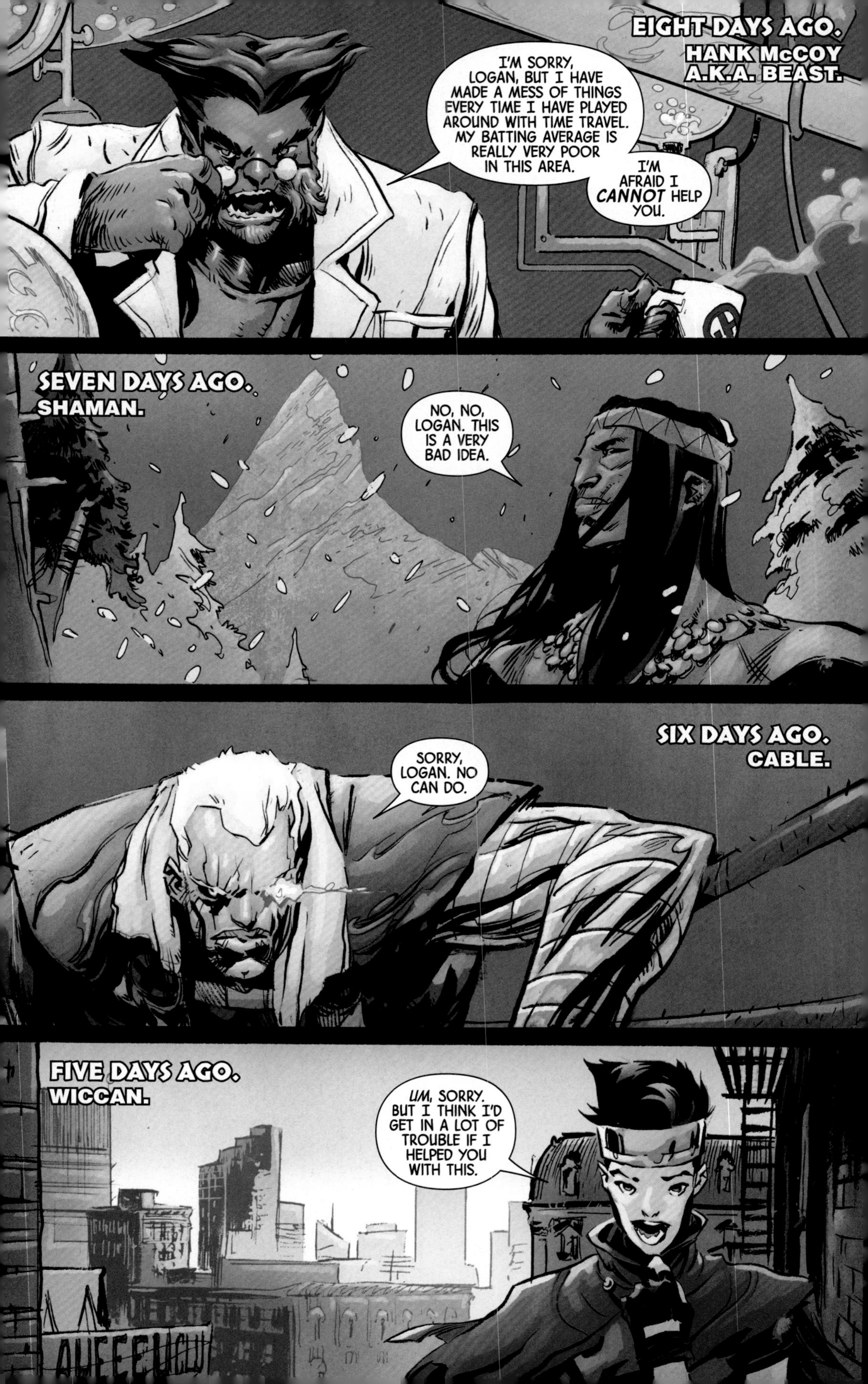
EIGHT DAYS AGO.
HANK McCOY A.K.A. BEAST.
I'M SORRY, LOGAN, BUT I HAVE MADE A MESS OF THINGS EVERY TIME I HAVE PLAYED AROUND WITH TIME TRAVEL. MY BATTING AVERAGE IS REALLY VERY POOR IN THIS AREA.
I'M AFRAID I *CANNOT* HELP YOU.
SEVEN DAYS AGO.
SHAMAN.
NO, NO, LOGAN. THIS IS A VERY BAD IDEA.
SIX DAYS AGO.
CABLE.
SORRY, LOGAN. NO CAN DO.
FIVE DAYS AGO.
WICCAN.
UM, SORRY. BUT I THINK I'D GET IN A LOT OF TROUBLE IF I HELPED YOU WITH THIS.

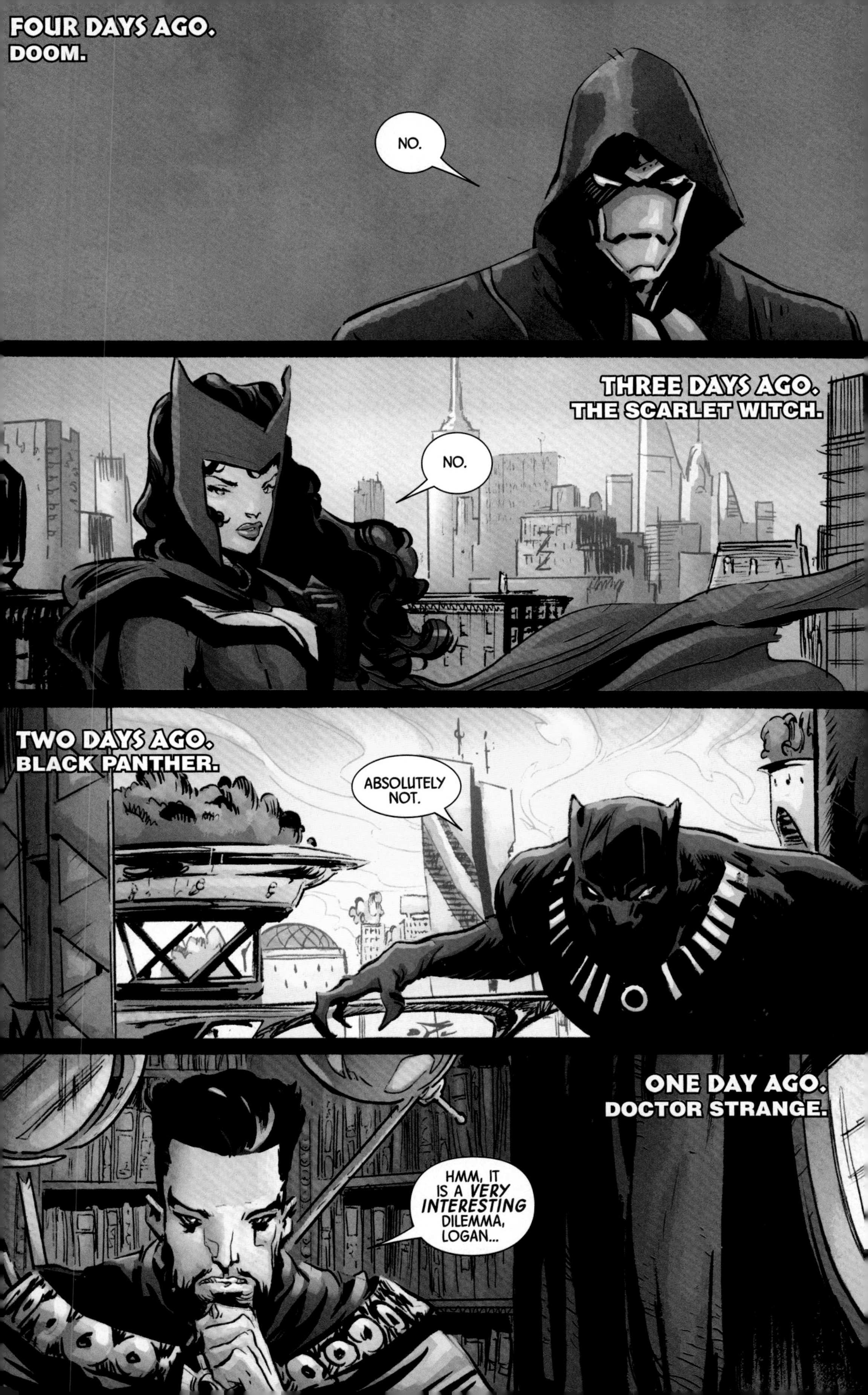
FOUR DAYS AGO.
DOOM.
NO.
THREE DAYS AGO.
THE SCARLET WITCH.
NO.
TWO DAYS AGO.
BLACK PANTHER.
ABSOLUTELY NOT.
ONE DAY AGO.
DOCTOR STRANGE.
HMM, IT IS A *VERY INTERESTING* DILEMMA, LOGAN...

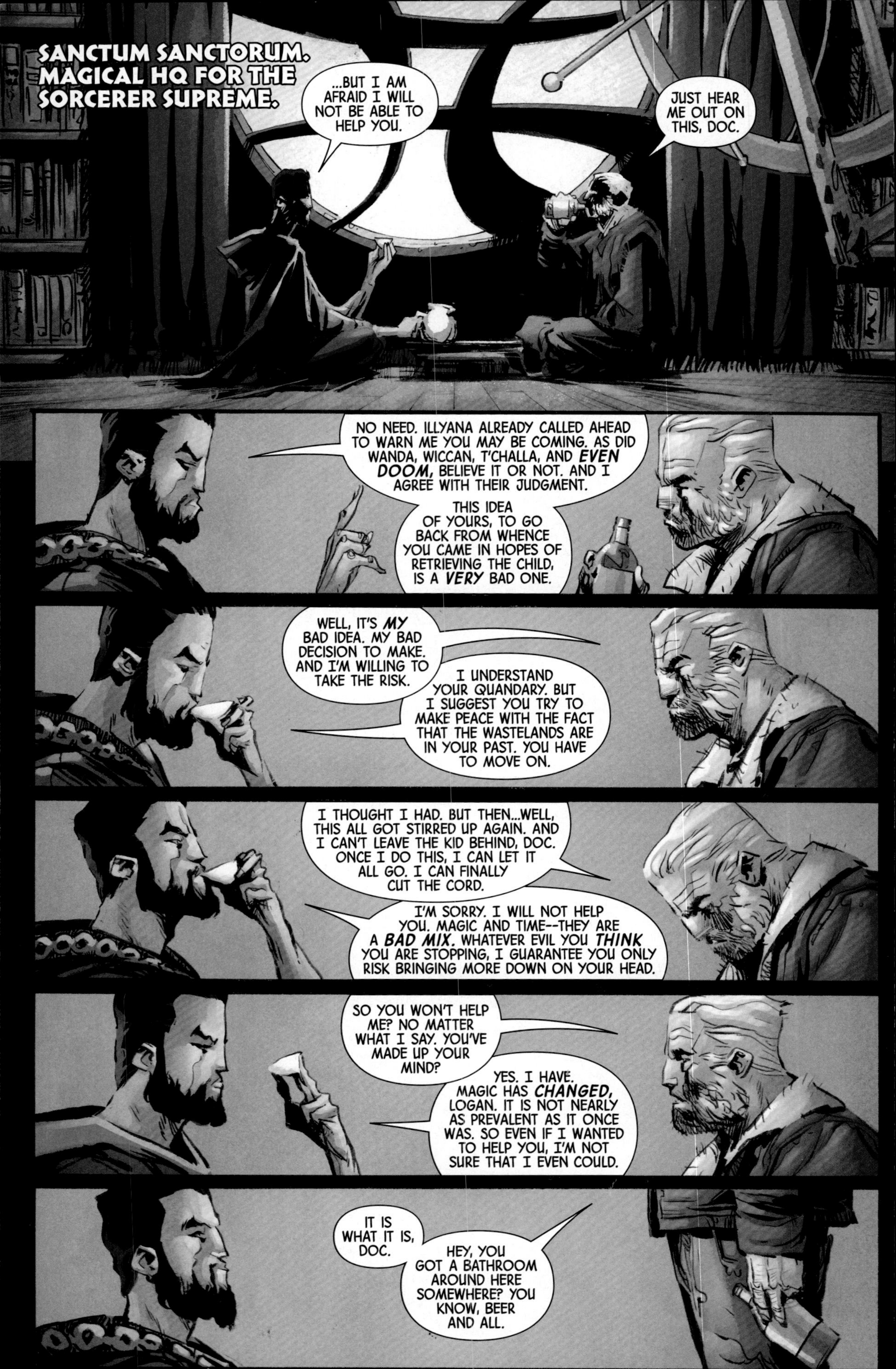
SANCTUM SANCTORUM. MAGICAL HQ FOR THE SORCERER SUPREME.
...BUT I AM AFRAID I WILL NOT BE ABLE TO HELP YOU.
JUST HEAR ME OUT ON THIS, DOC.
NO NEED. ILLYANA ALREADY CALLED AHEAD TO WARN ME YOU MAY BE COMING. AS DID WANDA, WICCAN, T'CHALLA, AND EVEN DOOM, BELIEVE IT OR NOT. AND I AGREE WITH THEIR JUDGMENT.
THIS IDEA OF YOURS, TO GO BACK FROM WHENCE YOU CAME IN HOPES OF RETRIEVING THE CHILD, IS A VERY BAD ONE.
WELL, IT'S MY BAD IDEA. MY BAD DECISION TO MAKE. AND I'M WILLING TO TAKE THE RISK.
I UNDERSTAND YOUR QUANDARY. BUT I SUGGEST YOU TRY TO MAKE PEACE WITH THE FACT THAT THE WASTELANDS ARE IN YOUR PAST. YOU HAVE TO MOVE ON.
I THOUGHT I HAD. BUT THEN...WELL, THIS ALL GOT STIRRED UP AGAIN. AND I CAN'T LEAVE THE KID BEHIND, DOC. ONCE I DO THIS, I CAN LET IT ALL GO. I CAN FINALLY CUT THE CORD.
I'M SORRY. I WILL NOT HELP YOU. MAGIC AND TIME--THEY ARE A BAD MIX. WHATEVER EVIL YOU THINK YOU ARE STOPPING, I GUARANTEE YOU ONLY RISK BRINGING MORE DOWN ON YOUR HEAD.
SO YOU WON'T HELP ME? NO MATTER WHAT I SAY. YOU'VE MADE UP YOUR MIND?
YES. I HAVE. MAGIC HAS CHANGED, LOGAN. IT IS NOT NEARLY AS PREVALENT AS IT ONCE WAS. SO EVEN IF I WANTED TO HELP YOU, I'M NOT SURE THAT I EVEN COULD.
IT IS WHAT IT IS, DOC.
HEY, YOU GOT A BATHROOM AROUND HERE SOMEWHERE? YOU KNOW, BEER AND ALL.

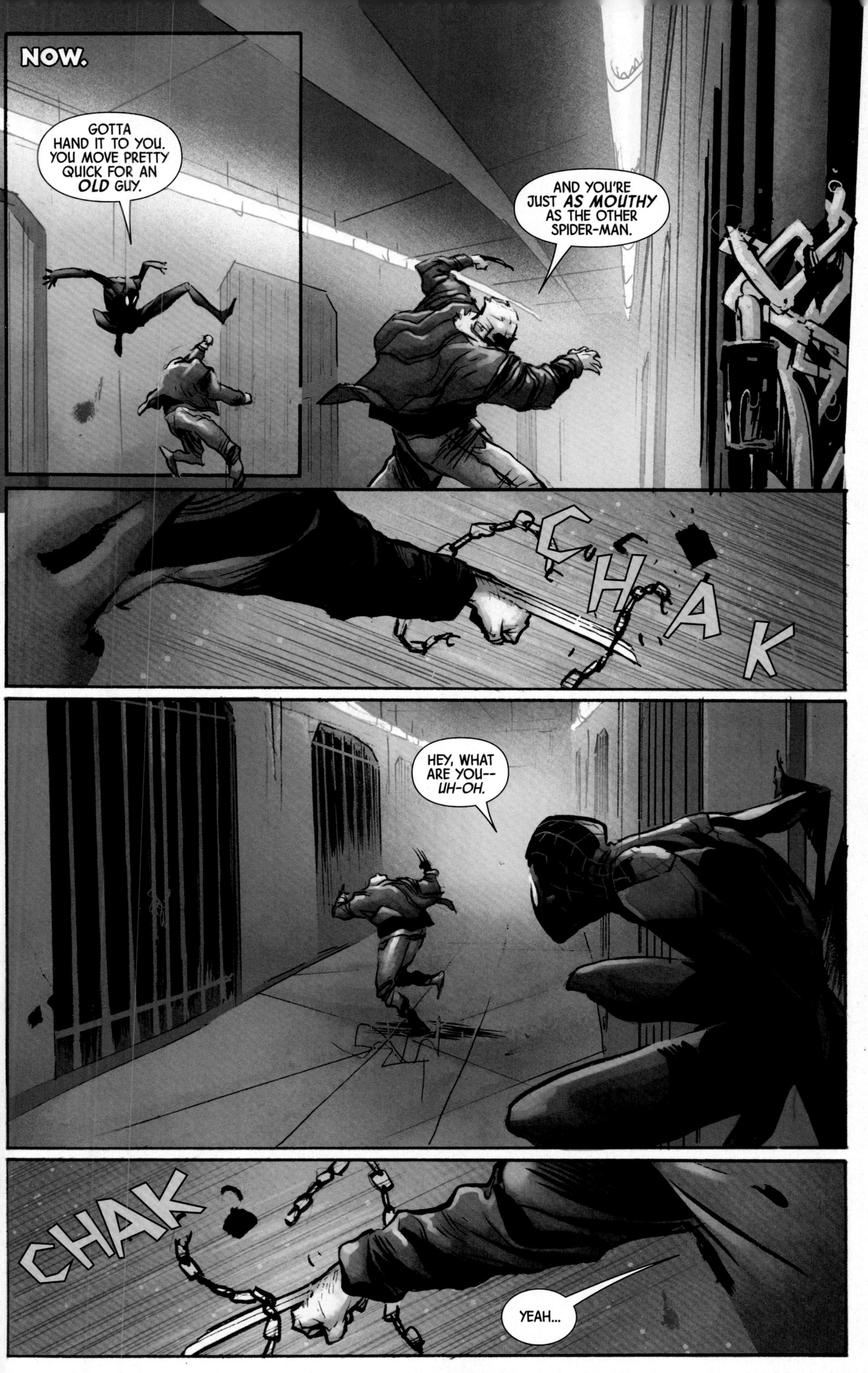
NOW.
GOTTA HAND IT TO YOU. YOU MOVE PRETTY QUICK FOR AN OLD GUY.
AND YOU'RE JUST AS MOUTHY AS THE OTHER SPIDER-MAN.
CHAK
HEY, WHAT ARE YOU-- UH-OH.
CHAK
YEAH...

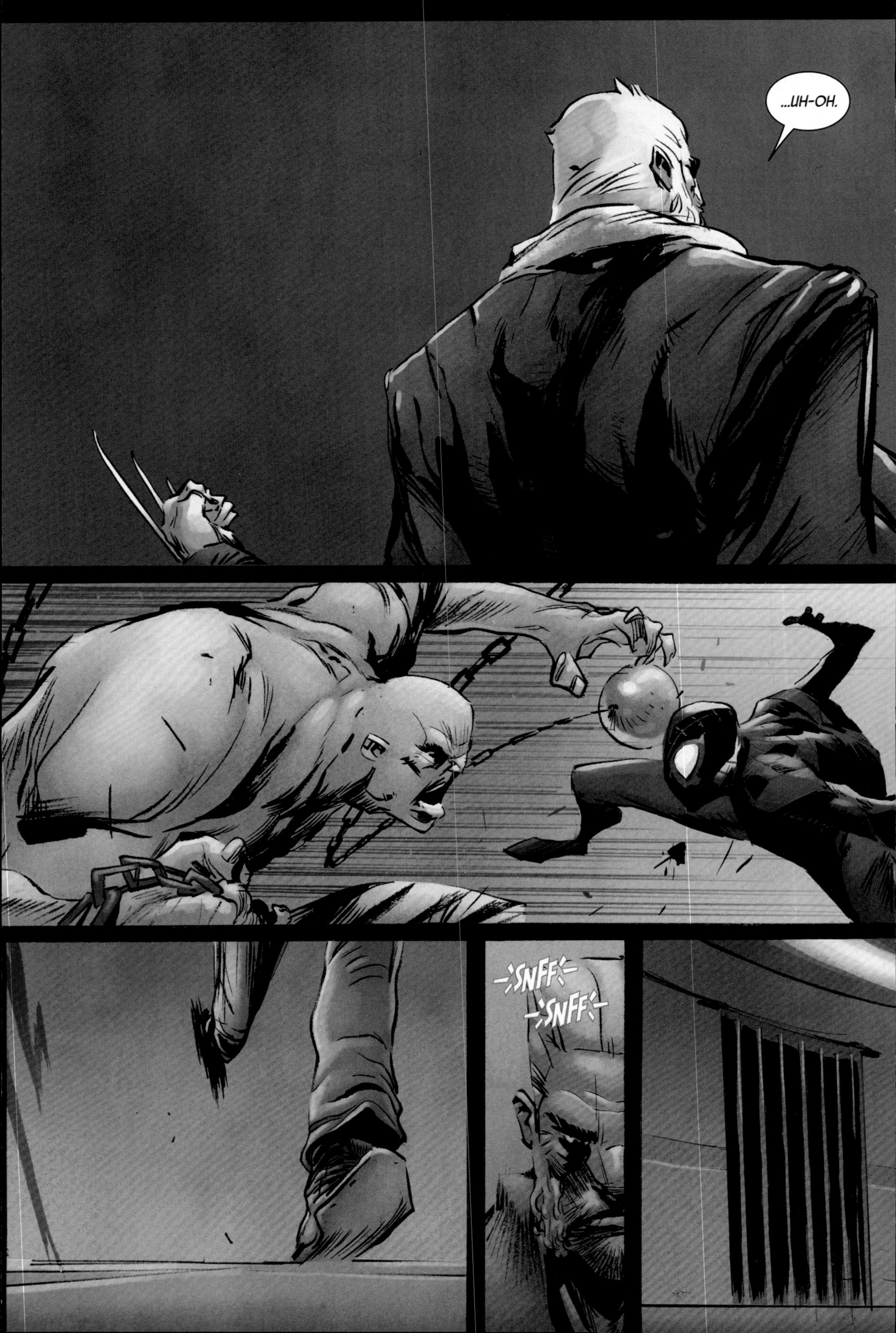
...UH-OH.
SNFF
SNFF

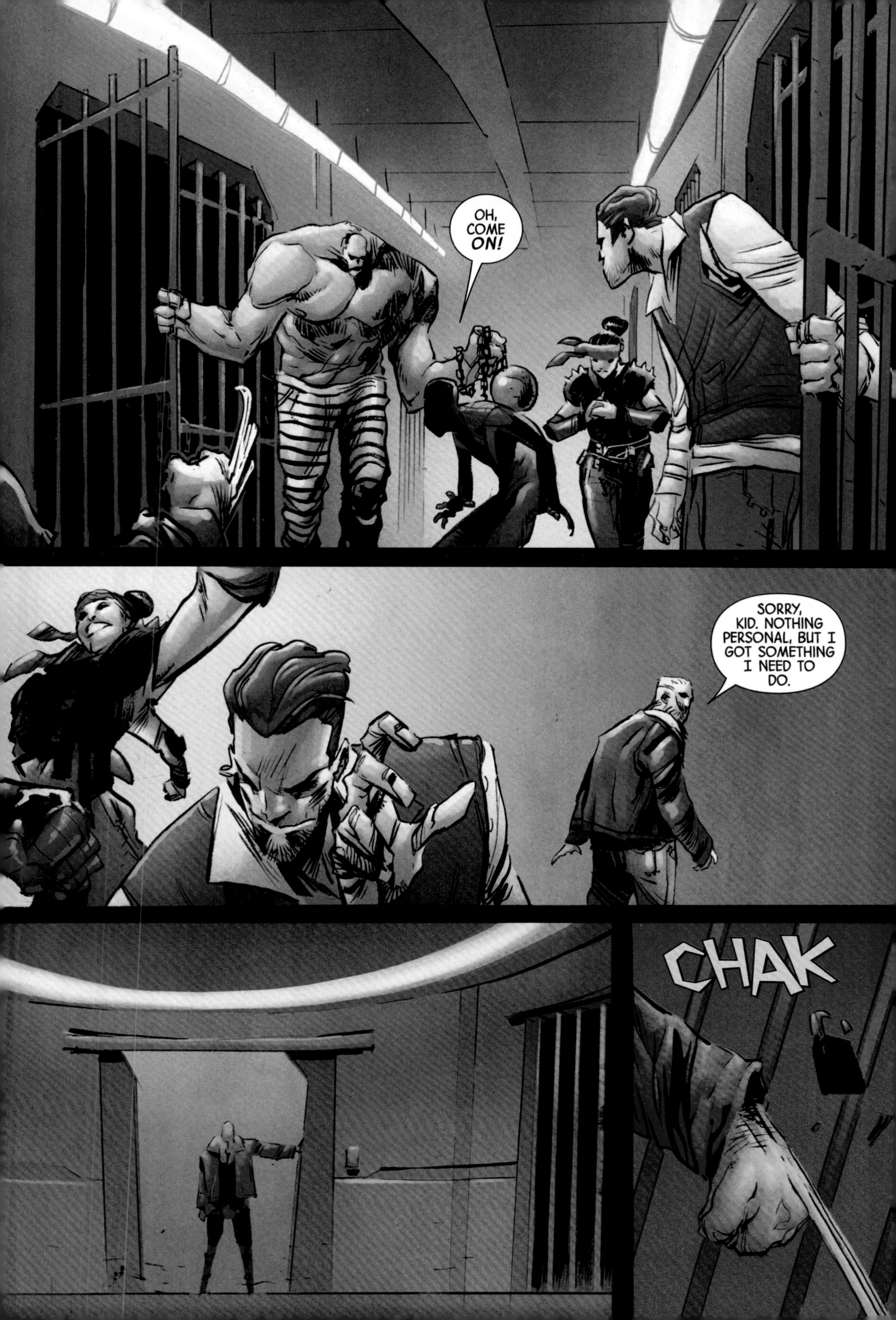
OH, COME ON!
SORRY, KID. NOTHING PERSONAL, BUT I GOT SOMETHING I NEED TO DO.
CHAK

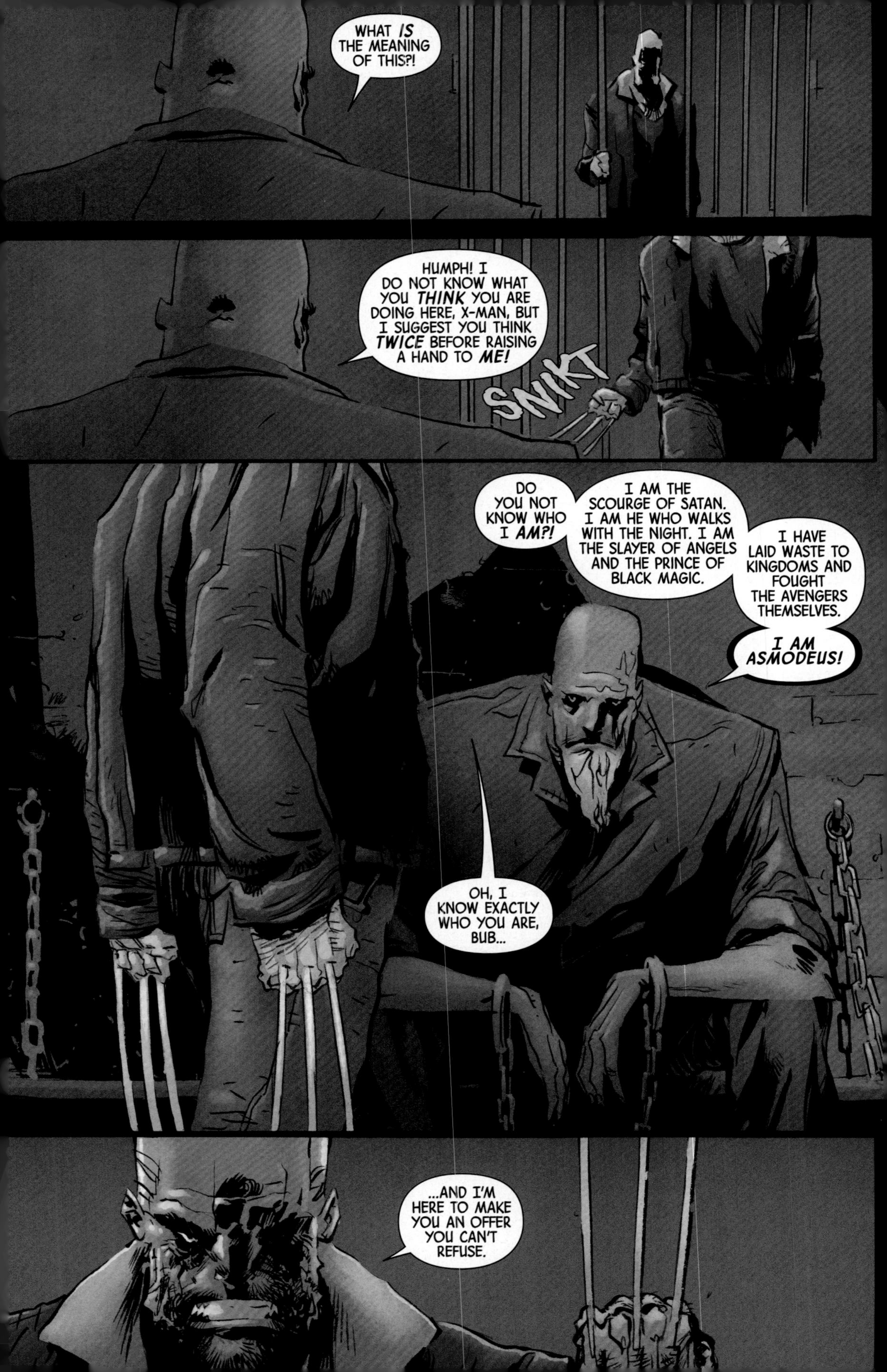
WHAT *IS* THE MEANING OF THIS?!
HUMPH! I DO NOT KNOW WHAT YOU *THINK* YOU ARE DOING HERE, X-MAN, BUT I SUGGEST YOU THINK *TWICE* BEFORE RAISING A HAND TO *ME!*
SNIKT
DO YOU NOT KNOW WHO I *AM?!*
I AM THE SCOURGE OF SATAN. I AM HE WHO WALKS WITH THE NIGHT. I AM THE SLAYER OF ANGELS AND THE PRINCE OF BLACK MAGIC.
I HAVE LAID WASTE TO KINGDOMS AND FOUGHT THE AVENGERS THEMSELVES.
I AM ASMODEUS!
OH, I KNOW EXACTLY WHO YOU ARE, BUB...
...AND I'M HERE TO MAKE YOU AN OFFER YOU CAN'T REFUSE.

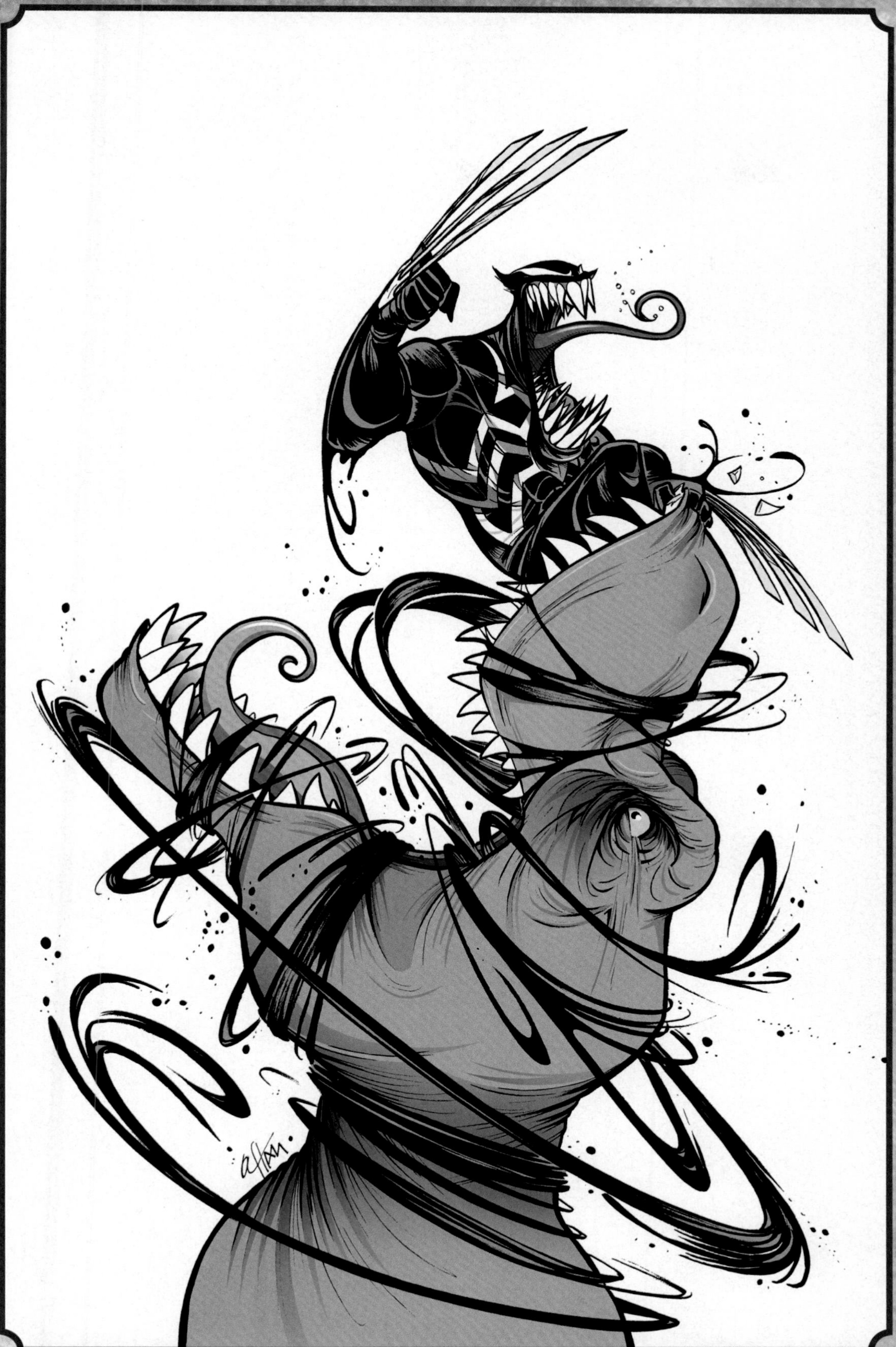

#19 VENOMIZED VARIANT
BY GUSTAVO DUARTE

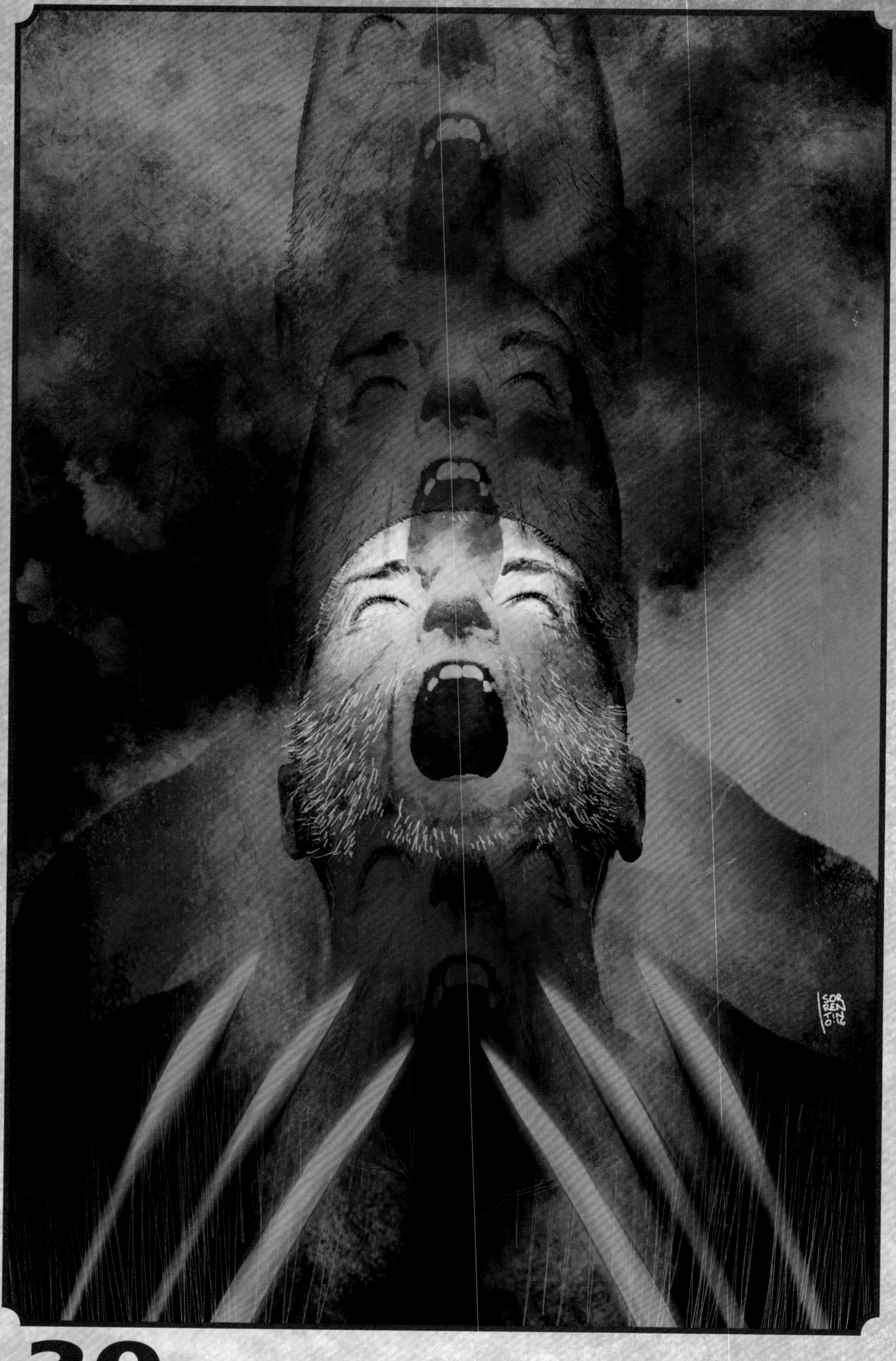

20

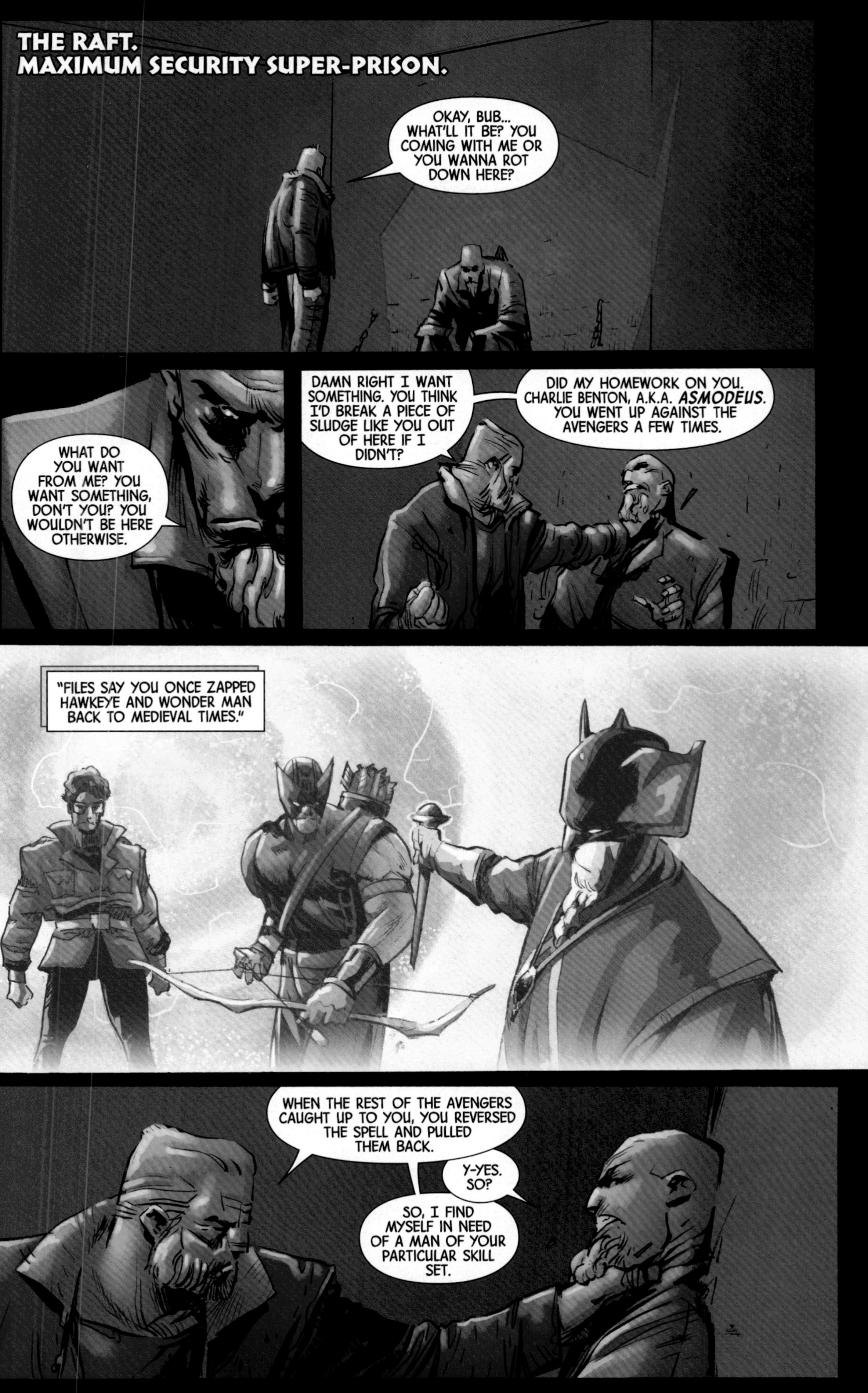
THE RAFT.
MAXIMUM SECURITY SUPER-PRISON.
OKAY, BUB... WHAT'LL IT BE? YOU COMING WITH ME OR YOU WANNA ROT DOWN HERE?
WHAT DO YOU WANT FROM ME? YOU WANT SOMETHING, DON'T YOU? YOU WOULDN'T BE HERE OTHERWISE.
DAMN RIGHT I WANT SOMETHING. YOU THINK I'D BREAK A PIECE OF SLUDGE LIKE YOU OUT OF HERE IF I DIDN'T?
DID MY HOMEWORK ON YOU. CHARLIE BENTON, A.K.A. ASMODEUS. YOU WENT UP AGAINST THE AVENGERS A FEW TIMES.
"FILES SAY YOU ONCE ZAPPED HAWKEYE AND WONDER MAN BACK TO MEDIEVAL TIMES."
WHEN THE REST OF THE AVENGERS CAUGHT UP TO YOU, YOU REVERSED THE SPELL AND PULLED THEM BACK.
Y-YES. SO?
SO, I FIND MYSELF IN NEED OF A MAN OF YOUR PARTICULAR SKILL SET.

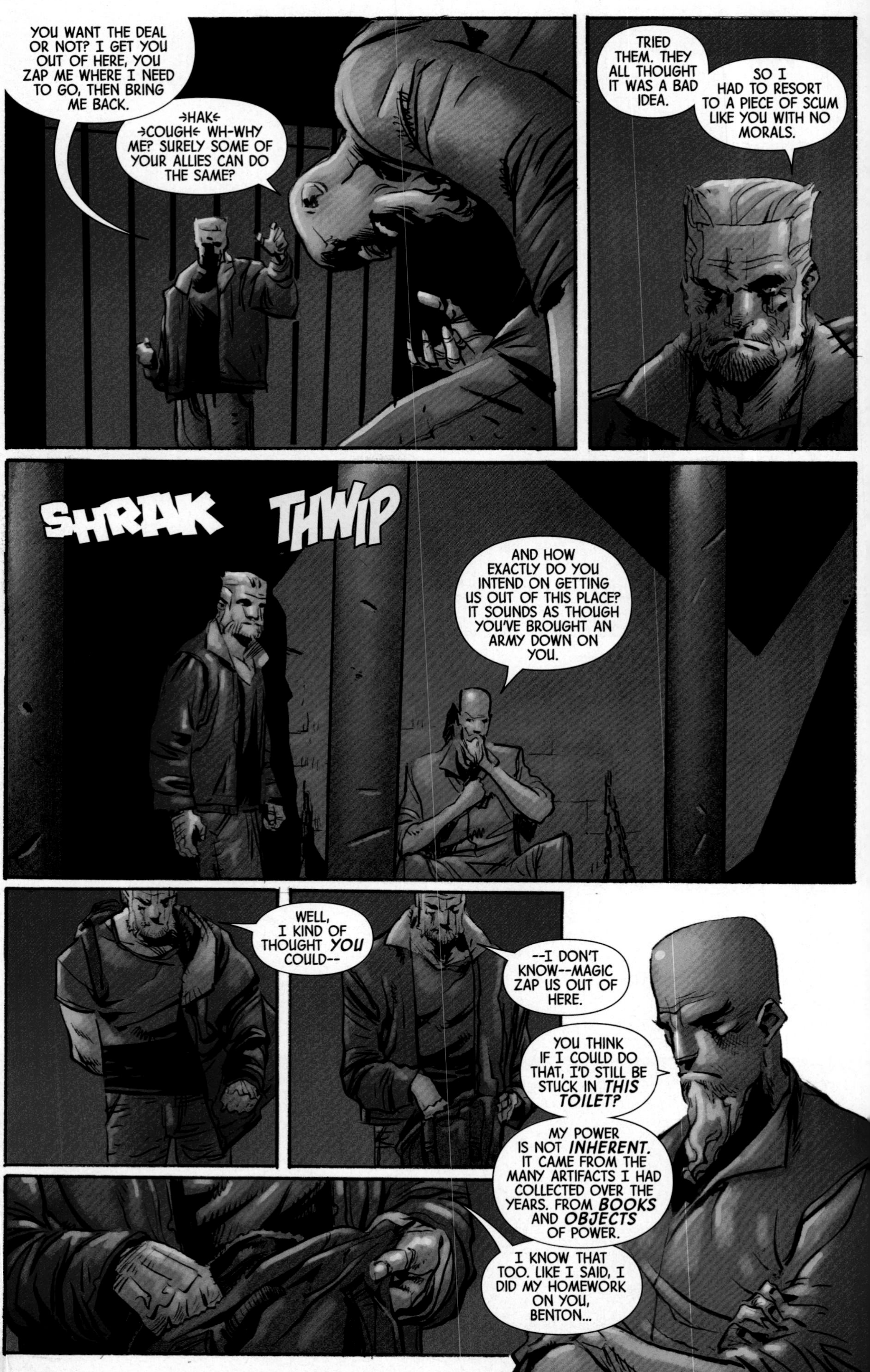
YOU WANT THE DEAL OR NOT? I GET YOU OUT OF HERE, YOU ZAP ME WHERE I NEED TO GO, THEN BRING ME BACK.
→HAK← →COUGH← WH-WHY ME? SURELY SOME OF YOUR ALLIES CAN DO THE SAME?
TRIED THEM. THEY ALL THOUGHT IT WAS A BAD IDEA.
SO I HAD TO RESORT TO A PIECE OF SCUM LIKE YOU WITH NO MORALS.
SHRAK
THWIP
AND HOW EXACTLY DO YOU INTEND ON GETTING US OUT OF THIS PLACE? IT SOUNDS AS THOUGH YOU'VE BROUGHT AN ARMY DOWN ON YOU.
WELL, I KIND OF THOUGHT *YOU* COULD--
--I DON'T KNOW--MAGIC ZAP US OUT OF HERE.
YOU THINK IF I COULD DO THAT, I'D STILL BE STUCK IN *THIS* TOILET?
MY POWER IS NOT *INHERENT.* IT CAME FROM THE MANY ARTIFACTS I HAD COLLECTED OVER THE YEARS. FROM *BOOKS* AND *OBJECTS* OF POWER.
I KNOW THAT TOO. LIKE I SAID, I DID MY HOMEWORK ON YOU, BENTON...

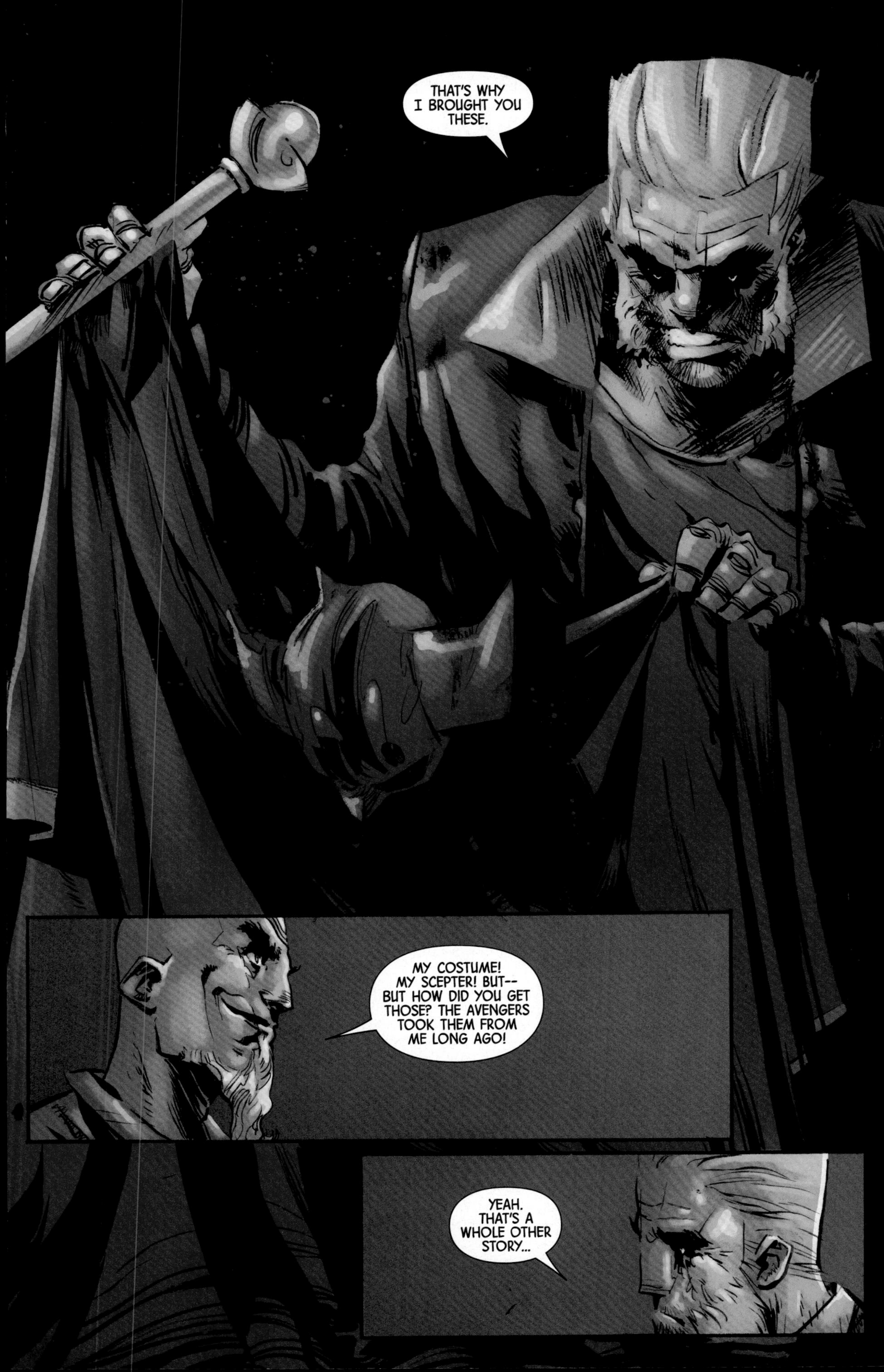
THAT'S WHY I BROUGHT YOU THESE.
MY COSTUME! MY SCEPTER! BUT-- BUT HOW DID YOU GET THOSE? THE AVENGERS TOOK THEM FROM ME LONG AGO!
YEAH. THAT'S A WHOLE OTHER STORY...

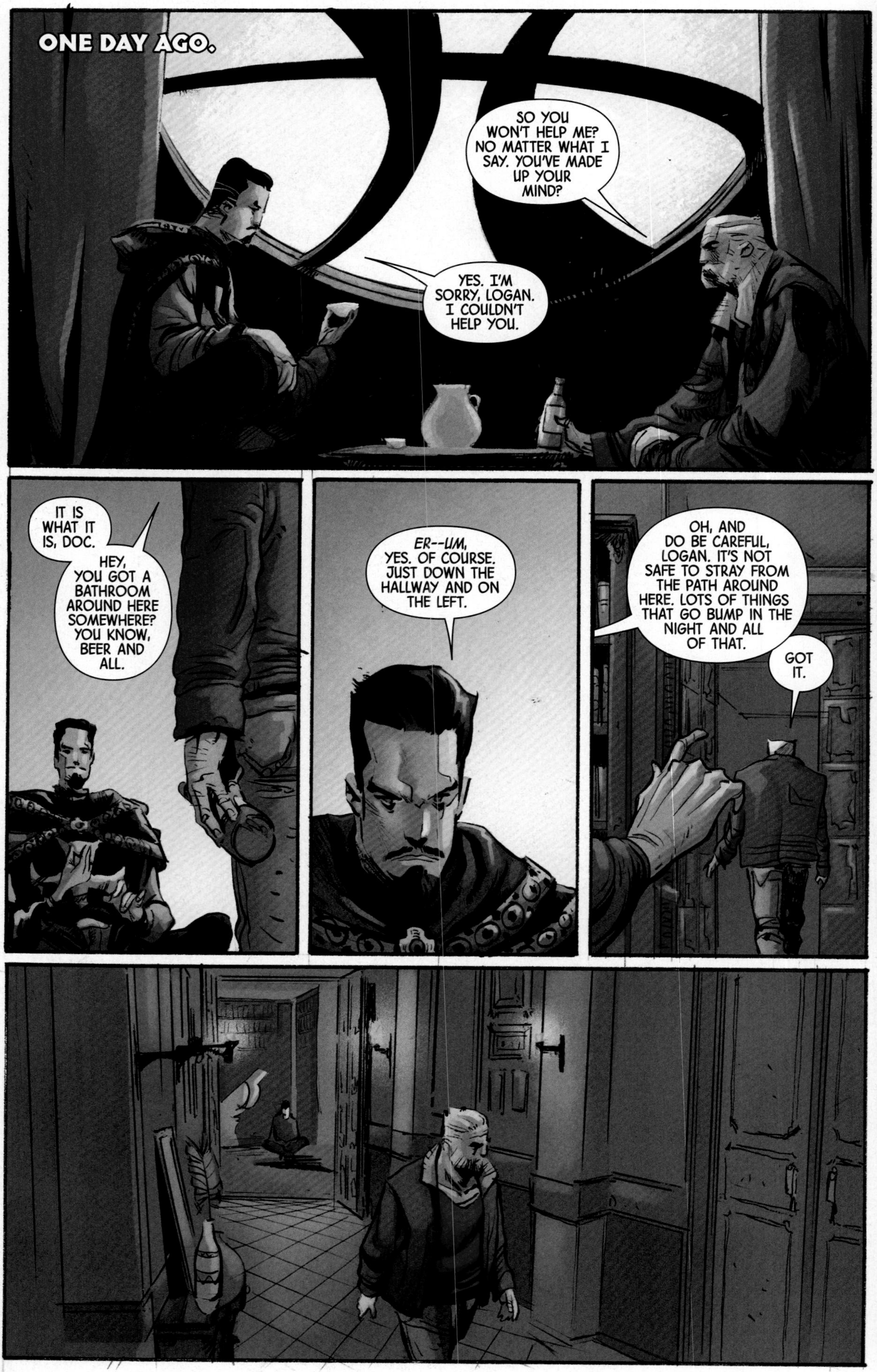
ONE DAY AGO.
SO YOU WON'T HELP ME? NO MATTER WHAT I SAY. YOU'VE MADE UP YOUR MIND?
YES. I'M SORRY, LOGAN. I COULDN'T HELP YOU.
IT IS WHAT IT IS, DOC.
HEY, YOU GOT A BATHROOM AROUND HERE SOMEWHERE? YOU KNOW, BEER AND ALL.
ER--UM, YES. OF COURSE. JUST DOWN THE HALLWAY AND ON THE LEFT.
OH, AND DO BE CAREFUL, LOGAN. IT'S NOT SAFE TO STRAY FROM THE PATH AROUND HERE. LOTS OF THINGS THAT GO BUMP IN THE NIGHT AND ALL OF THAT.
GOT IT.

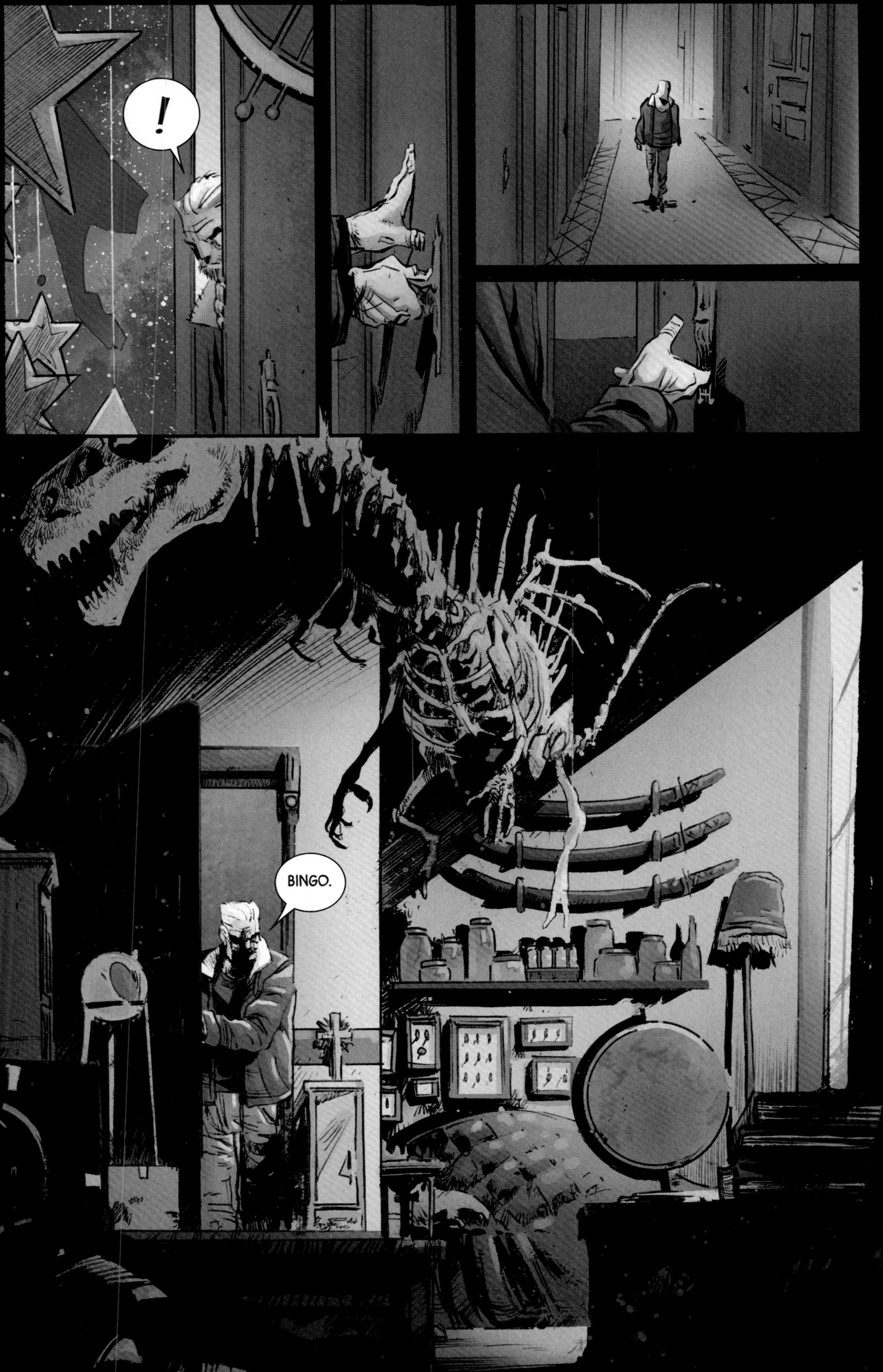
!
BINGO.

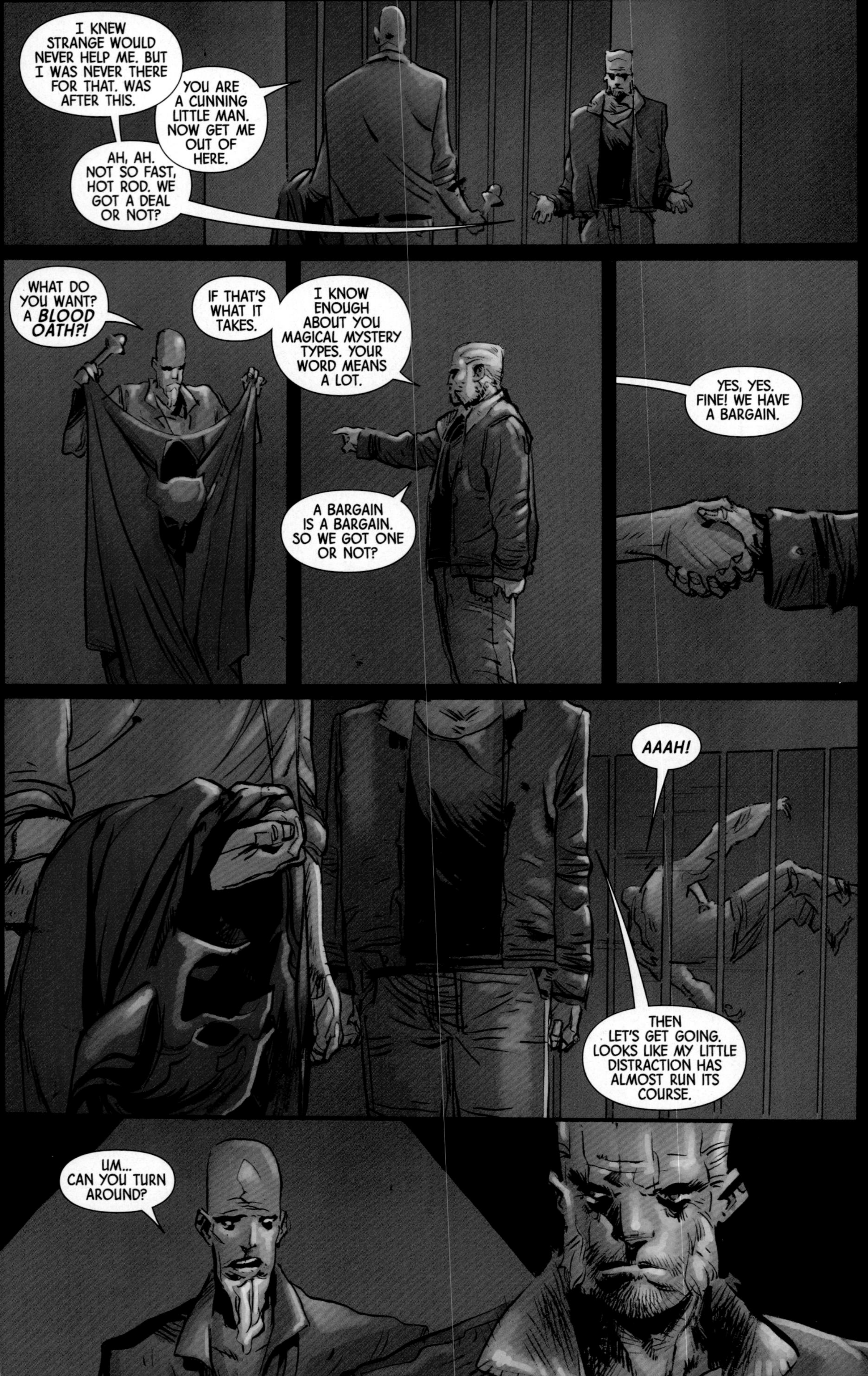
I KNEW STRANGE WOULD NEVER HELP ME. BUT I WAS NEVER THERE FOR THAT. WAS AFTER THIS.
YOU ARE A CUNNING LITTLE MAN. NOW GET ME OUT OF HERE.
AH, AH. NOT SO FAST, HOT ROD. WE GOT A DEAL OR NOT?
WHAT DO YOU WANT? A BLOOD OATH?!
IF THAT'S WHAT IT TAKES.
I KNOW ENOUGH ABOUT YOU MAGICAL MYSTERY TYPES. YOUR WORD MEANS A LOT.
A BARGAIN IS A BARGAIN. SO WE GOT ONE OR NOT?
YES, YES. FINE! WE HAVE A BARGAIN.
AAAH!
THEN LET'S GET GOING. LOOKS LIKE MY LITTLE DISTRACTION HAS ALMOST RUN ITS COURSE.
UM... CAN YOU TURN AROUND?

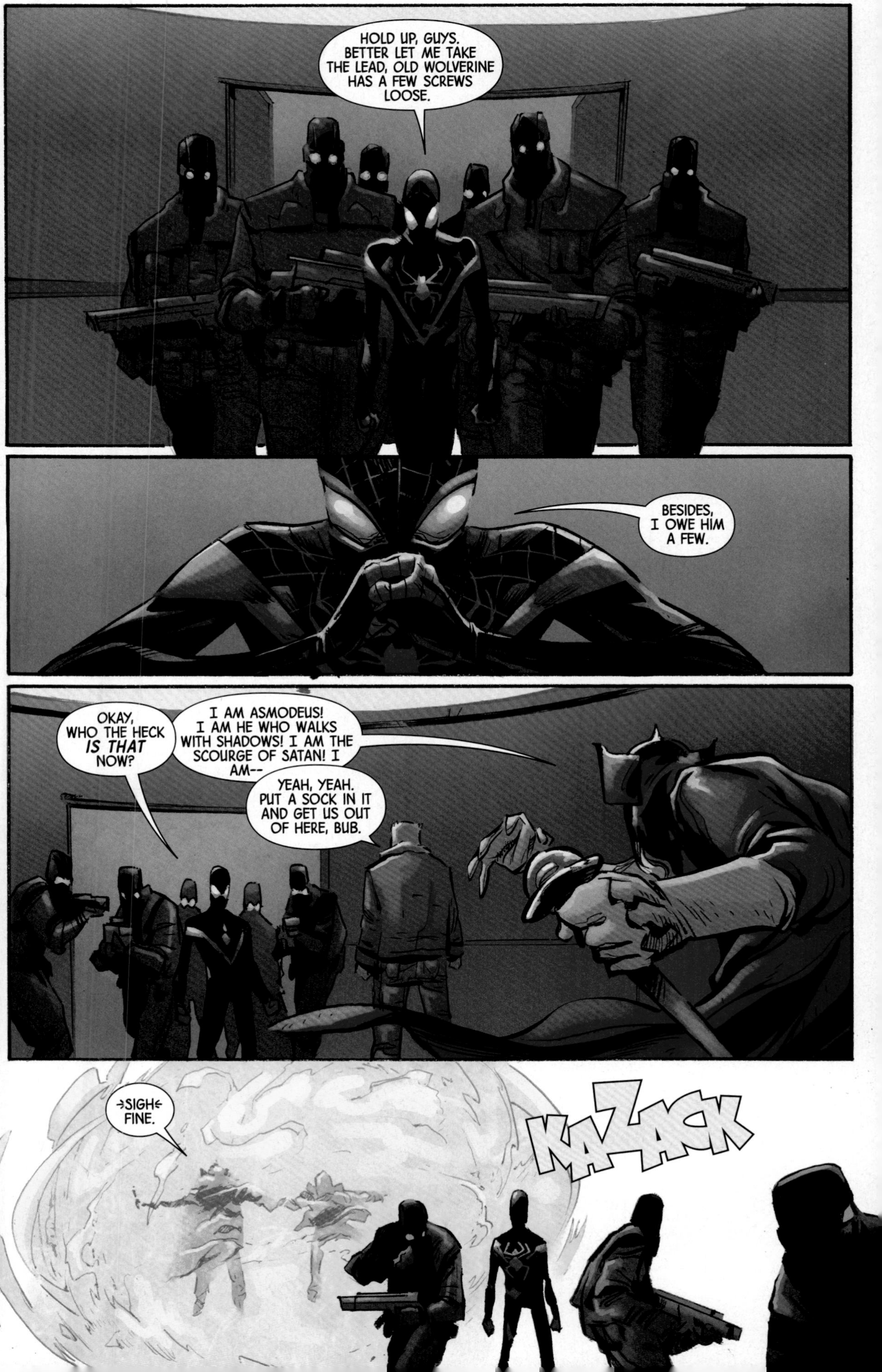
HOLD UP, GUYS. BETTER LET ME TAKE THE LEAD, OLD WOLVERINE HAS A FEW SCREWS LOOSE.
BESIDES, I OWE HIM A FEW.
OKAY, WHO THE HECK *IS THAT* NOW?
I AM ASMODEUS! I AM HE WHO WALKS WITH SHADOWS! I AM THE SCOURGE OF SATAN! I AM--
YEAH, YEAH. PUT A SOCK IN IT AND GET US OUT OF HERE, BUB.
SIGH FINE.
KAZACK

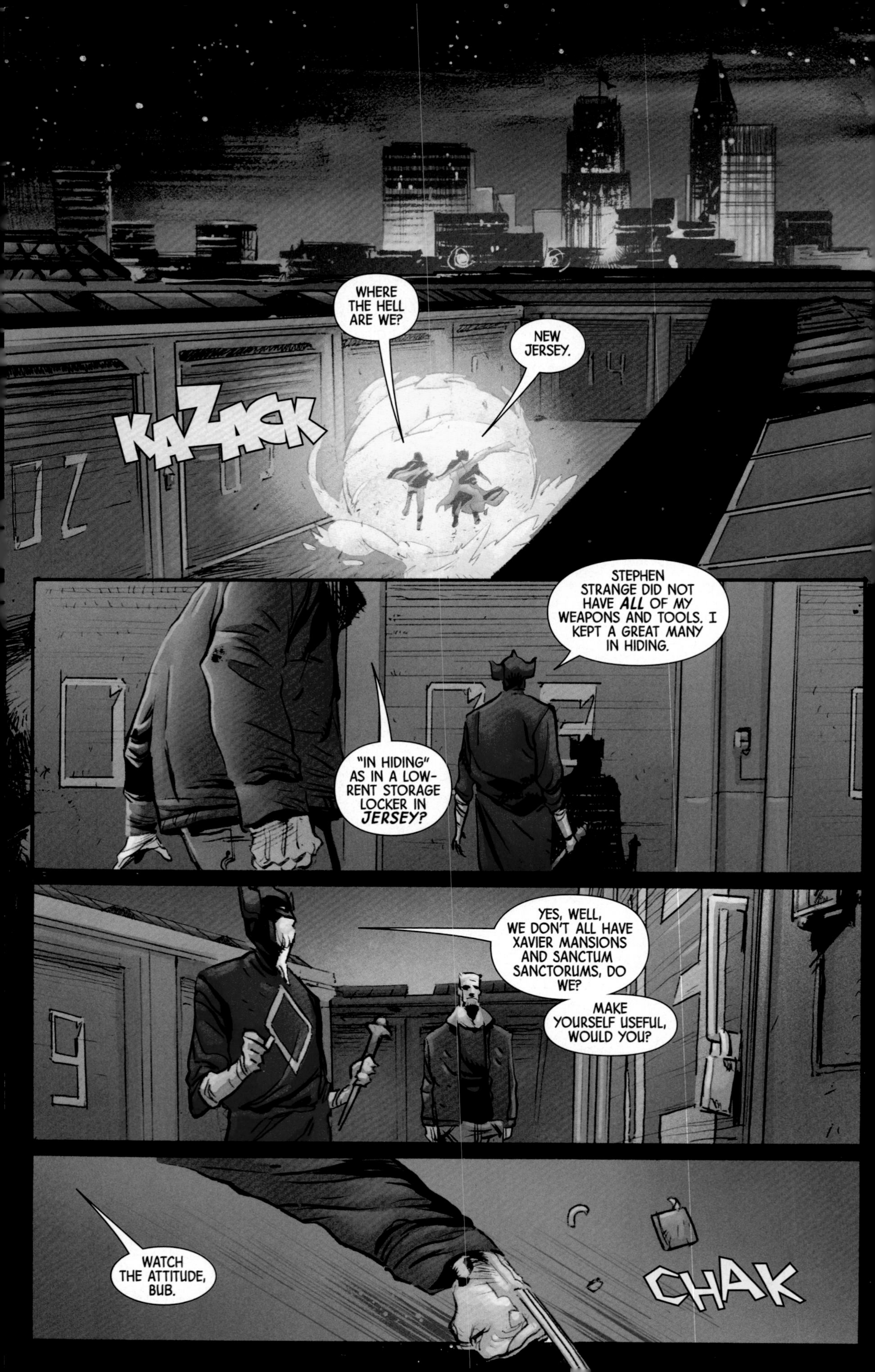
KAZACK
WHERE THE HELL ARE WE?
NEW JERSEY.
STEPHEN STRANGE DID NOT HAVE *ALL* OF MY WEAPONS AND TOOLS. I KEPT A GREAT MANY IN HIDING.
"IN HIDING" AS IN A LOW-RENT STORAGE LOCKER IN *JERSEY?*
YES, WELL, WE DON'T ALL HAVE XAVIER MANSIONS AND SANCTUM SANCTORUMS, DO WE?
MAKE YOURSELF USEFUL, WOULD YOU?
WATCH THE ATTITUDE, BUB.
CHAK

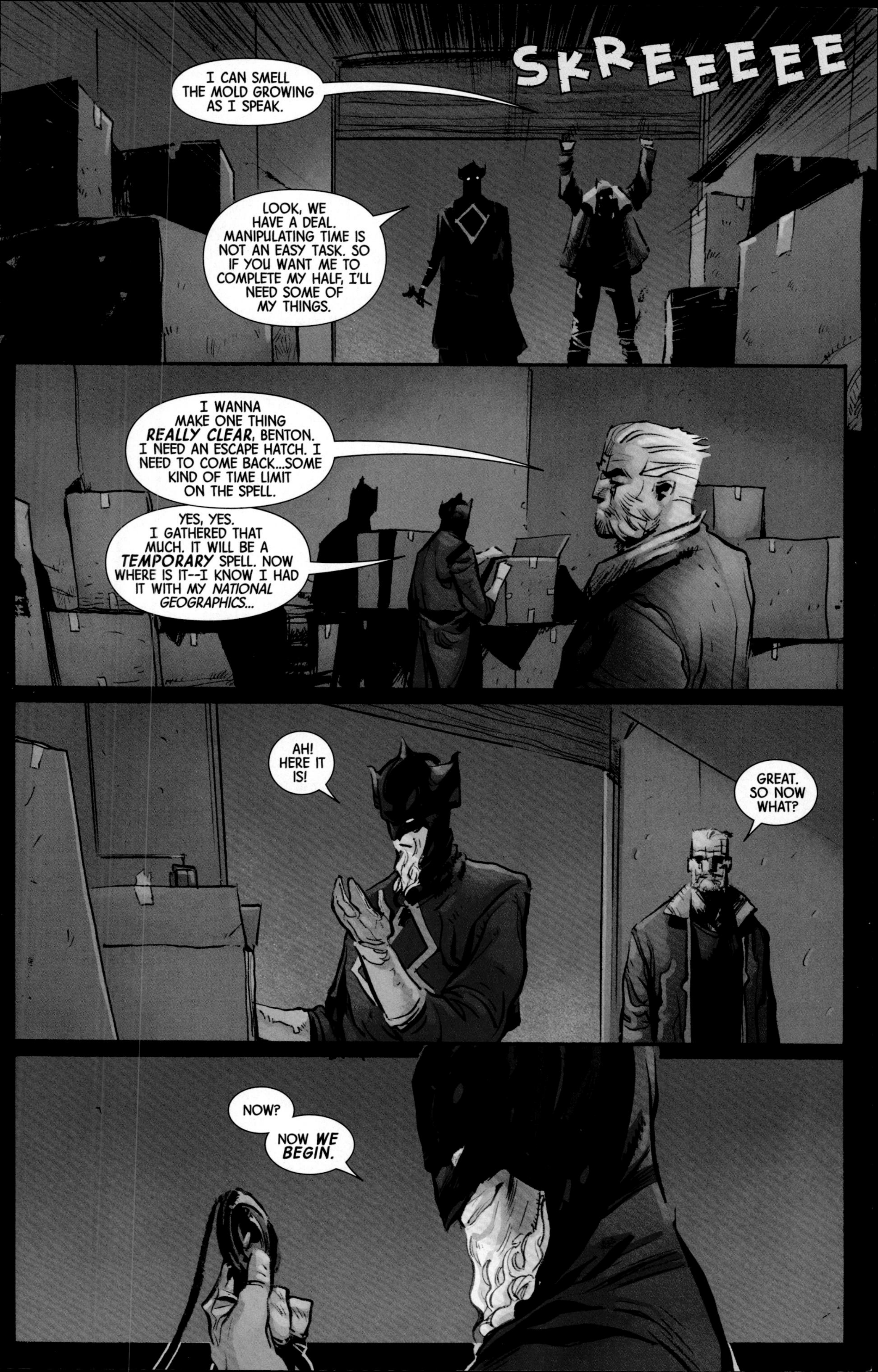

SKREEEEEE
I CAN SMELL THE MOLD GROWING AS I SPEAK.
LOOK, WE HAVE A DEAL. MANIPULATING TIME IS NOT AN EASY TASK. SO IF YOU WANT ME TO COMPLETE MY HALF, I'LL NEED SOME OF MY THINGS.
I WANNA MAKE ONE THING REALLY CLEAR, BENTON. I NEED AN ESCAPE HATCH. I NEED TO COME BACK...SOME KIND OF TIME LIMIT ON THE SPELL.
YES, YES. I GATHERED THAT MUCH. IT WILL BE A TEMPORARY SPELL. NOW WHERE IS IT--I KNOW I HAD IT WITH MY NATIONAL GEOGRAPHICS...
AH! HERE IT IS!
GREAT. SO NOW WHAT?
NOW?
NOW WE BEGIN.

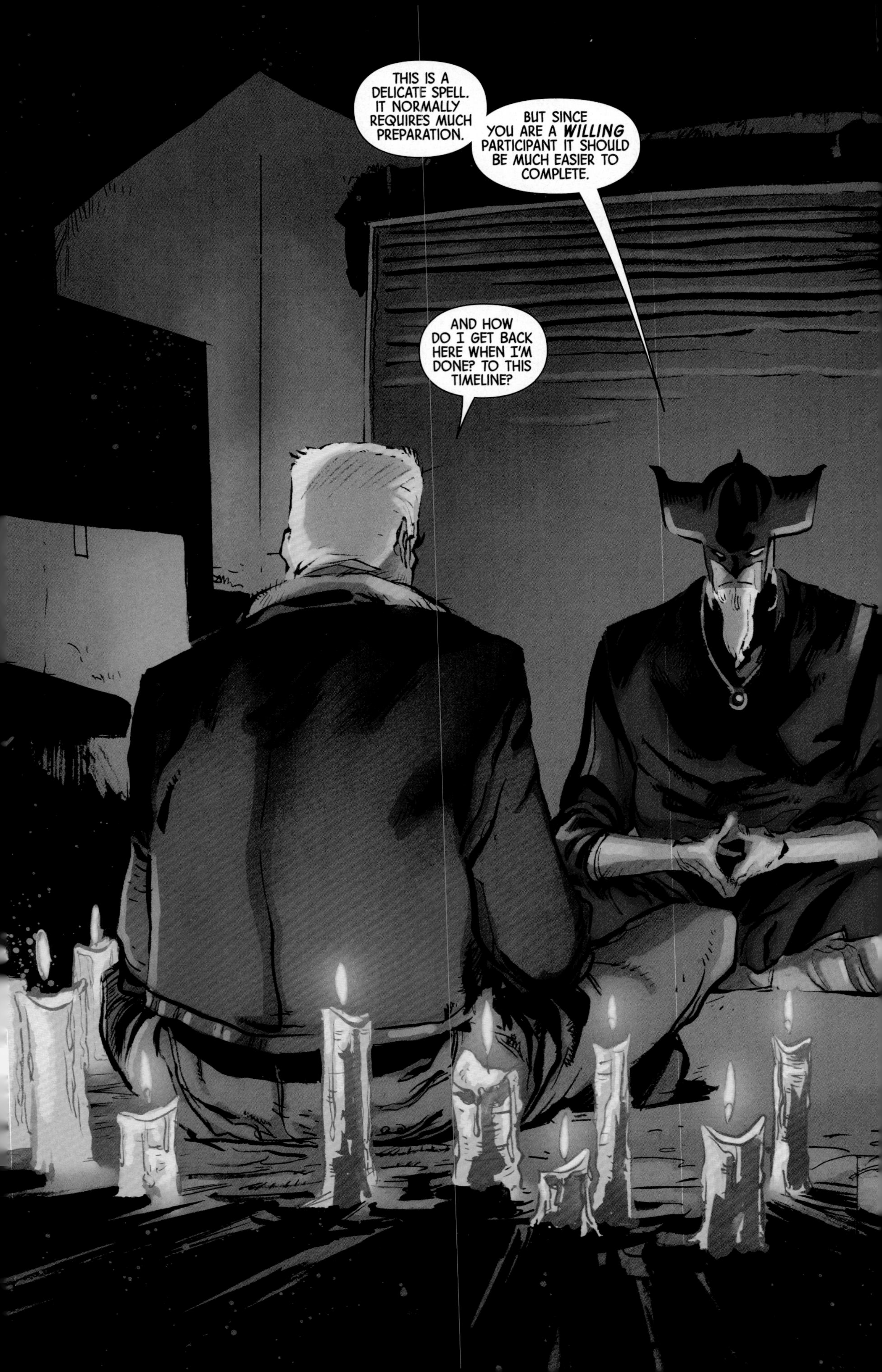
THIS IS A DELICATE SPELL. IT NORMALLY REQUIRES MUCH PREPARATION.
BUT SINCE YOU ARE A *WILLING* PARTICIPANT IT SHOULD BE MUCH EASIER TO COMPLETE.
AND HOW DO I GET BACK HERE WHEN I'M DONE? TO THIS TIMELINE?

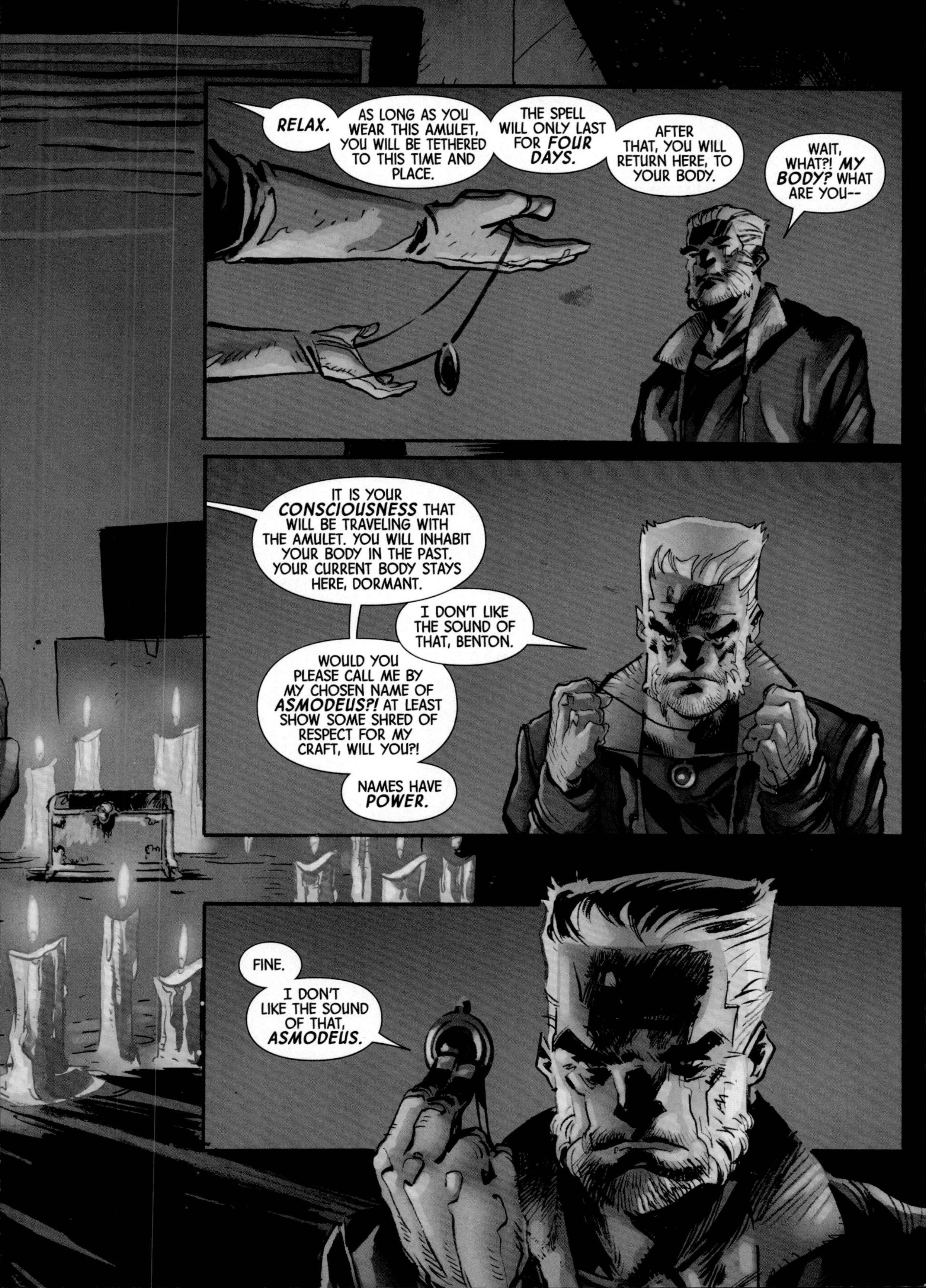
RELAX.
AS LONG AS YOU WEAR THIS AMULET, YOU WILL BE TETHERED TO THIS TIME AND PLACE.
THE SPELL WILL ONLY LAST FOR FOUR DAYS.
AFTER THAT, YOU WILL RETURN HERE, TO YOUR BODY.
WAIT, WHAT?! MY BODY? WHAT ARE YOU--
IT IS YOUR CONSCIOUSNESS THAT WILL BE TRAVELING WITH THE AMULET. YOU WILL INHABIT YOUR BODY IN THE PAST. YOUR CURRENT BODY STAYS HERE, DORMANT.
I DON'T LIKE THE SOUND OF THAT, BENTON.
WOULD YOU PLEASE CALL ME BY MY CHOSEN NAME OF ASMODEUS?! AT LEAST SHOW SOME SHRED OF RESPECT FOR MY CRAFT, WILL YOU?!
NAMES HAVE POWER.
FINE.
I DON'T LIKE THE SOUND OF THAT, ASMODEUS.

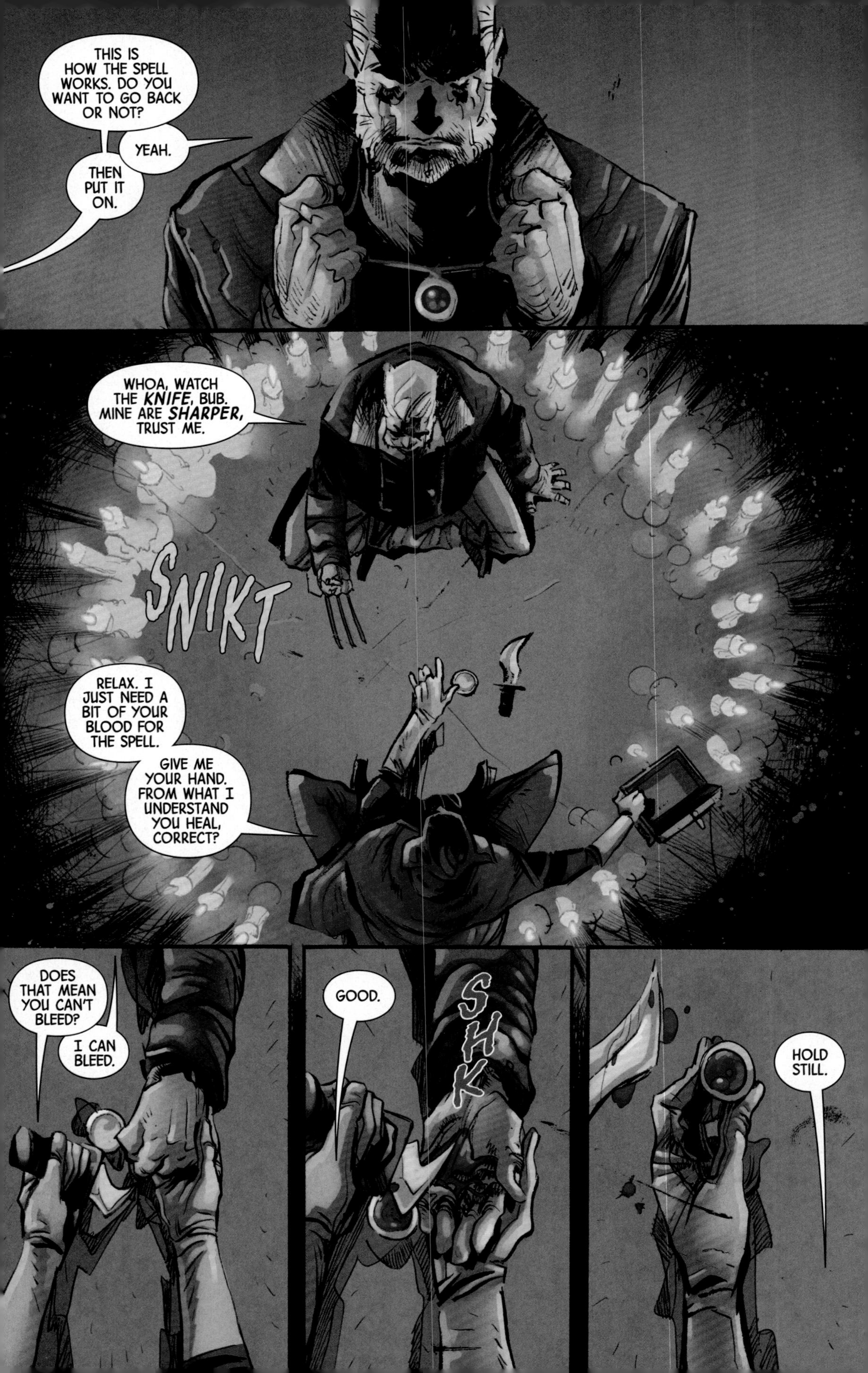
THIS IS HOW THE SPELL WORKS. DO YOU WANT TO GO BACK OR NOT?
YEAH.
THEN PUT IT ON.
WHOA, WATCH THE KNIFE, BUB. MINE ARE SHARPER, TRUST ME.
SNIKT
RELAX. I JUST NEED A BIT OF YOUR BLOOD FOR THE SPELL.
GIVE ME YOUR HAND. FROM WHAT I UNDERSTAND YOU HEAL, CORRECT?
DOES THAT MEAN YOU CAN'T BLEED?
I CAN BLEED.
GOOD.
SHK
HOLD STILL.

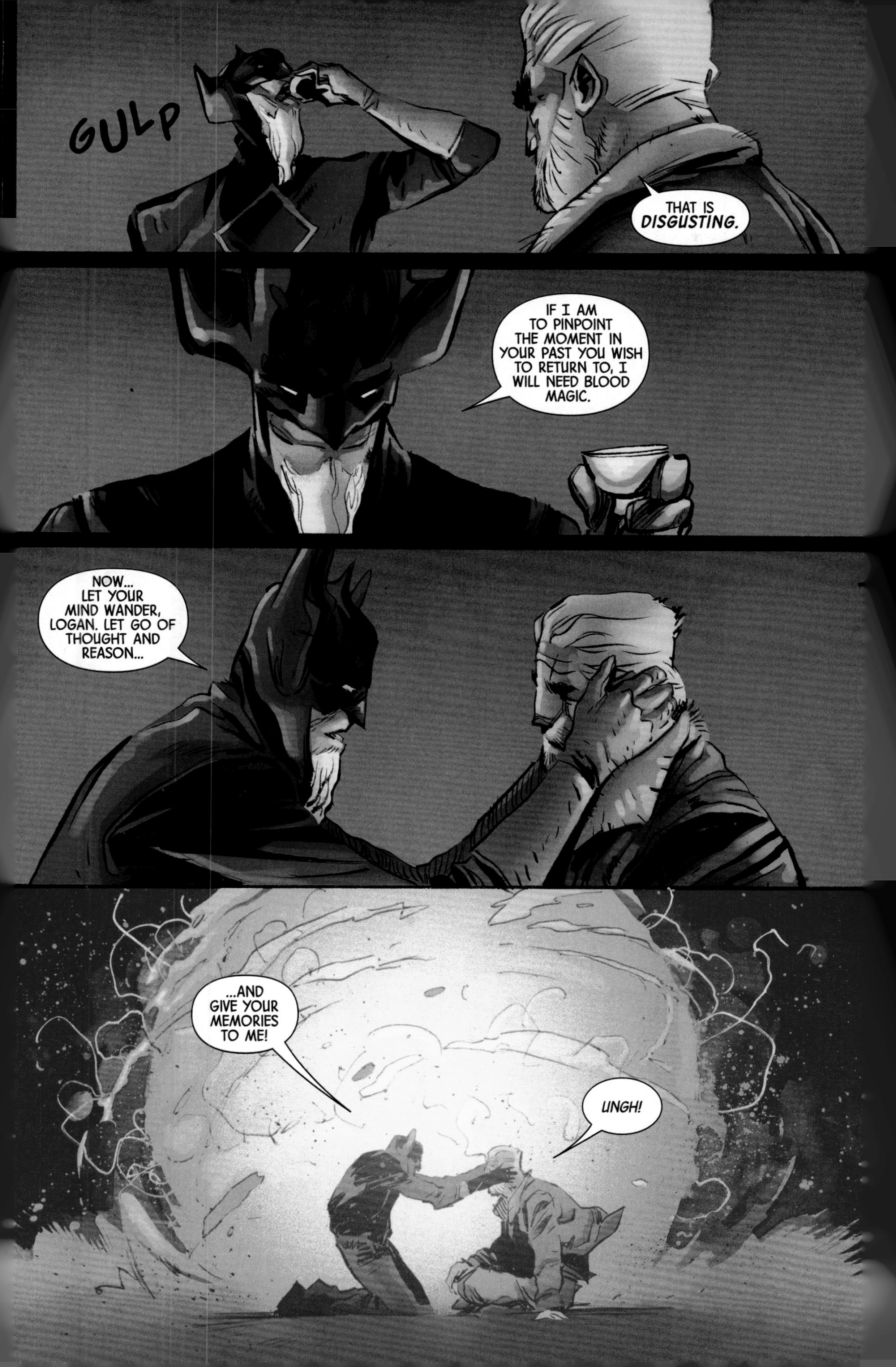
GULP
THAT IS DISGUSTING.
IF I AM TO PINPOINT THE MOMENT IN YOUR PAST YOU WISH TO RETURN TO, I WILL NEED BLOOD MAGIC.
NOW... LET YOUR MIND WANDER, LOGAN. LET GO OF THOUGHT AND REASON...
...AND GIVE YOUR MEMORIES TO ME!
UNGH!

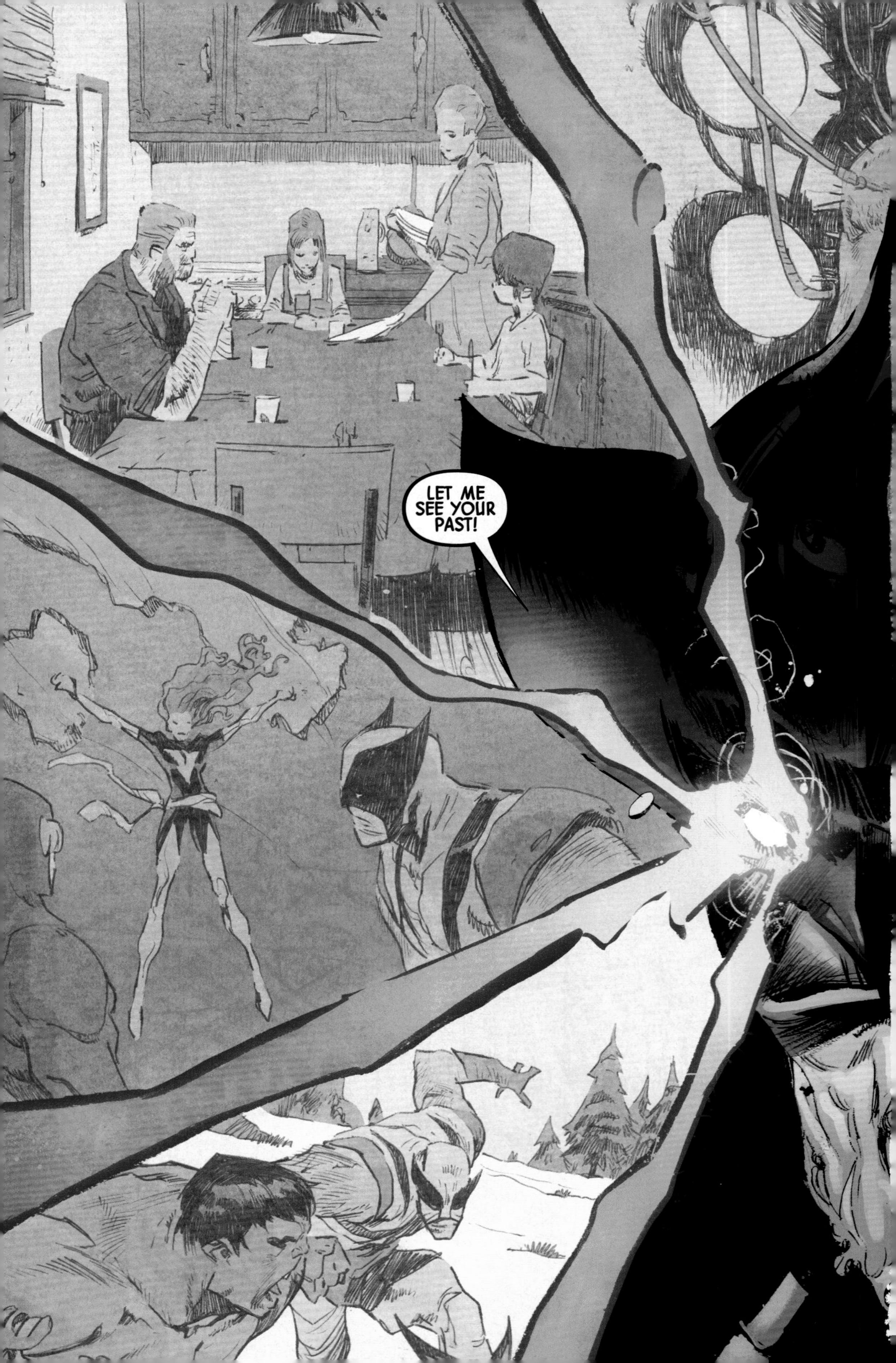
LET ME SEE YOUR PAST!

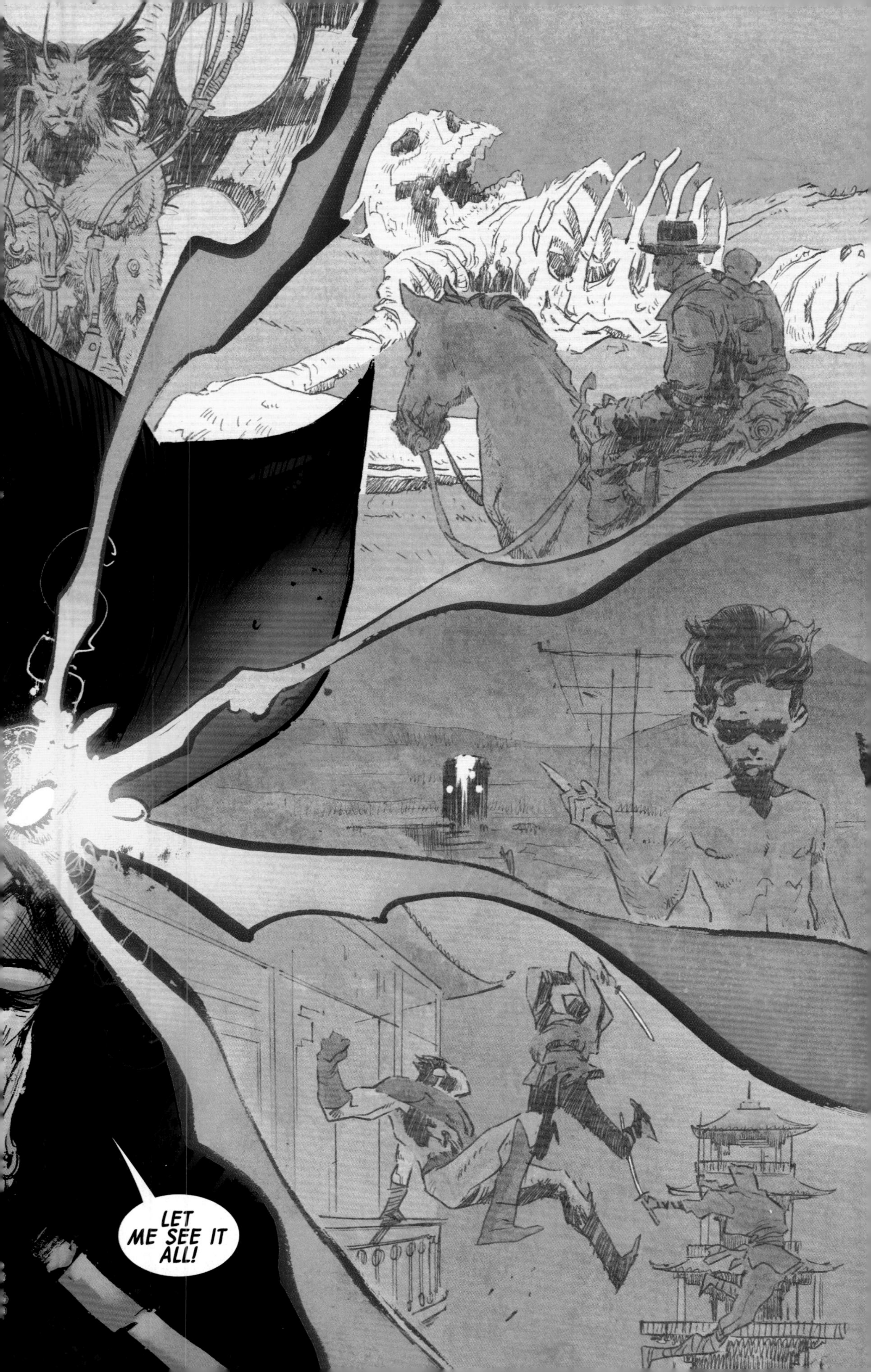
LET ME SEE IT ALL!

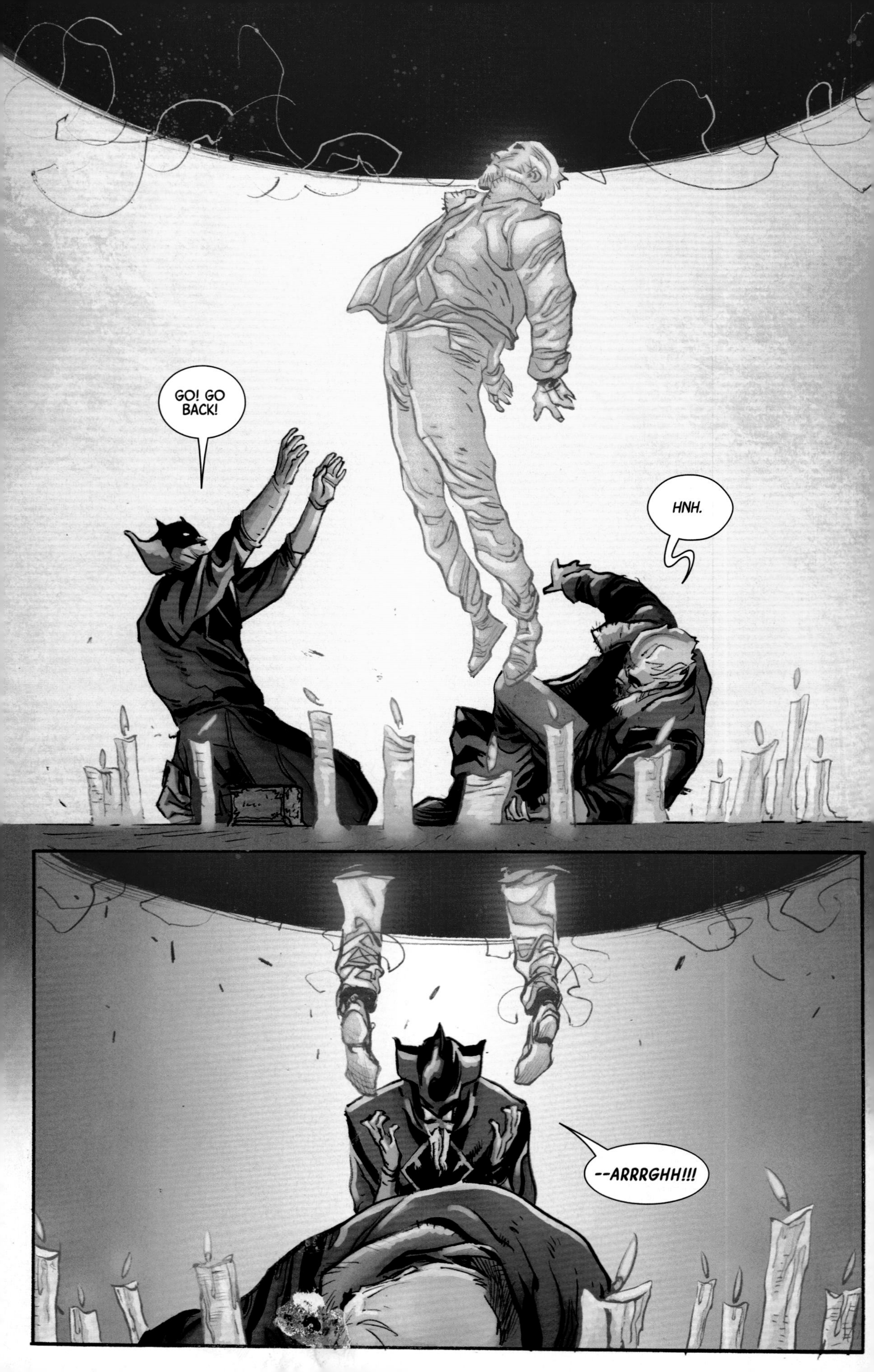
GO! GO BACK!
HNH.
--ARRRGHH!!!

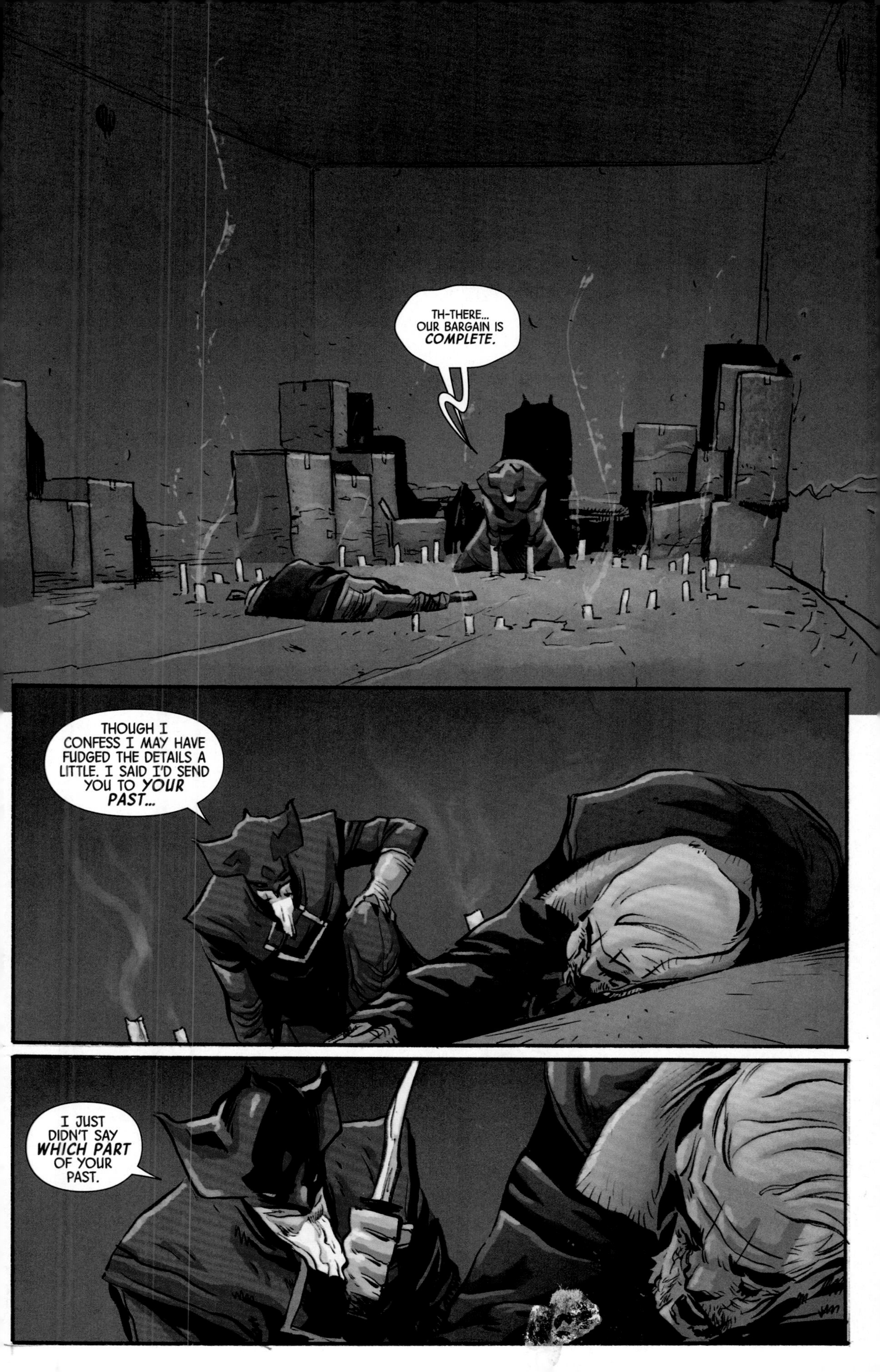
TH-THERE... OUR BARGAIN IS COMPLETE.
THOUGH I CONFESS I MAY HAVE FUDGED THE DETAILS A LITTLE. I SAID I'D SEND YOU TO YOUR PAST...
I JUST DIDN'T SAY WHICH PART OF YOUR PAST.

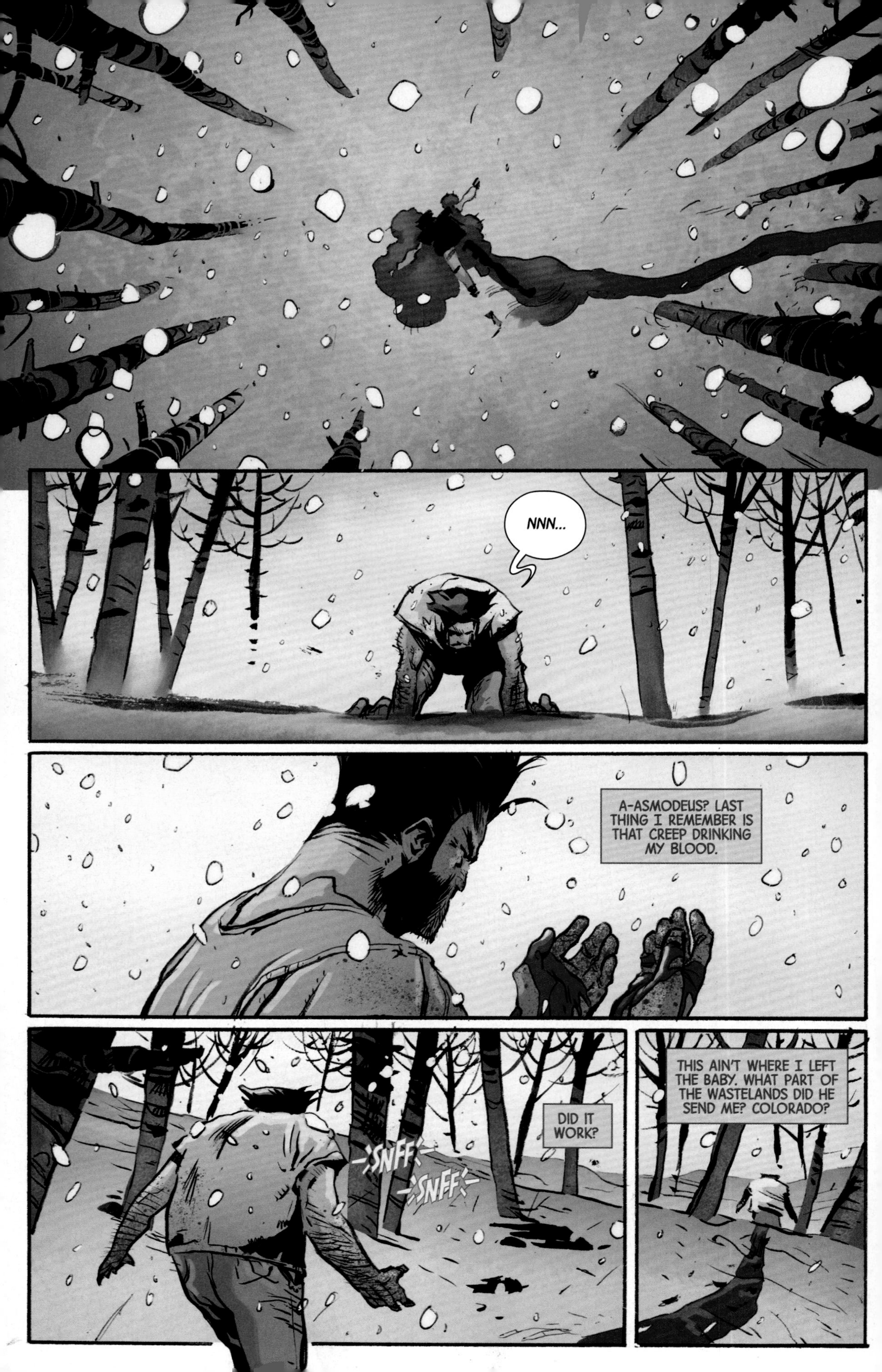
NNN...
A-ASMODEUS? LAST THING I REMEMBER IS THAT CREEP DRINKING MY BLOOD.
DID IT WORK?
SNFF
SNFF
THIS AIN'T WHERE I LEFT THE BABY. WHAT PART OF THE WASTELANDS DID HE SEND ME? COLORADO?

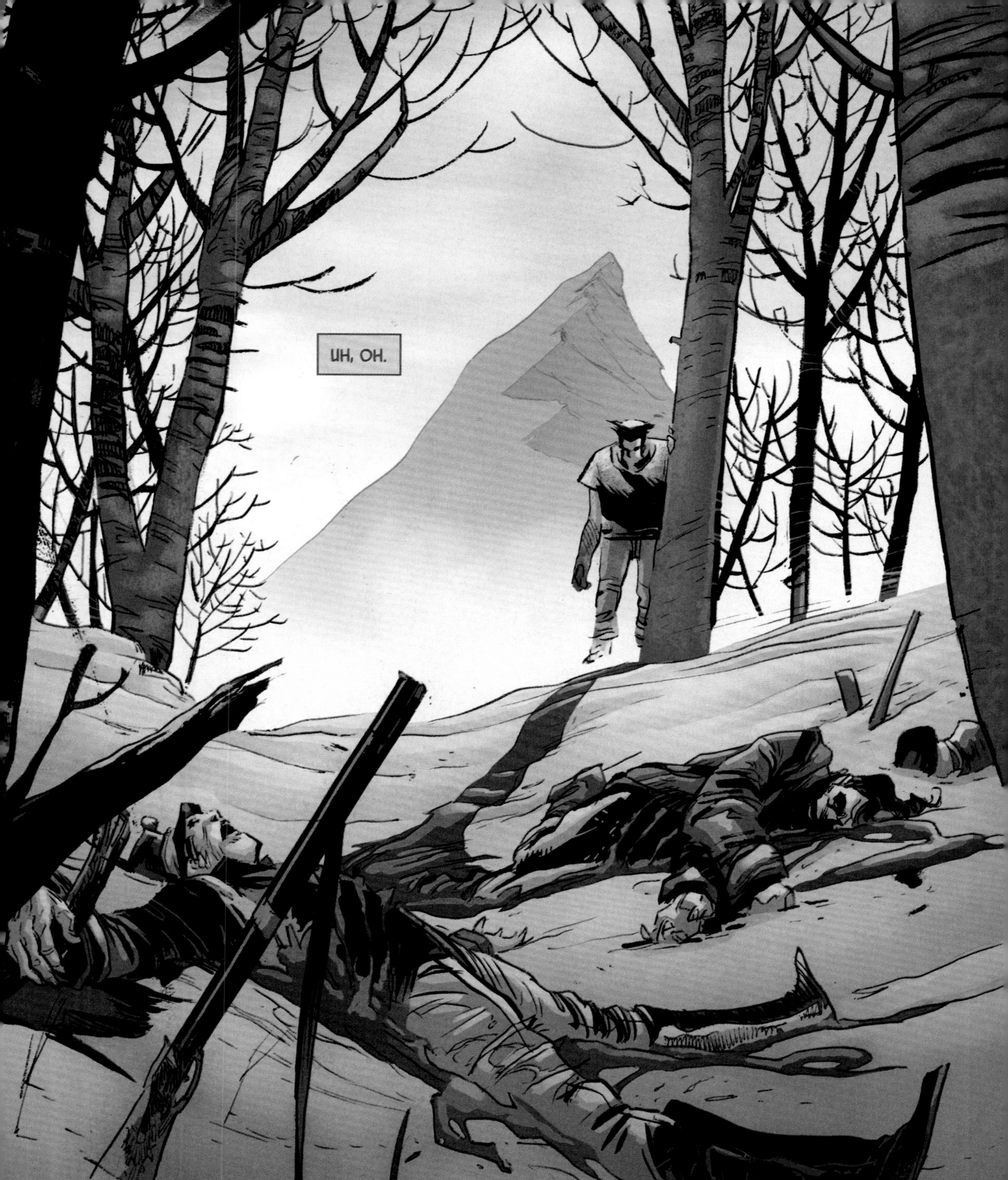
UH, OH.

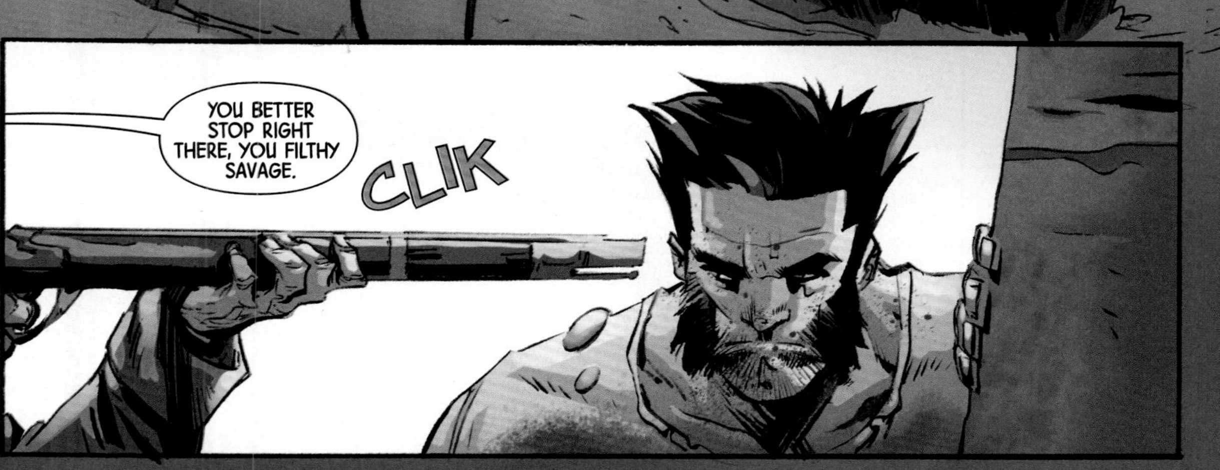
YOU BETTER STOP RIGHT THERE, YOU FILTHY SAVAGE.
CLIK

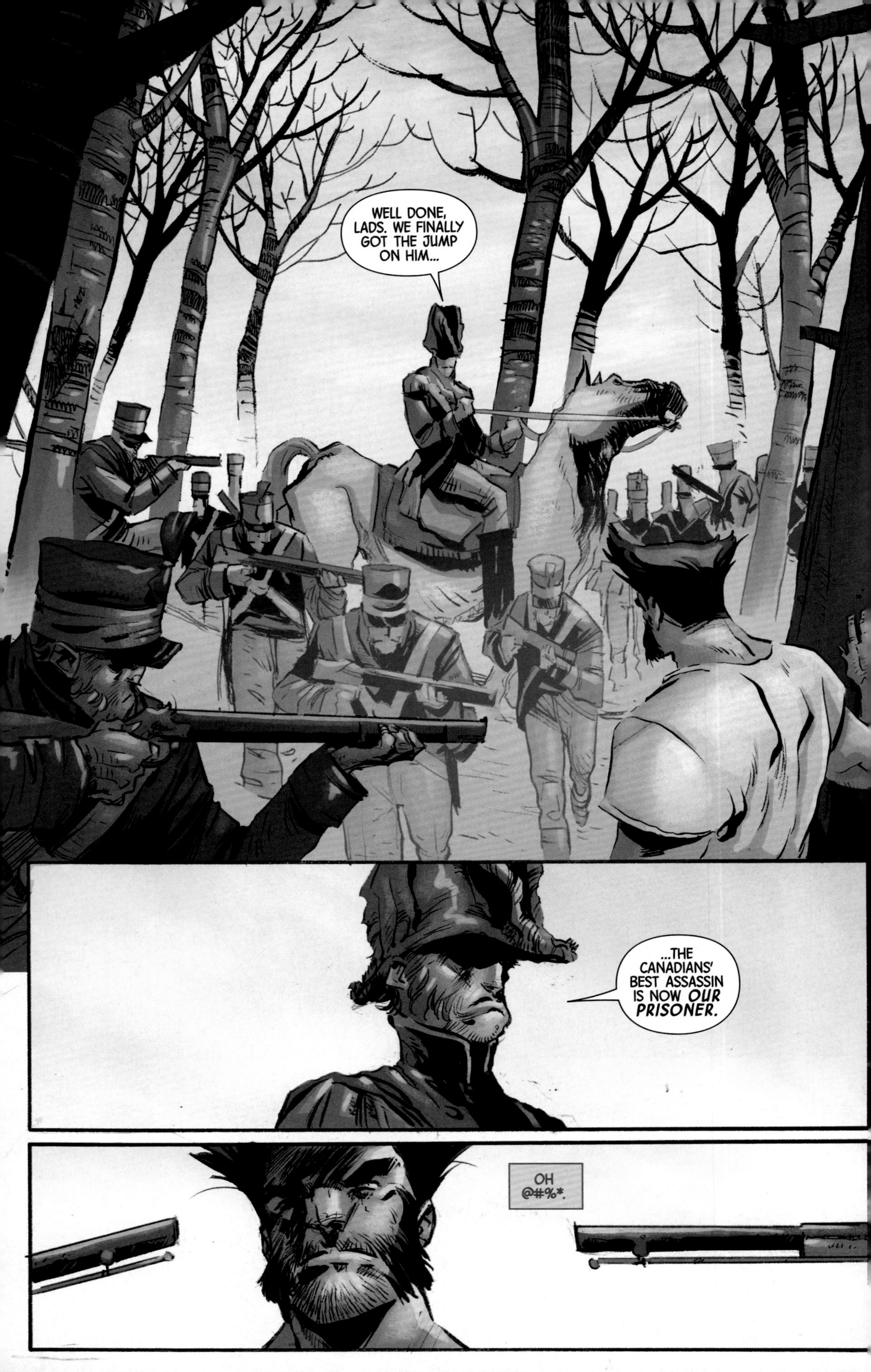
WELL DONE, LADS. WE FINALLY GOT THE JUMP ON HIM...
...THE CANADIANS' BEST ASSASSIN IS NOW *OUR PRISONER.*
OH @#%*.

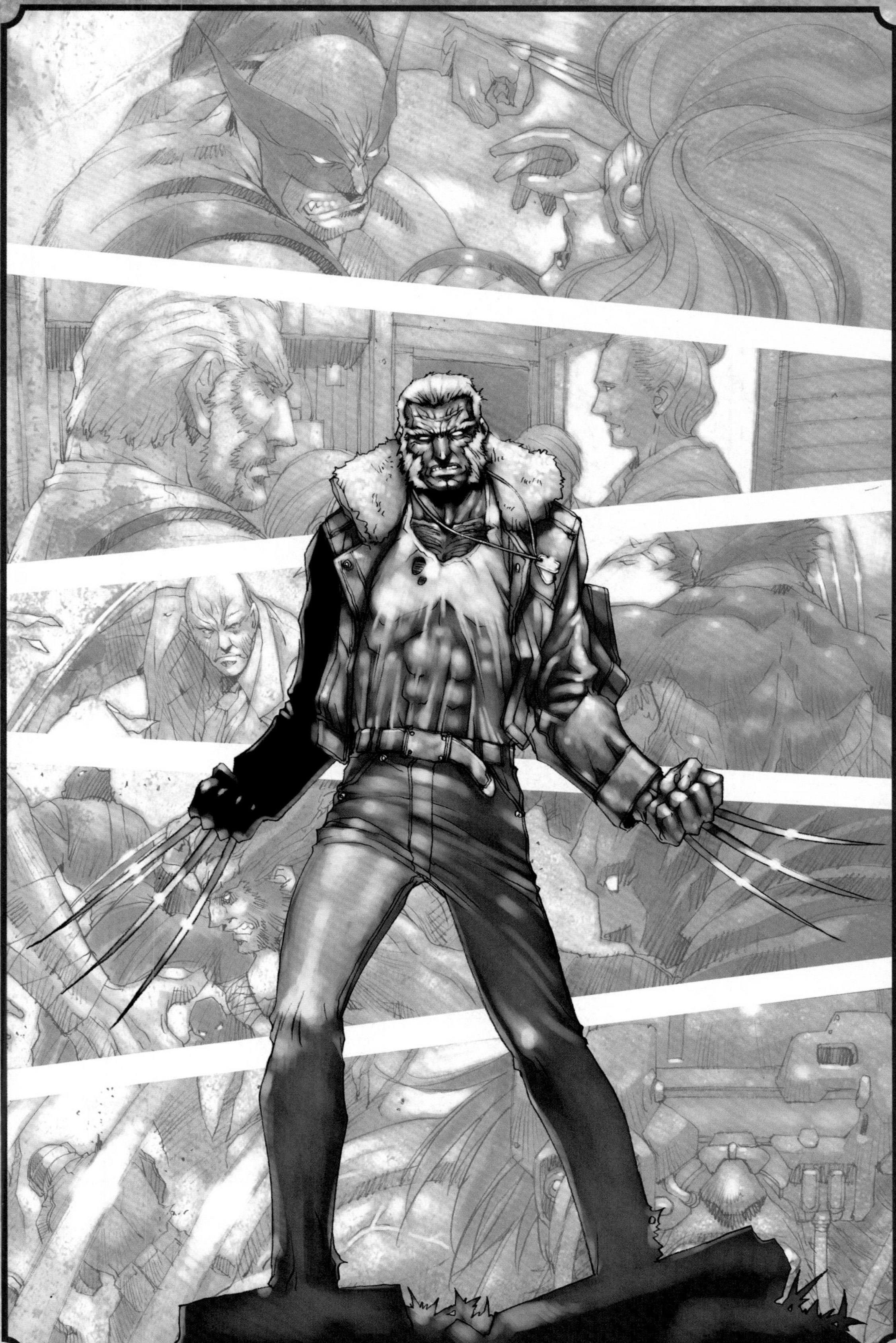

#19 VARIANT
BY KIA ASAMIYA

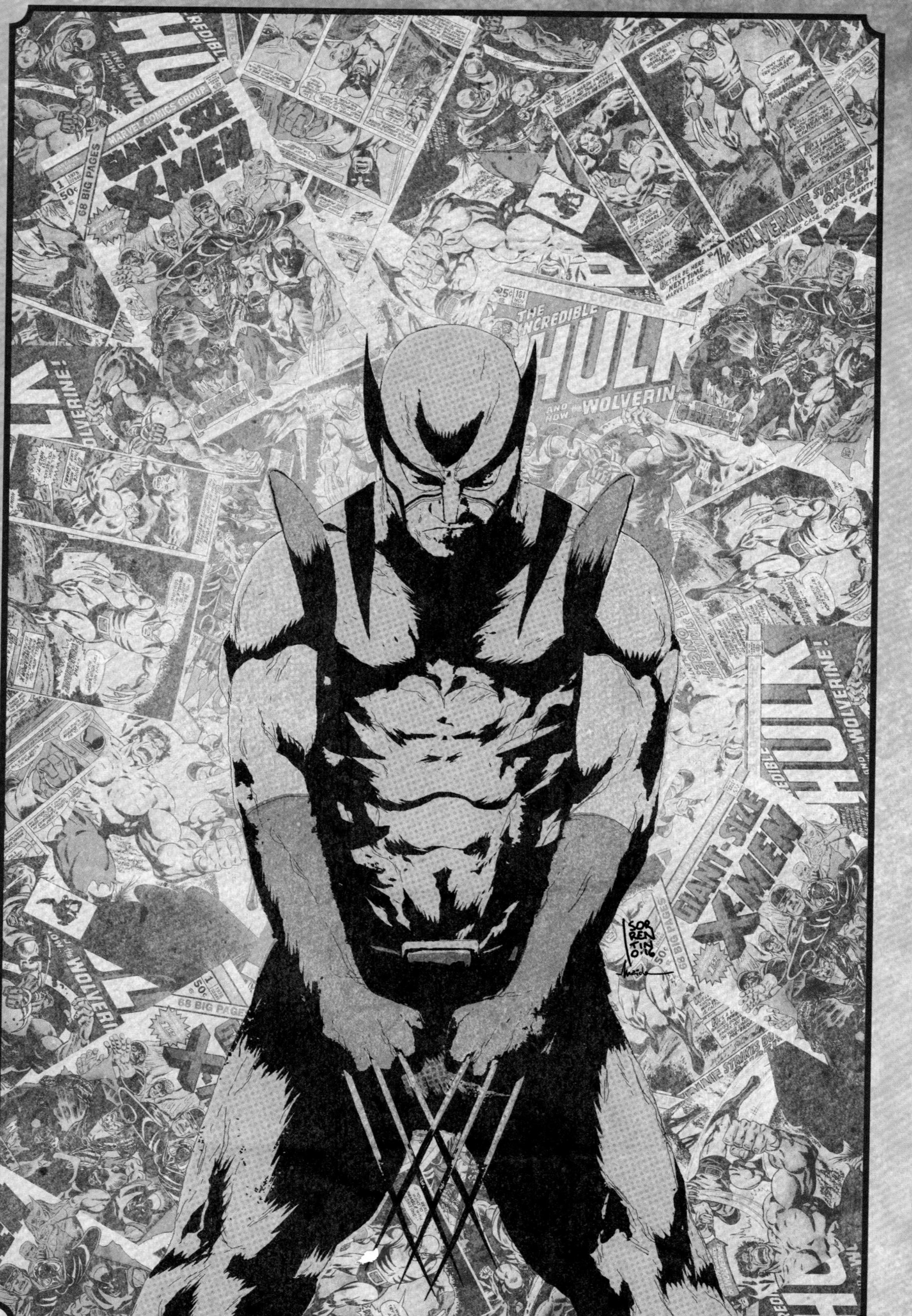
MARVEL COMICS GROUP
GIANT-SIZE X-MEN
68 BIG PAGES
THE INCREDIBLE HULK
AND NOW the WOLVERINE
The WOLVERINE STRIKES BUT ONCE!

21

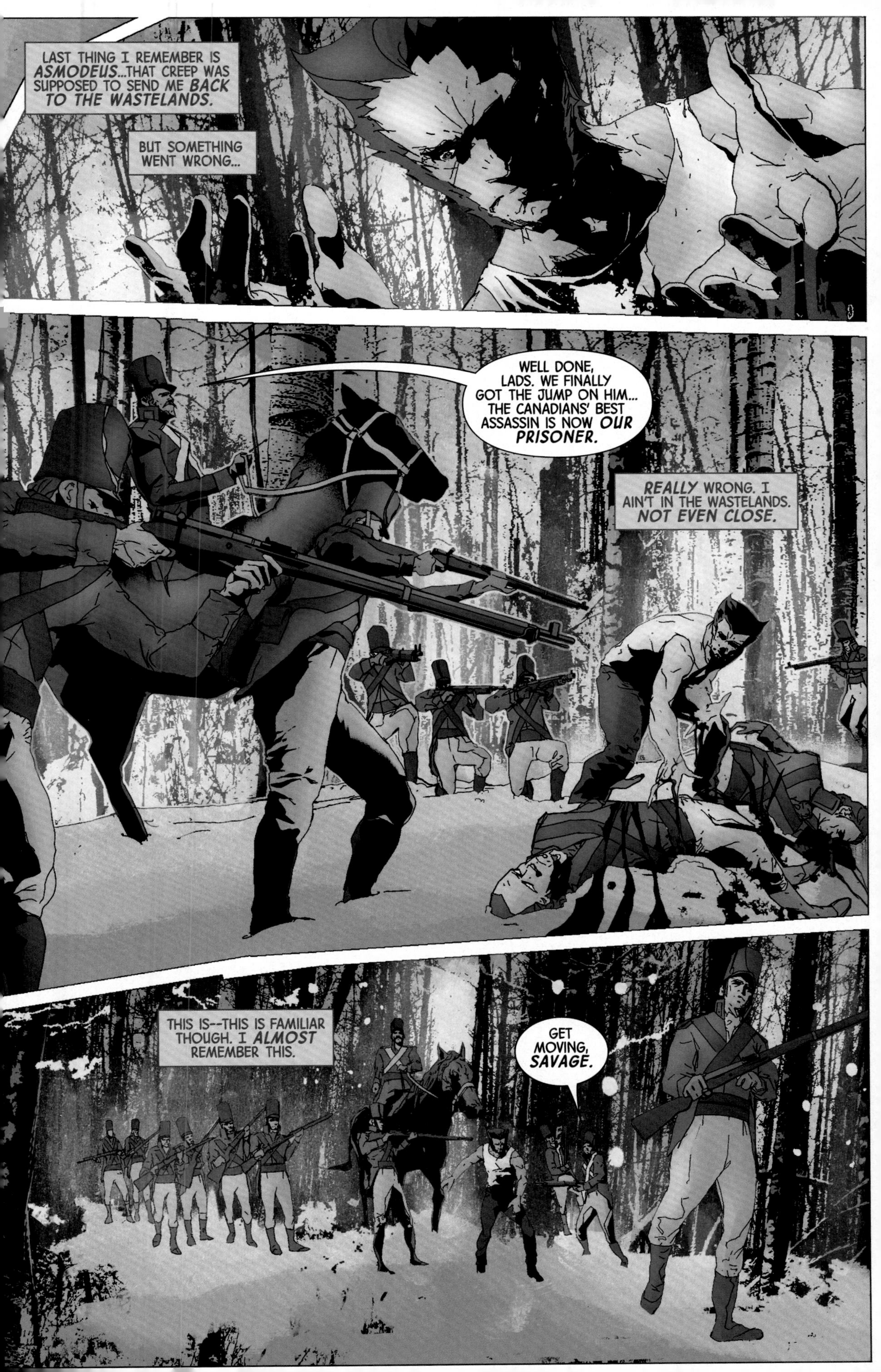
LAST THING I REMEMBER IS ASMODEUS...THAT CREEP WAS SUPPOSED TO SEND ME BACK TO THE WASTELANDS.
BUT SOMETHING WENT WRONG...
WELL DONE, LADS. WE FINALLY GOT THE JUMP ON HIM... THE CANADIANS' BEST ASSASSIN IS NOW OUR PRISONER.
REALLY WRONG. I AIN'T IN THE WASTELANDS. NOT EVEN CLOSE.
THIS IS--THIS IS FAMILIAR THOUGH. I ALMOST REMEMBER THIS.
GET MOVING, SAVAGE.

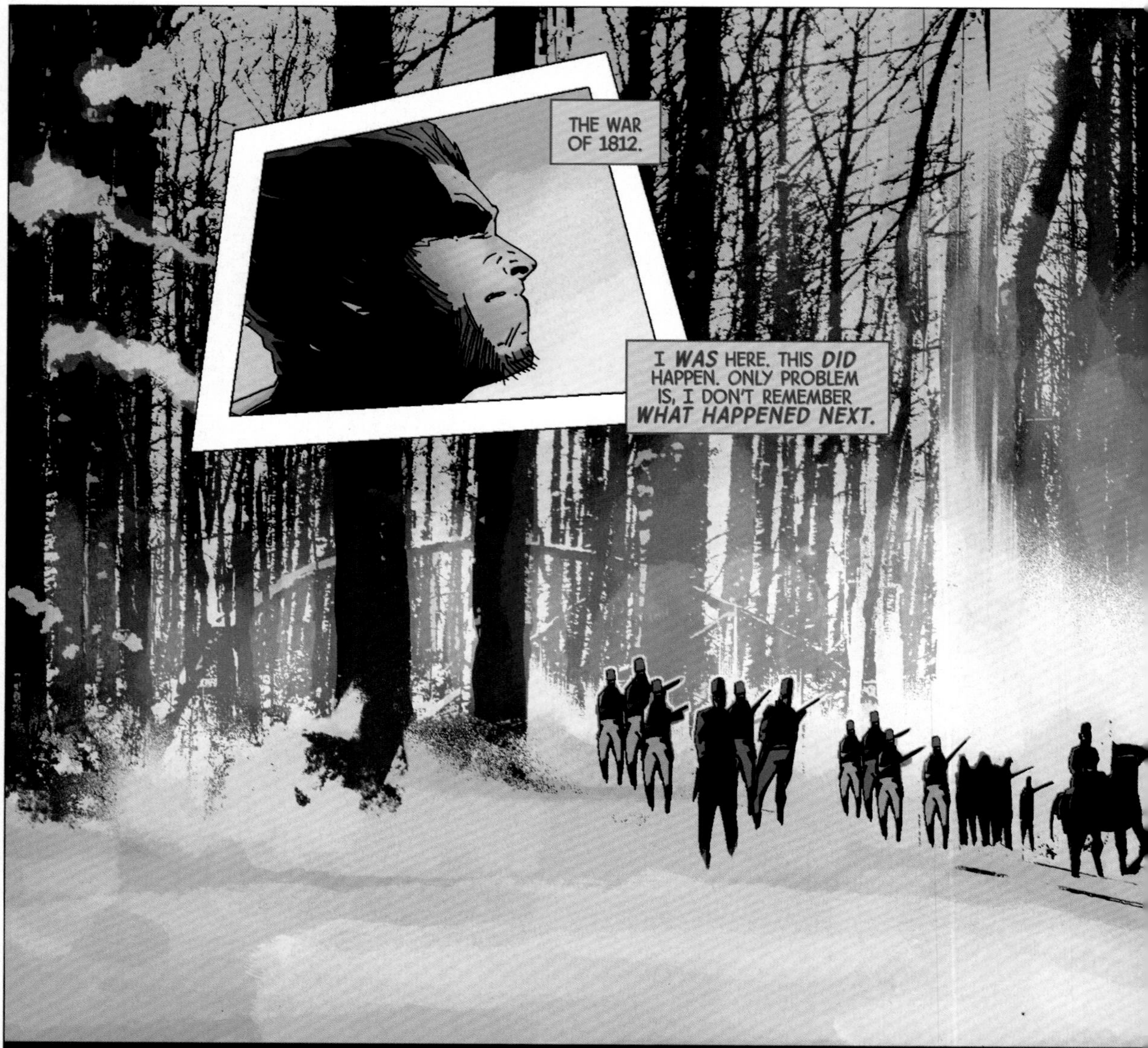
THE WAR OF 1812.
I WAS HERE. THIS DID HAPPEN. ONLY PROBLEM IS, I DON'T REMEMBER WHAT HAPPENED NEXT.

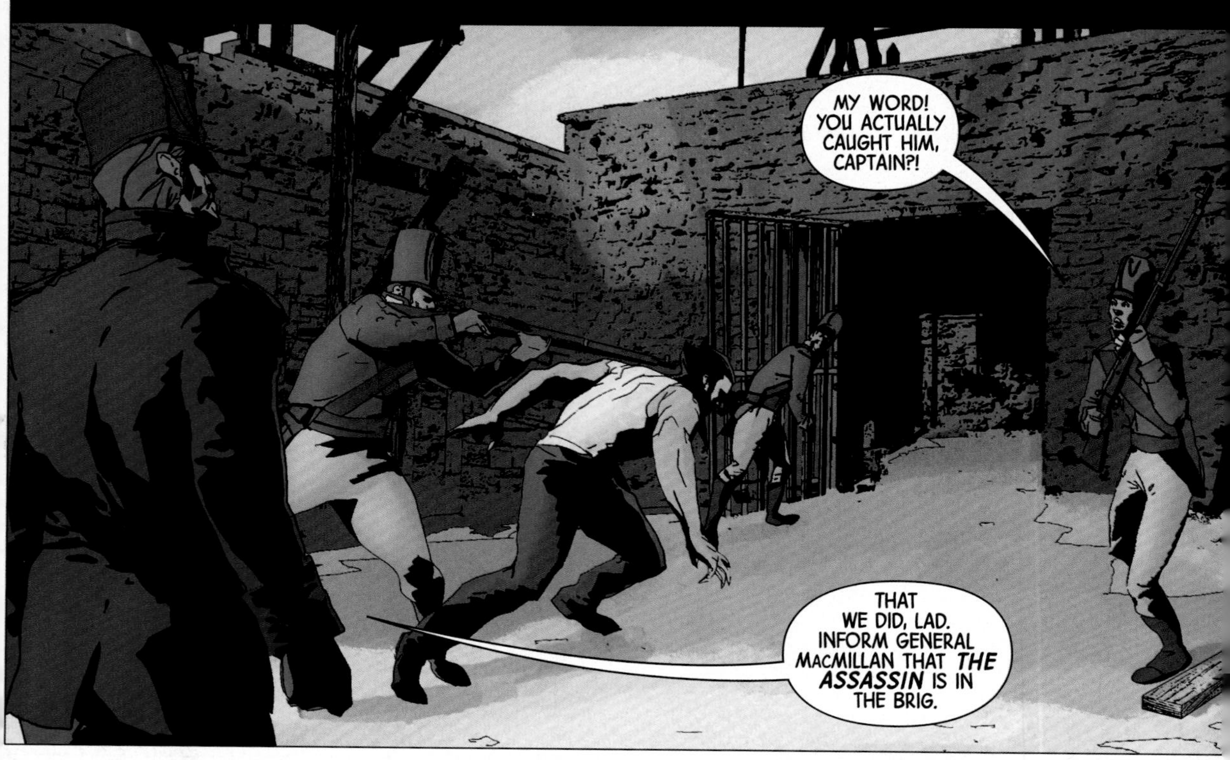
MY WORD! YOU ACTUALLY CAUGHT HIM, CAPTAIN?!
THAT WE DID, LAD. INFORM GENERAL MACMILLAN THAT THE ASSASSIN IS IN THE BRIG.

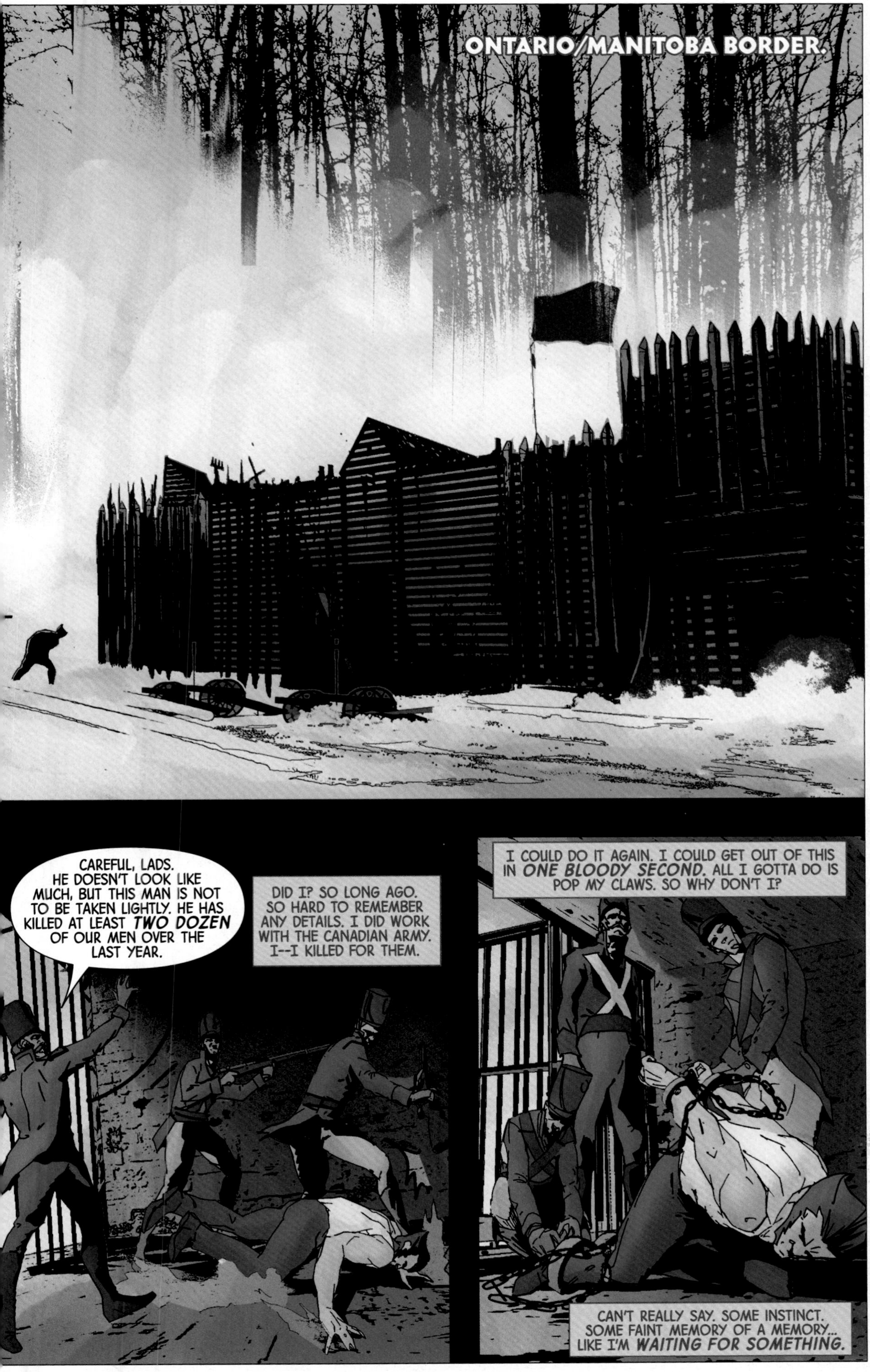
ONTARIO/MANITOBA BORDER.
CAREFUL, LADS. HE DOESN'T LOOK LIKE MUCH, BUT THIS MAN IS NOT TO BE TAKEN LIGHTLY. HE HAS KILLED AT LEAST *TWO DOZEN* OF OUR MEN OVER THE LAST YEAR.
DID I? SO LONG AGO. SO HARD TO REMEMBER ANY DETAILS. I DID WORK WITH THE CANADIAN ARMY. I--I KILLED FOR THEM.
I COULD DO IT AGAIN. I COULD GET OUT OF THIS IN *ONE BLOODY SECOND.* ALL I GOTTA DO IS POP MY CLAWS. SO WHY DON'T I?
CAN'T REALLY SAY. SOME INSTINCT. SOME FAINT MEMORY OF A MEMORY... LIKE I'M *WAITING FOR SOMETHING.*

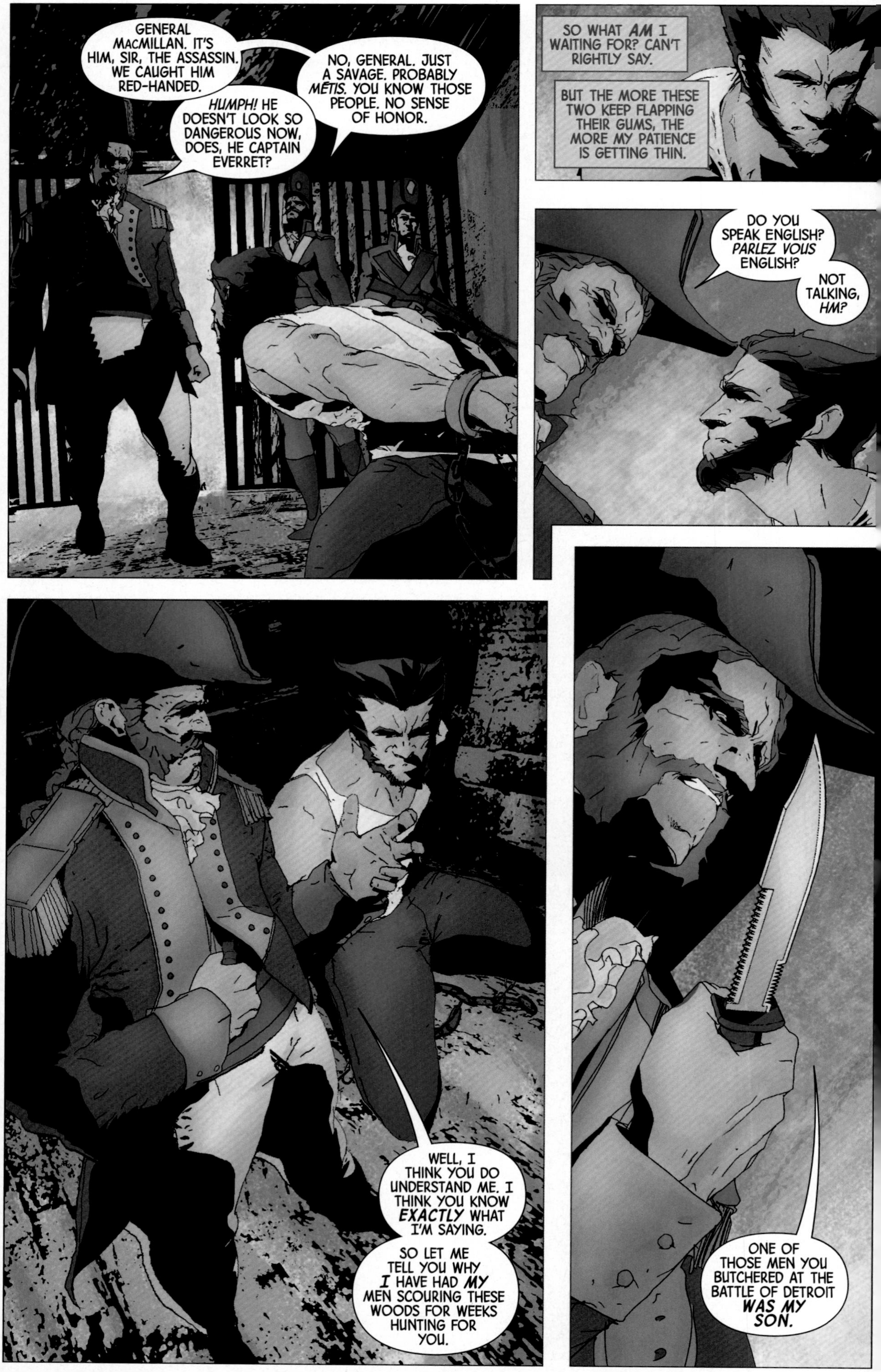
GENERAL MacMILLAN. IT'S HIM, SIR, THE ASSASSIN. WE CAUGHT HIM RED-HANDED.
HUMPH! HE DOESN'T LOOK SO DANGEROUS NOW, DOES, HE CAPTAIN EVERRET?
NO, GENERAL. JUST A SAVAGE. PROBABLY MÉTIS. YOU KNOW THOSE PEOPLE. NO SENSE OF HONOR.
SO WHAT AM I WAITING FOR? CAN'T RIGHTLY SAY.
BUT THE MORE THESE TWO KEEP FLAPPING THEIR GUMS, THE MORE MY PATIENCE IS GETTING THIN.
DO YOU SPEAK ENGLISH? PARLEZ VOUS ENGLISH?
NOT TALKING, HM?
WELL, I THINK YOU DO UNDERSTAND ME. I THINK YOU KNOW EXACTLY WHAT I'M SAYING.
SO LET ME TELL YOU WHY I HAVE HAD MY MEN SCOURING THESE WOODS FOR WEEKS HUNTING FOR YOU.
ONE OF THOSE MEN YOU BUTCHERED AT THE BATTLE OF DETROIT WAS MY SON.

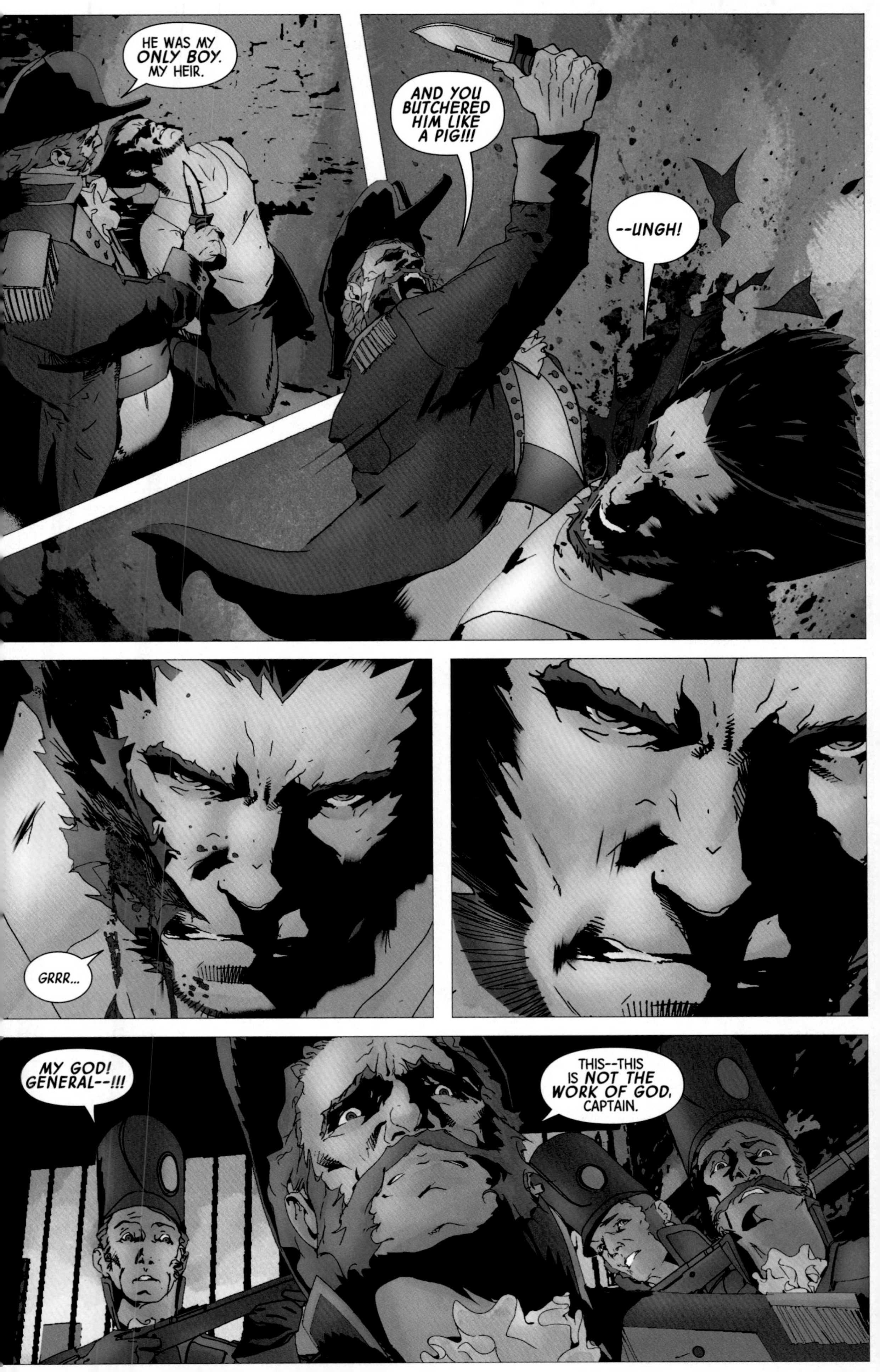
HE WAS MY ONLY BOY. MY HEIR.
AND YOU BUTCHERED HIM LIKE A PIG!!!
--UNGH!
GRRR...
MY GOD! GENERAL--!!!
THIS--THIS IS NOT THE WORK OF GOD, CAPTAIN.

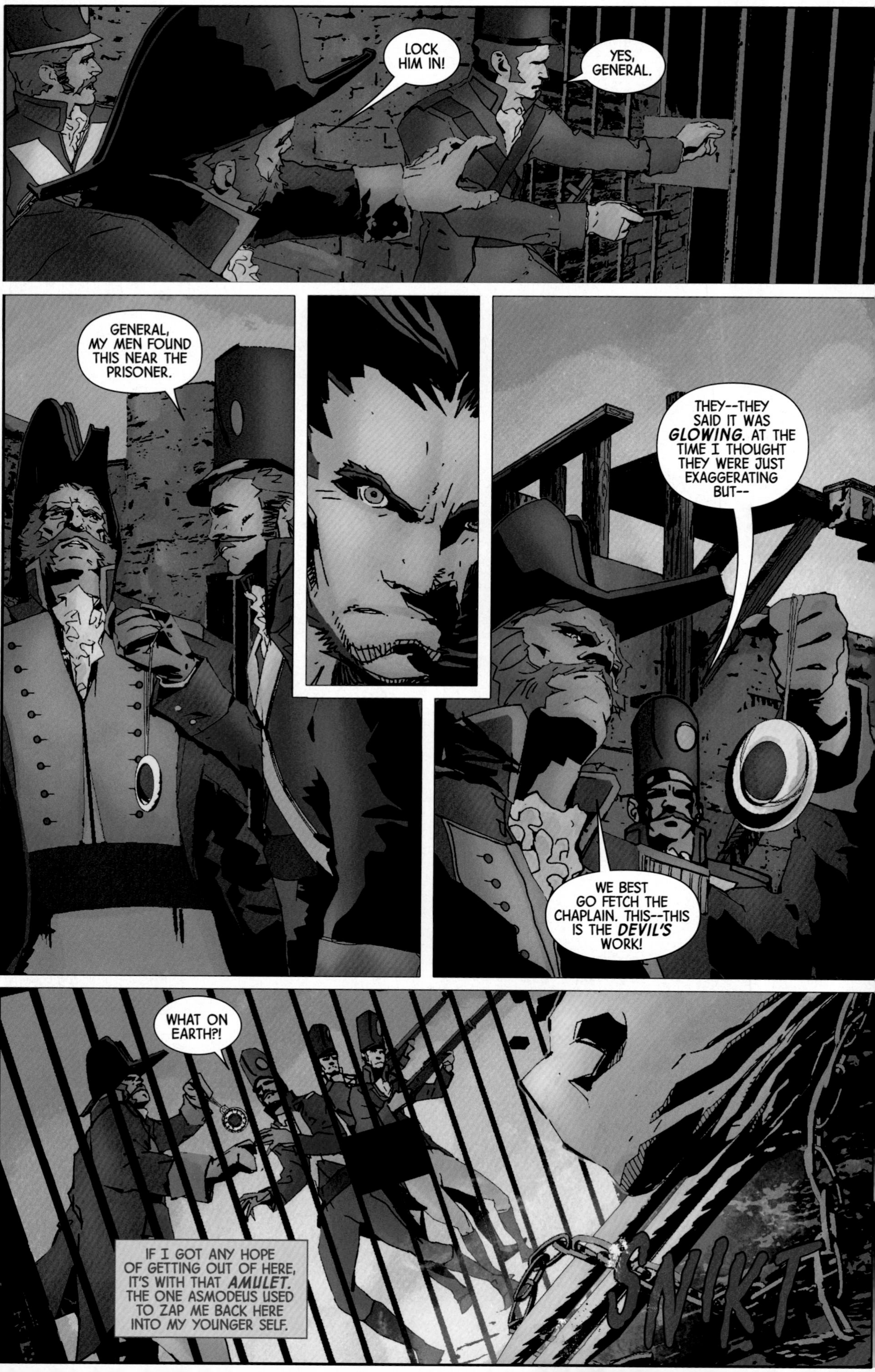
LOCK HIM IN!
YES, GENERAL.
GENERAL, MY MEN FOUND THIS NEAR THE PRISONER.
THEY--THEY SAID IT WAS GLOWING. AT THE TIME I THOUGHT THEY WERE JUST EXAGGERATING BUT--
WE BEST GO FETCH THE CHAPLAIN. THIS--THIS IS THE DEVIL'S WORK!
WHAT ON EARTH?!
IF I GOT ANY HOPE OF GETTING OUT OF HERE, IT'S WITH THAT AMULET. THE ONE ASMODEUS USED TO ZAP ME BACK HERE INTO MY YOUNGER SELF.
SNIKT

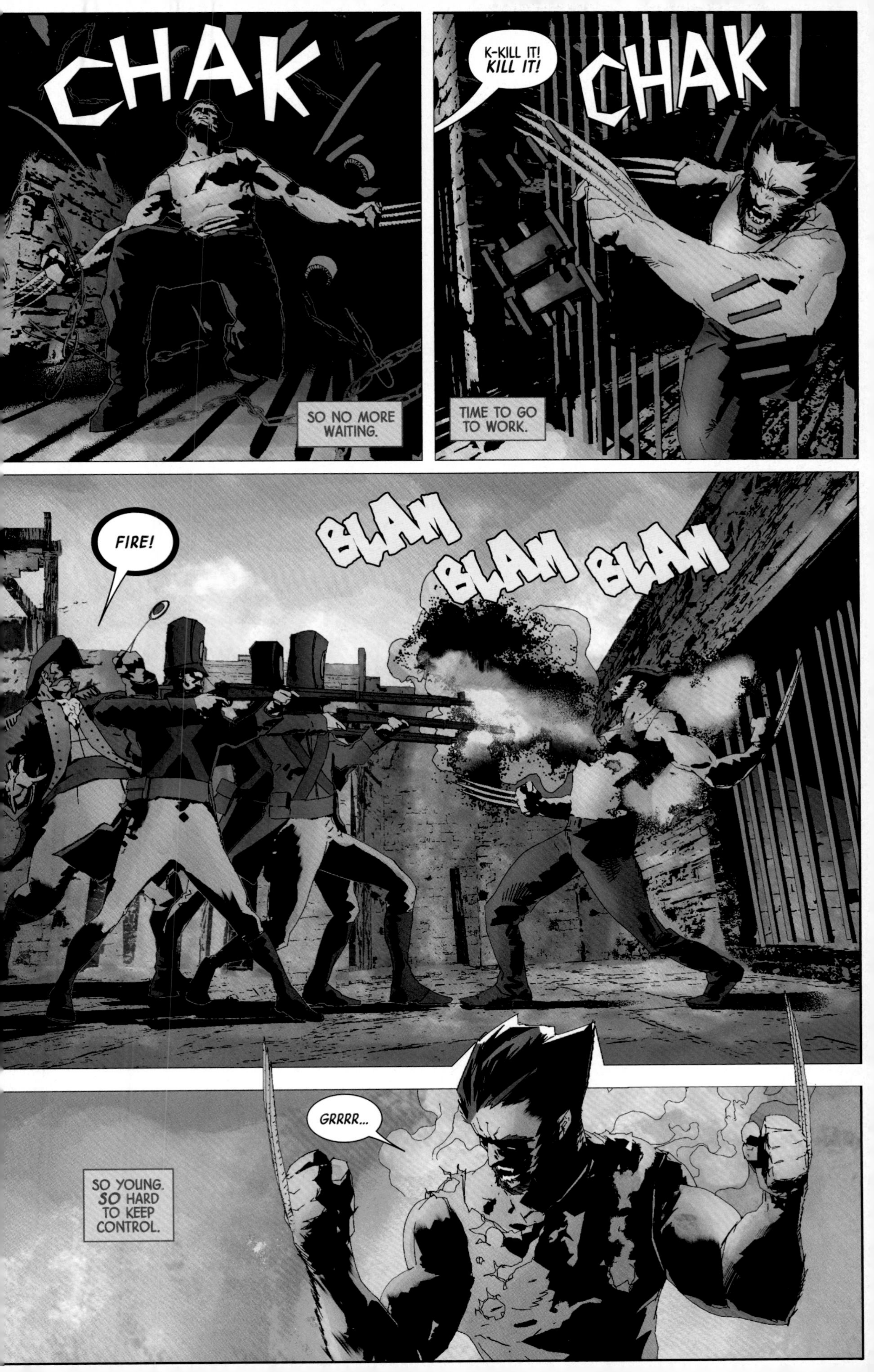

CHAK
SO NO MORE WAITING.
K-KILL IT! KILL IT!
CHAK
TIME TO GO TO WORK.
FIRE!
BLAM
BLAM
BLAM
GRRRR...
SO YOUNG. SO HARD TO KEEP CONTROL.

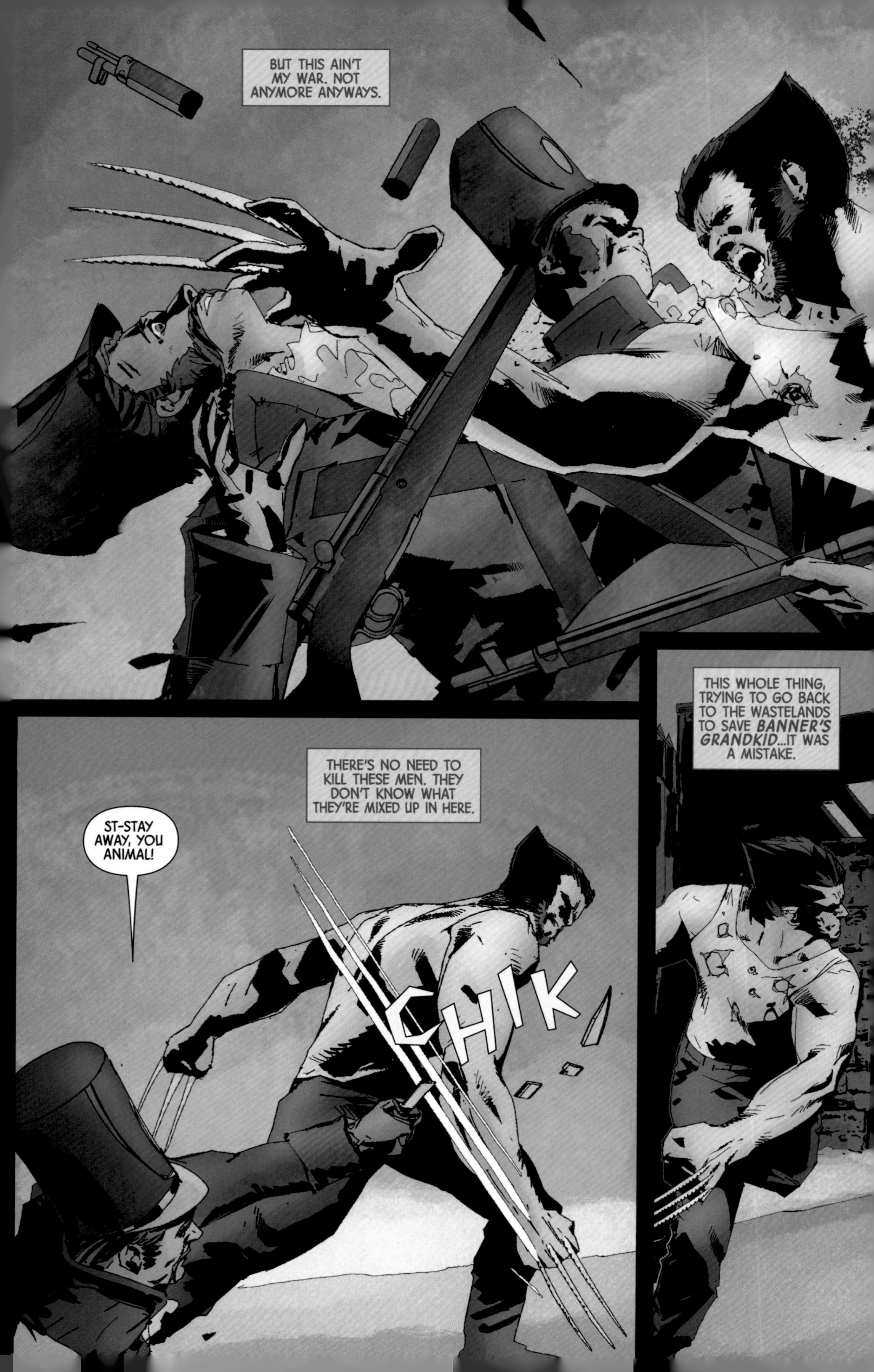
BUT THIS AIN'T MY WAR. NOT ANYMORE ANYWAYS.
THIS WHOLE THING, TRYING TO GO BACK TO THE WASTELANDS TO SAVE BANNER'S GRANDKID...IT WAS A MISTAKE.
THERE'S NO NEED TO KILL THESE MEN. THEY DON'T KNOW WHAT THEY'RE MIXED UP IN HERE.
ST-STAY AWAY, YOU ANIMAL!
CHIK

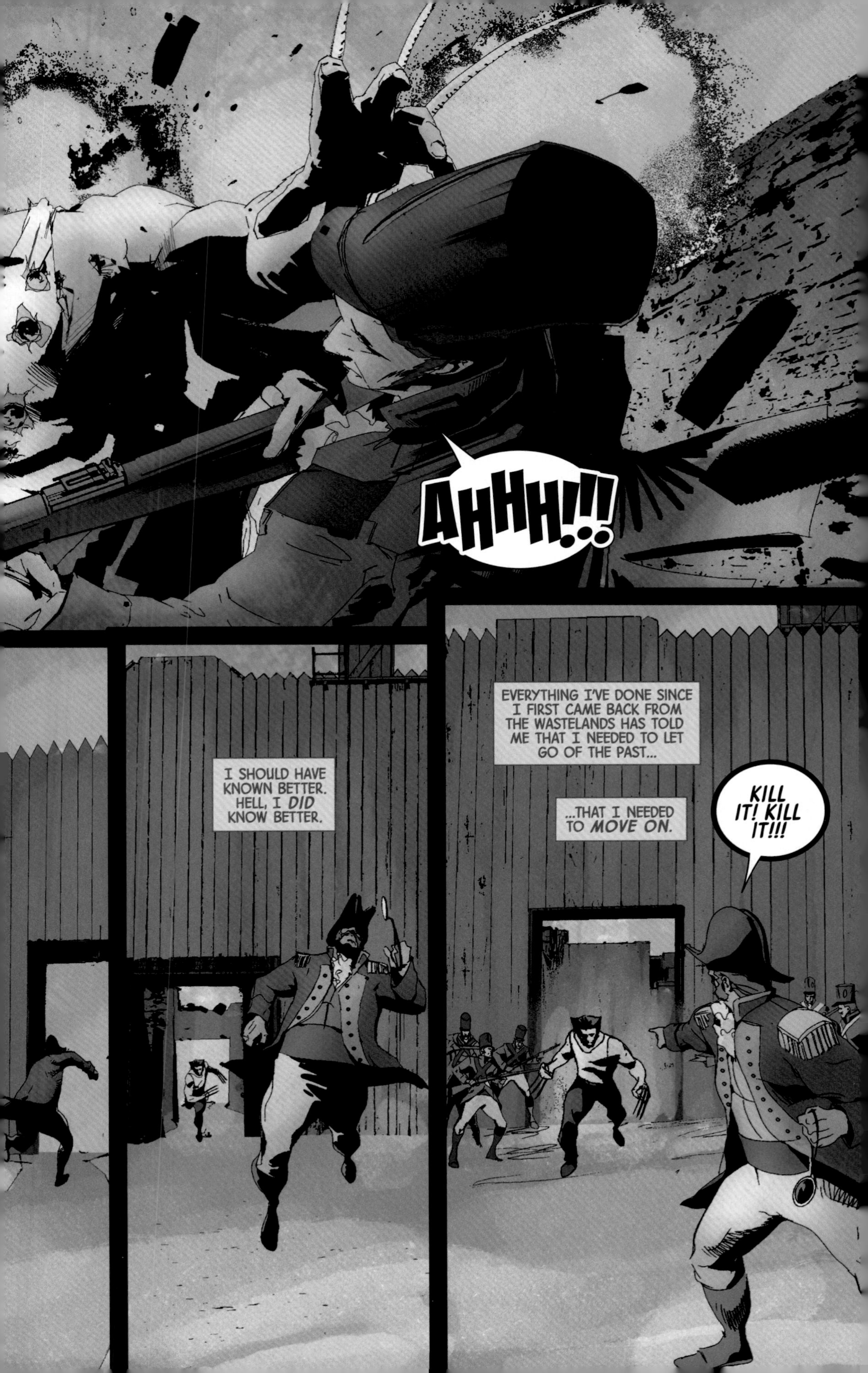
AHHH!!!
I SHOULD HAVE KNOWN BETTER. HELL, I *DID* KNOW BETTER.
EVERYTHING I'VE DONE SINCE I FIRST CAME BACK FROM THE WASTELANDS HAS TOLD ME THAT I NEEDED TO LET GO OF THE PAST...
...THAT I NEEDED TO *MOVE ON*.
KILL IT! KILL IT!!!

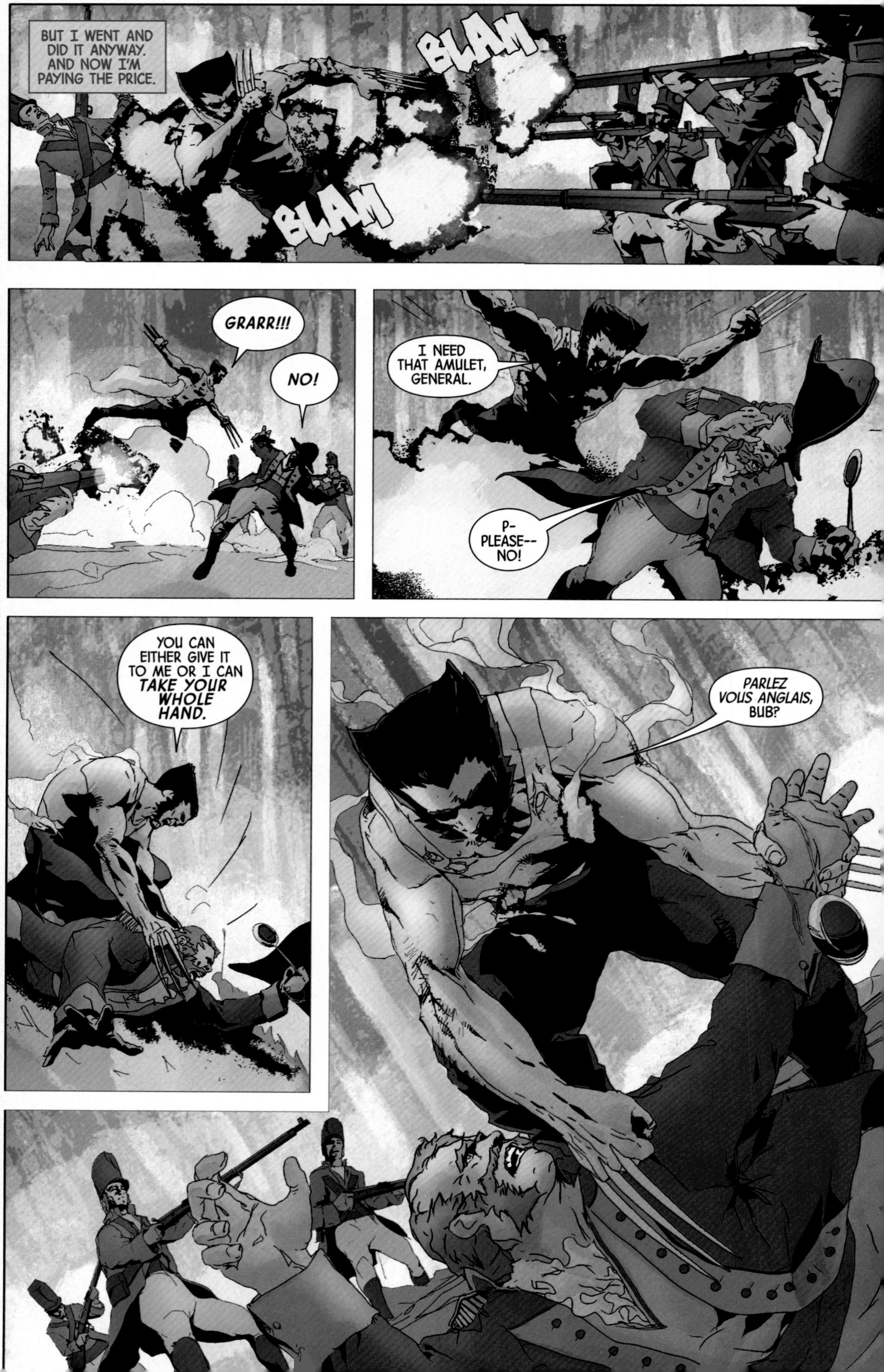
BUT I WENT AND DID IT ANYWAY. AND NOW I'M PAYING THE PRICE.
BLAM
BLAM
GRARR!!!
NO!
I NEED THAT AMULET, GENERAL.
P-PLEASE--NO!
YOU CAN EITHER GIVE IT TO ME OR I CAN TAKE YOUR WHOLE HAND.
PARLEZ VOUS ANGLAIS, BUB?

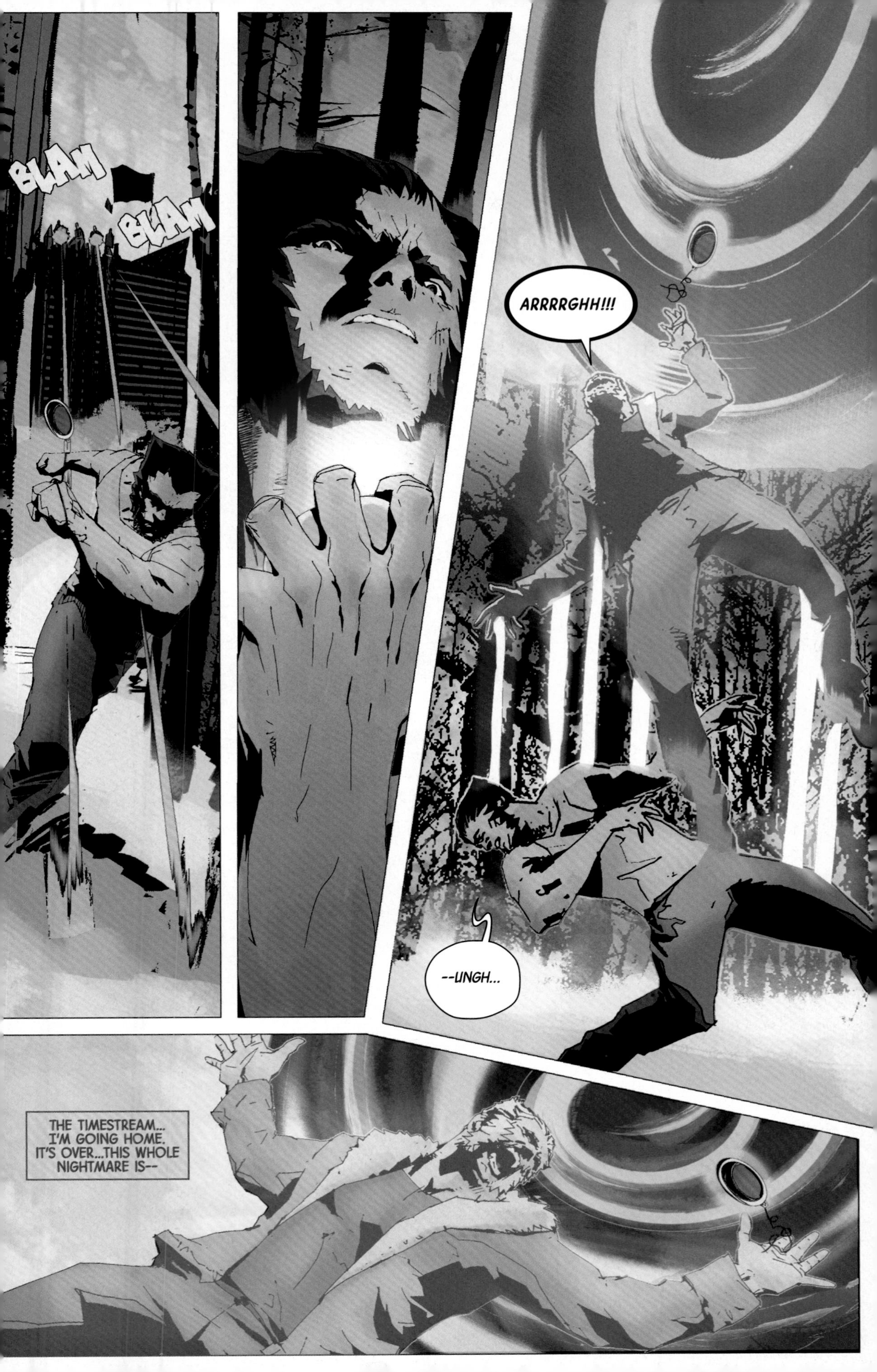
BLAM
BLAM
ARRRRGHH!!!
--UNGH...
THE TIMESTREAM... I'M GOING HOME. IT'S OVER...THIS WHOLE NIGHTMARE IS--

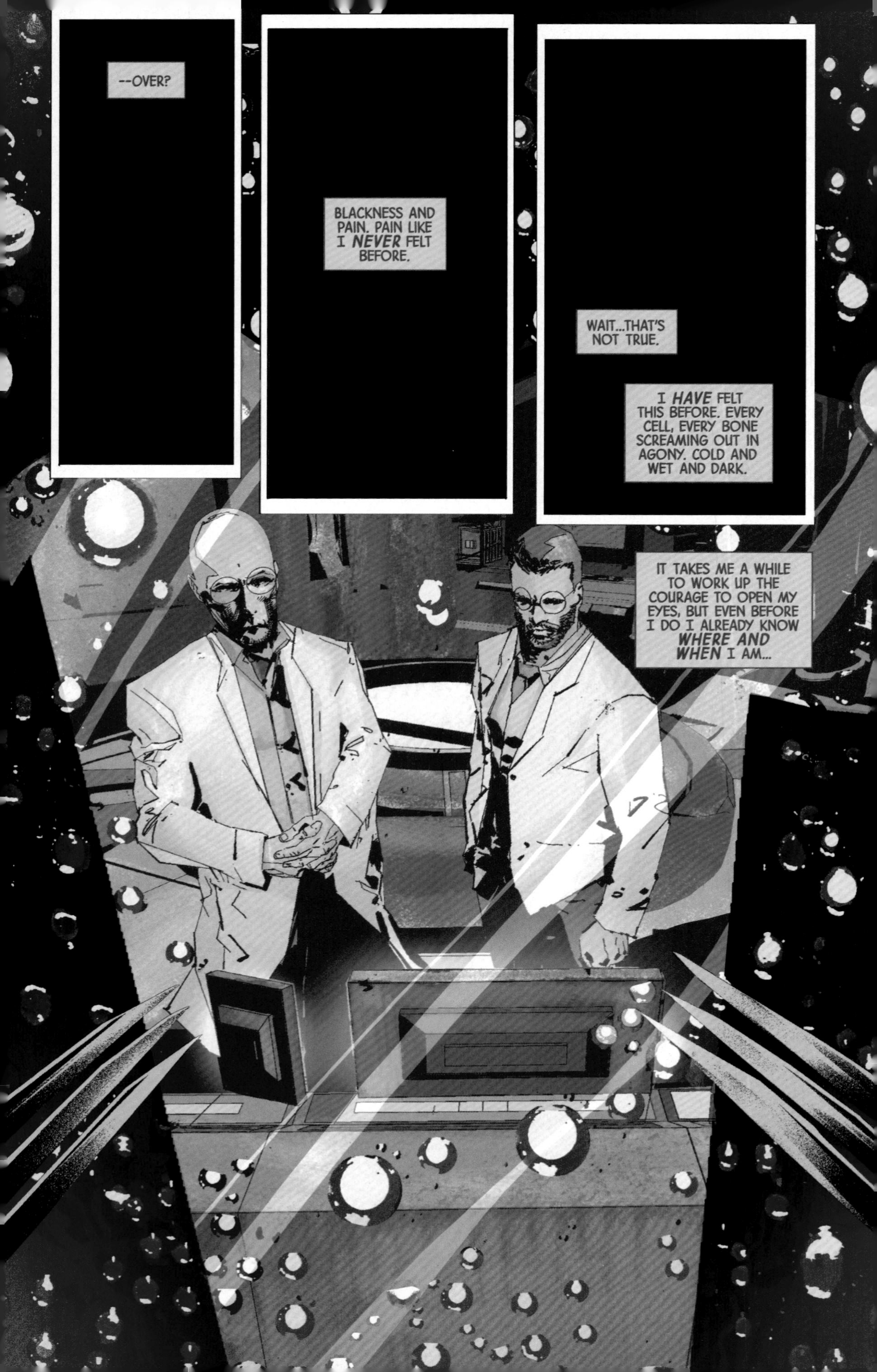
--OVER?
BLACKNESS AND PAIN. PAIN LIKE I NEVER FELT BEFORE.
WAIT...THAT'S NOT TRUE.
I HAVE FELT THIS BEFORE. EVERY CELL, EVERY BONE SCREAMING OUT IN AGONY. COLD AND WET AND DARK.
IT TAKES ME A WHILE TO WORK UP THE COURAGE TO OPEN MY EYES, BUT EVEN BEFORE I DO I ALREADY KNOW WHERE AND WHEN I AM...

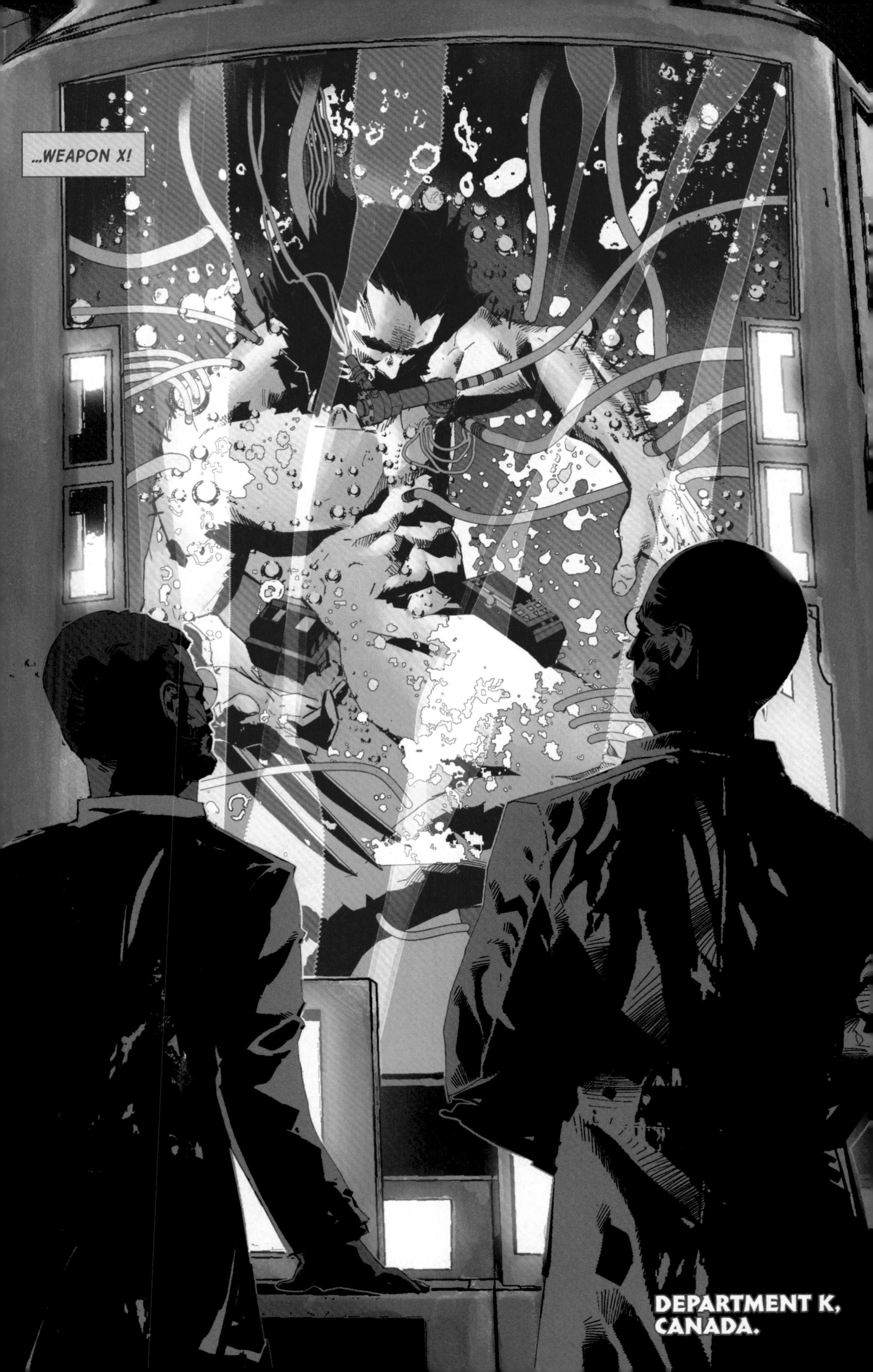
...WEAPON X!
DEPARTMENT K, CANADA.

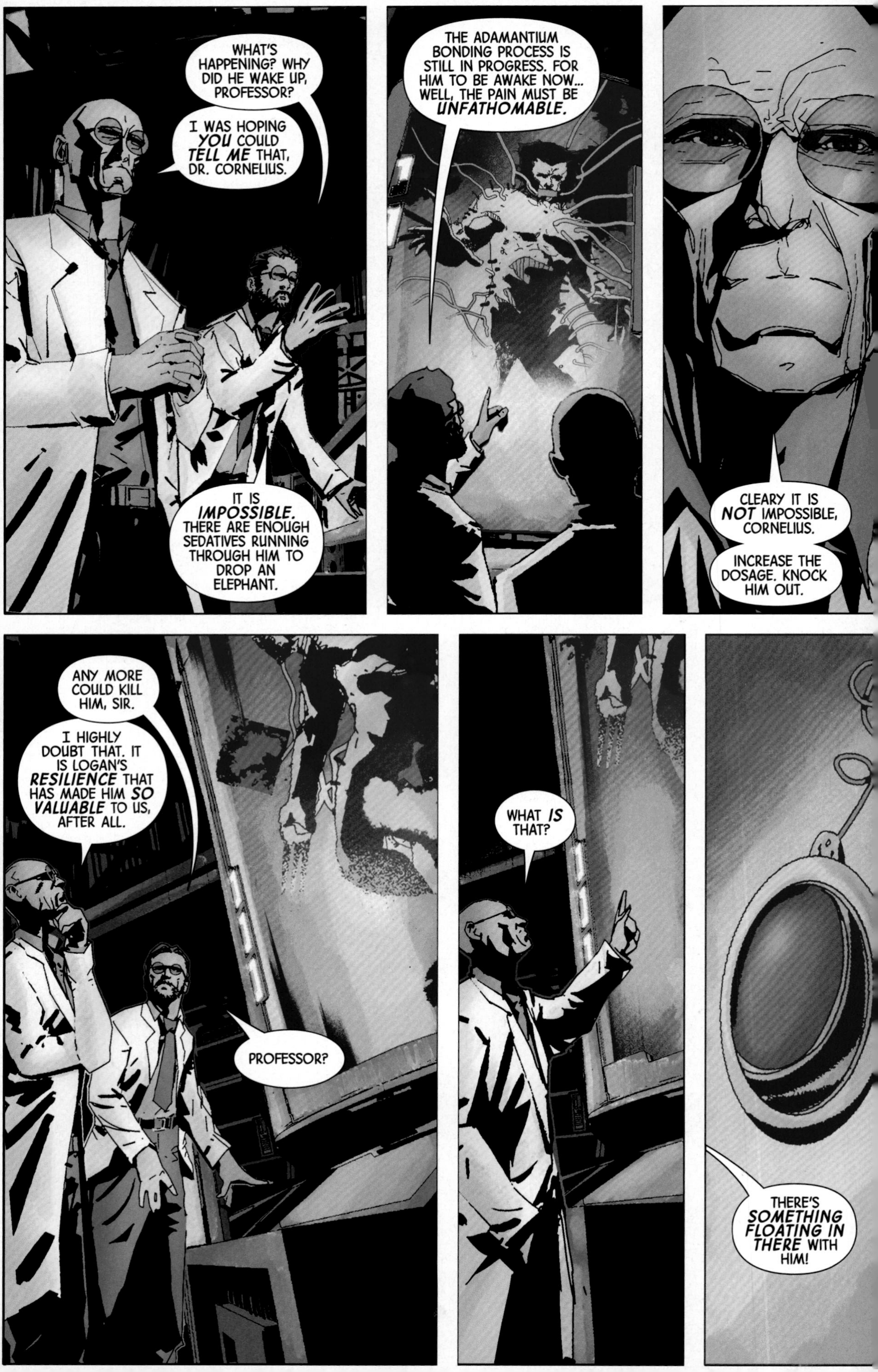
WHAT'S HAPPENING? WHY DID HE WAKE UP, PROFESSOR?
I WAS HOPING YOU COULD TELL ME THAT, DR. CORNELIUS.
IT IS IMPOSSIBLE. THERE ARE ENOUGH SEDATIVES RUNNING THROUGH HIM TO DROP AN ELEPHANT.
THE ADAMANTIUM BONDING PROCESS IS STILL IN PROGRESS. FOR HIM TO BE AWAKE NOW... WELL, THE PAIN MUST BE UNFATHOMABLE.
CLEARY IT IS NOT IMPOSSIBLE, CORNELIUS.
INCREASE THE DOSAGE. KNOCK HIM OUT.
ANY MORE COULD KILL HIM, SIR.
I HIGHLY DOUBT THAT. IT IS LOGAN'S RESILIENCE THAT HAS MADE HIM SO VALUABLE TO US, AFTER ALL.
PROFESSOR?
WHAT IS THAT?
THERE'S SOMETHING FLOATING IN THERE WITH HIM!

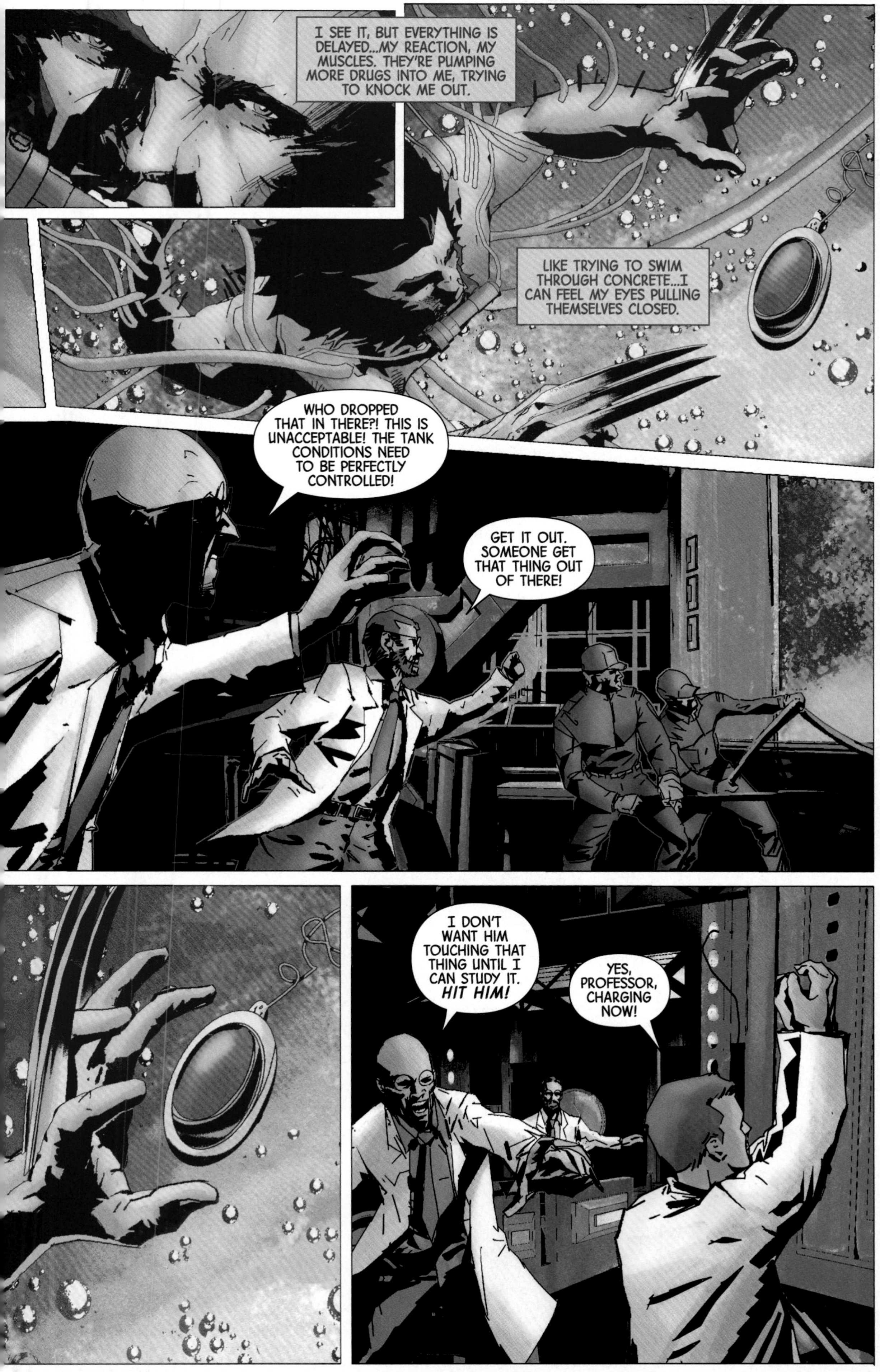
I SEE IT, BUT EVERYTHING IS DELAYED...MY REACTION, MY MUSCLES. THEY'RE PUMPING MORE DRUGS INTO ME, TRYING TO KNOCK ME OUT.
LIKE TRYING TO SWIM THROUGH CONCRETE...I CAN FEEL MY EYES PULLING THEMSELVES CLOSED.
WHO DROPPED THAT IN THERE?! THIS IS UNACCEPTABLE! THE TANK CONDITIONS NEED TO BE PERFECTLY CONTROLLED!
GET IT OUT. SOMEONE GET THAT THING OUT OF THERE!
I DON'T WANT HIM TOUCHING THAT THING UNTIL I CAN STUDY IT. HIT HIM!
YES, PROFESSOR, CHARGING NOW!

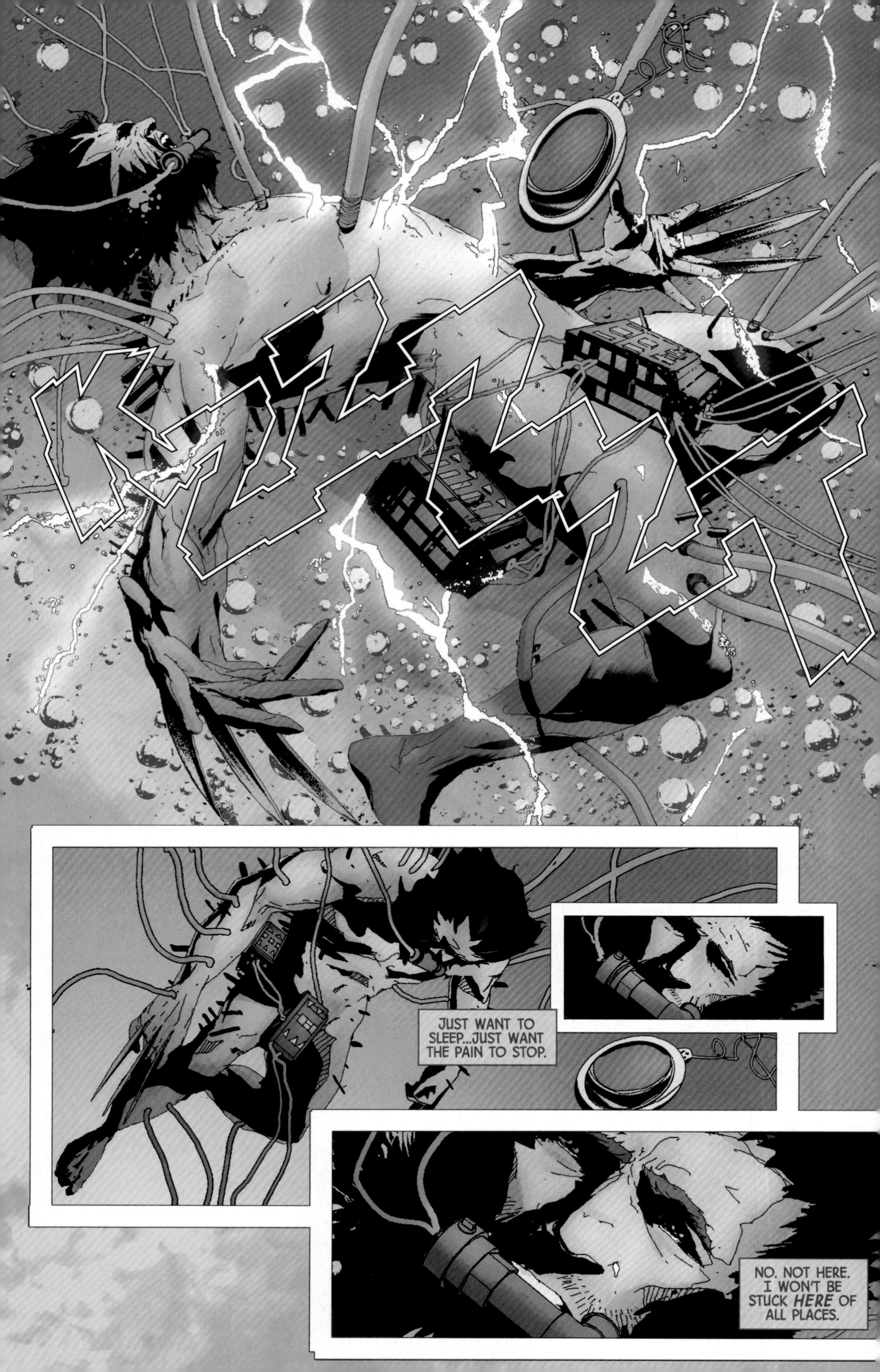
KZZZAK
JUST WANT TO SLEEP...JUST WANT THE PAIN TO STOP.
NO. NOT HERE. I WON'T BE STUCK *HERE* OF ALL PLACES.

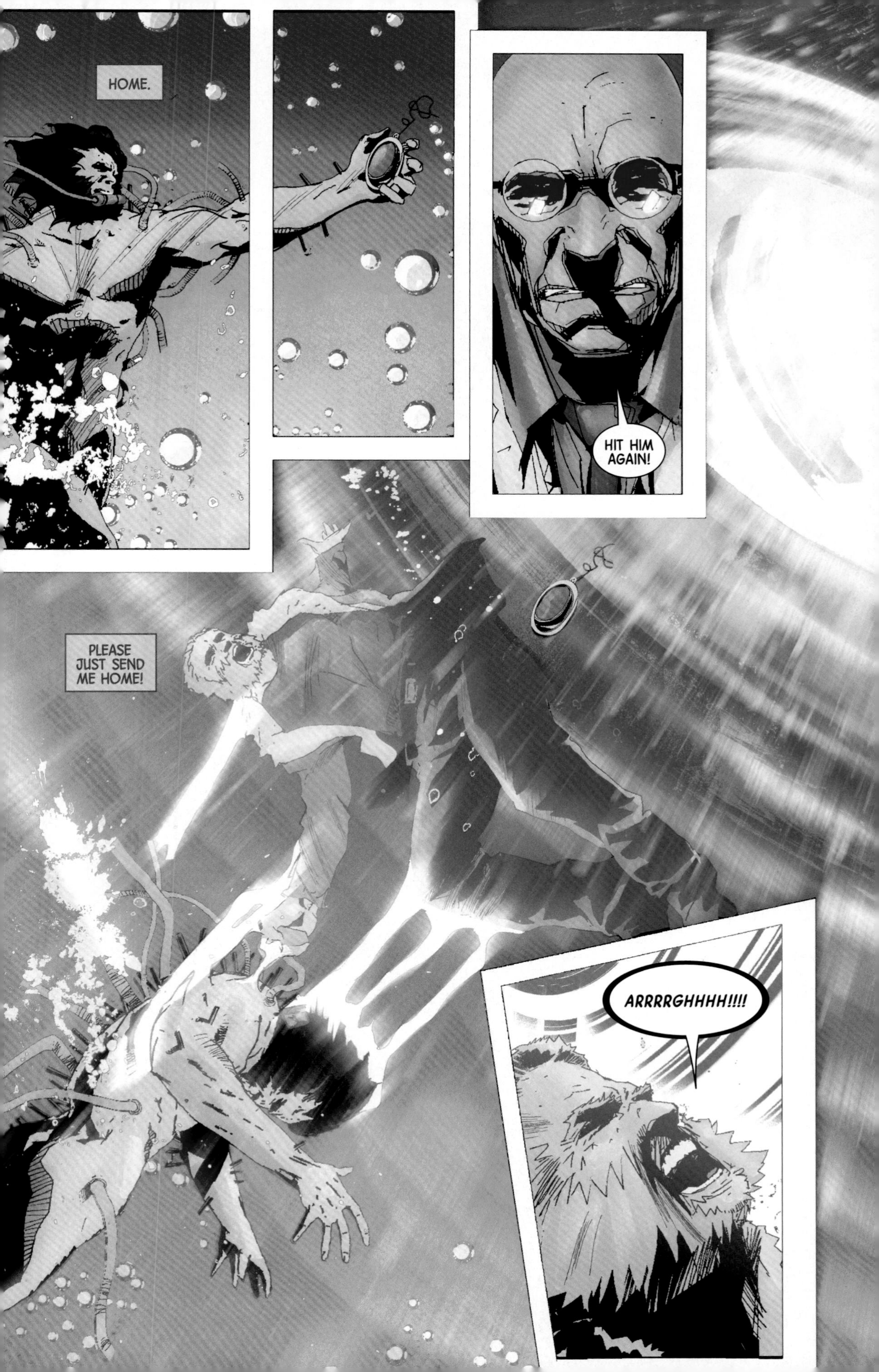
HOME.
HIT HIM AGAIN!
PLEASE JUST SEND ME HOME!
ARRRRGHHHH!!!!

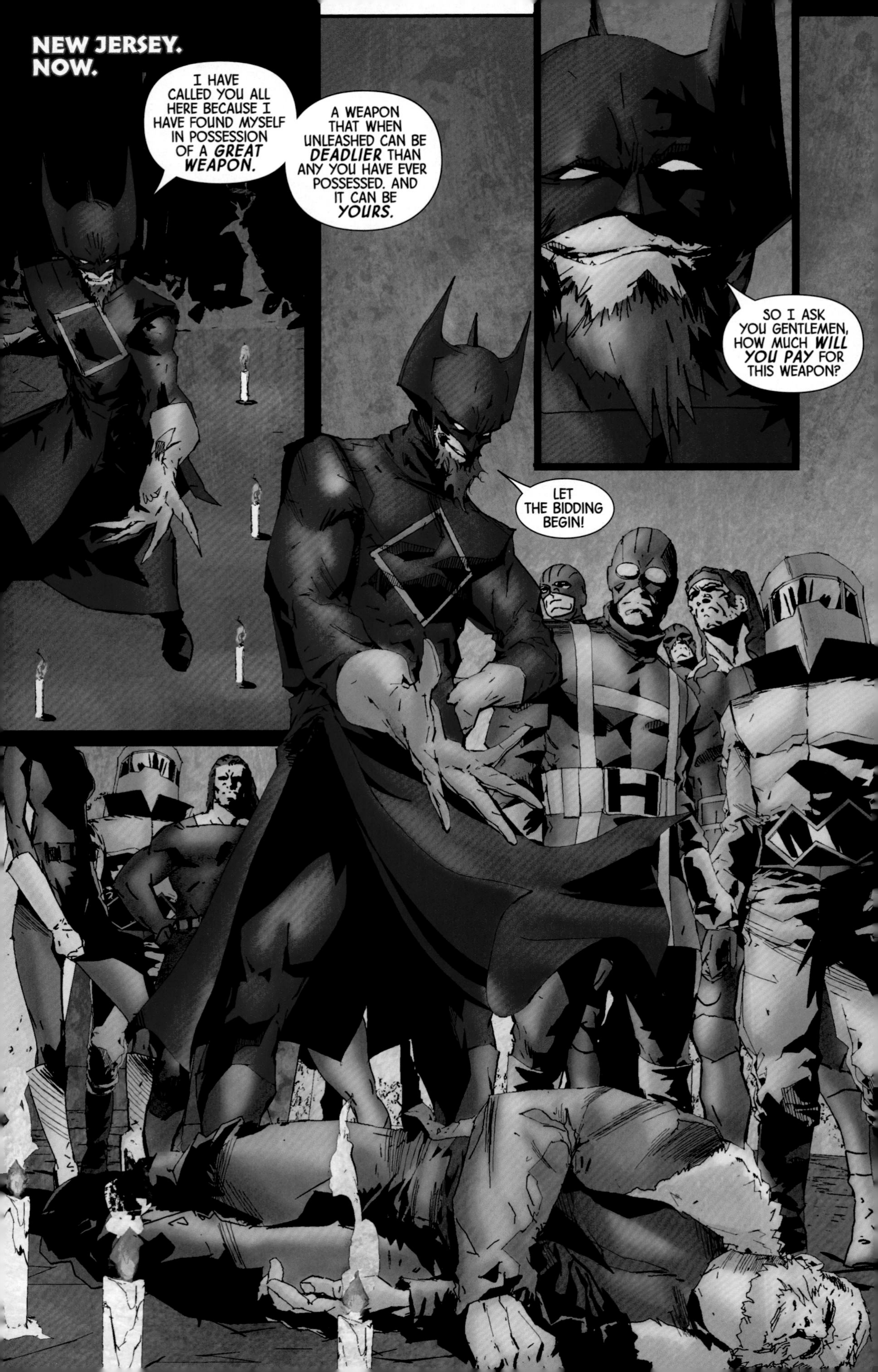

NEW JERSEY. NOW.
I HAVE CALLED YOU ALL HERE BECAUSE I HAVE FOUND MYSELF IN POSSESSION OF A GREAT WEAPON.
A WEAPON THAT WHEN UNLEASHED CAN BE DEADLIER THAN ANY YOU HAVE EVER POSSESSED. AND IT CAN BE YOURS.
SO I ASK YOU GENTLEMEN, HOW MUCH WILL YOU PAY FOR THIS WEAPON?
LET THE BIDDING BEGIN!

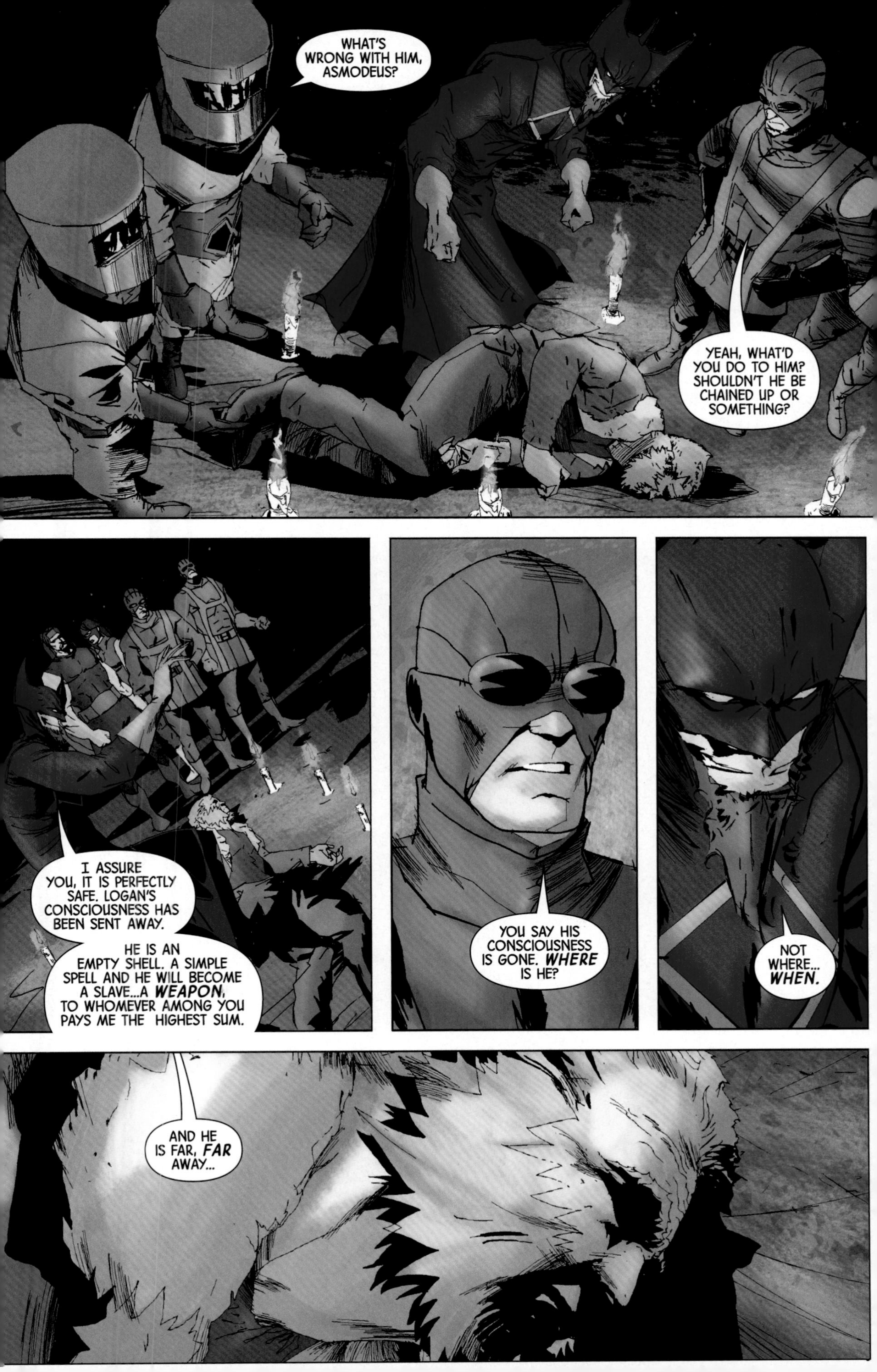
WHAT'S WRONG WITH HIM, ASMODEUS?
YEAH, WHAT'D YOU DO TO HIM? SHOULDN'T HE BE CHAINED UP OR SOMETHING?
I ASSURE YOU, IT IS PERFECTLY SAFE. LOGAN'S CONSCIOUSNESS HAS BEEN SENT AWAY.
HE IS AN EMPTY SHELL. A SIMPLE SPELL AND HE WILL BECOME A SLAVE...A WEAPON, TO WHOMEVER AMONG YOU PAYS ME THE HIGHEST SUM.
YOU SAY HIS CONSCIOUSNESS IS GONE. WHERE IS HE?
NOT WHERE... WHEN.
AND HE IS FAR, FAR AWAY...

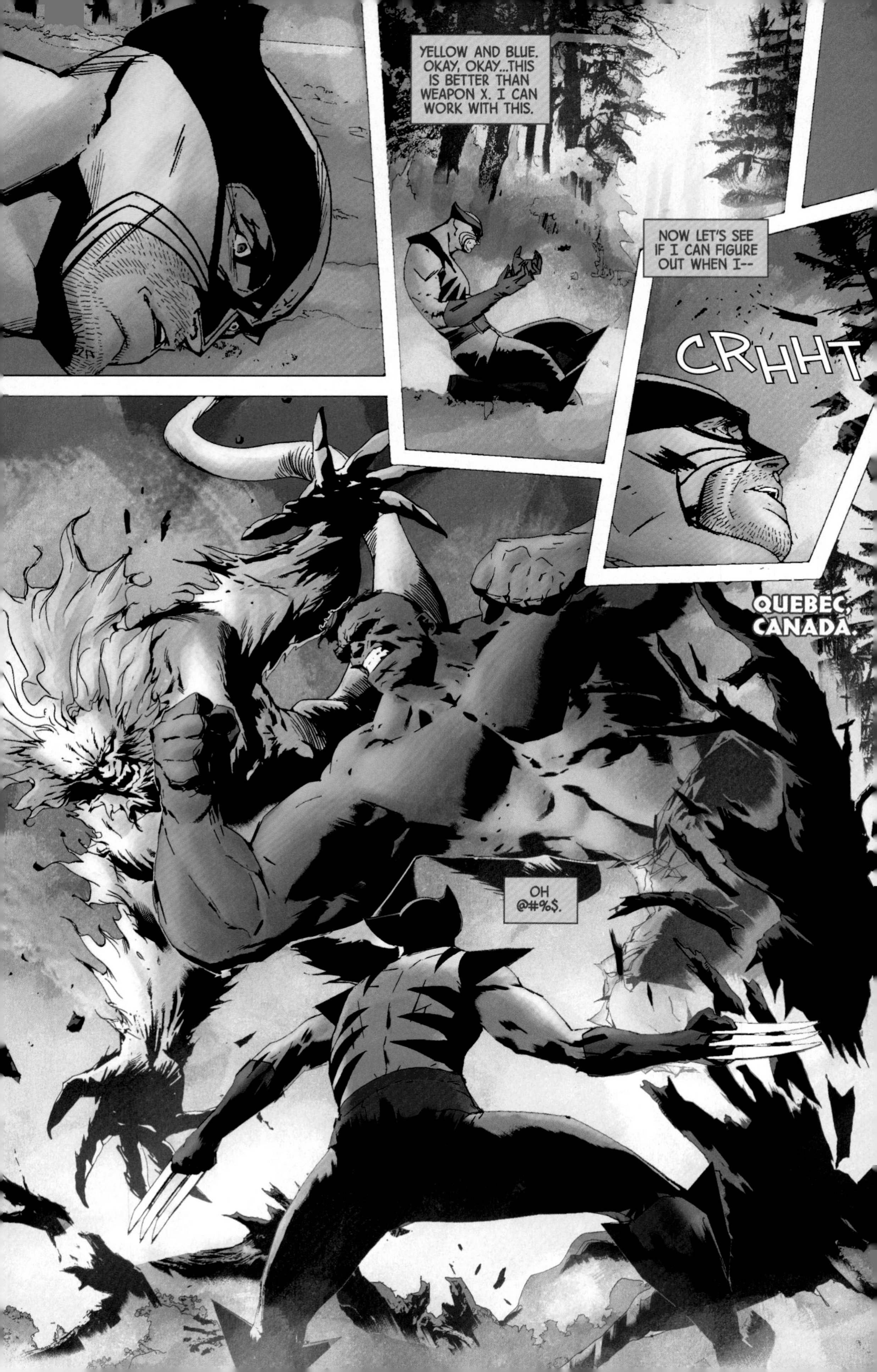
YELLOW AND BLUE. OKAY, OKAY...THIS IS BETTER THAN WEAPON X. I CAN WORK WITH THIS.
NOW LET'S SEE IF I CAN FIGURE OUT WHEN I--
CRHHT
QUEBEC, CANADA.
OH @#%$.

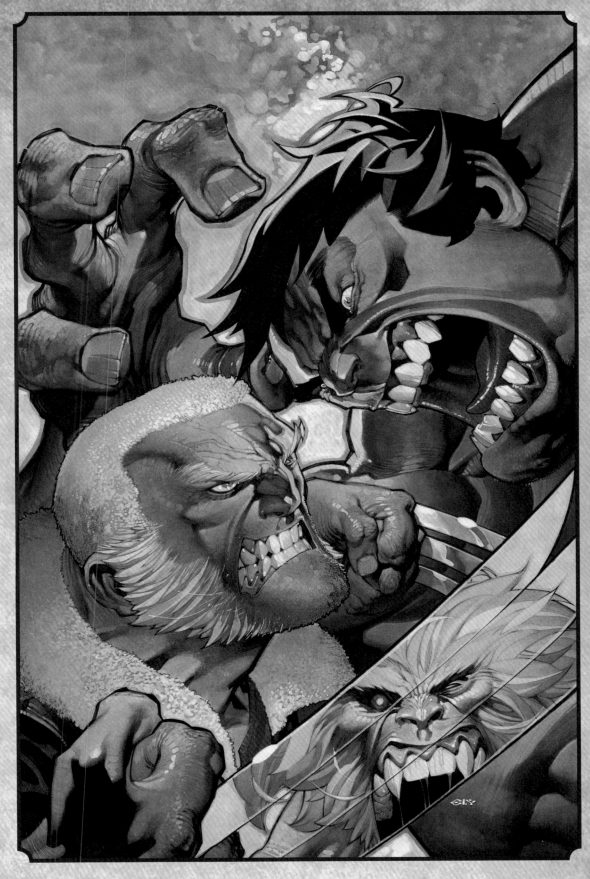

**#22 VARIANT
BY CHRISTOPHER STEVENS**

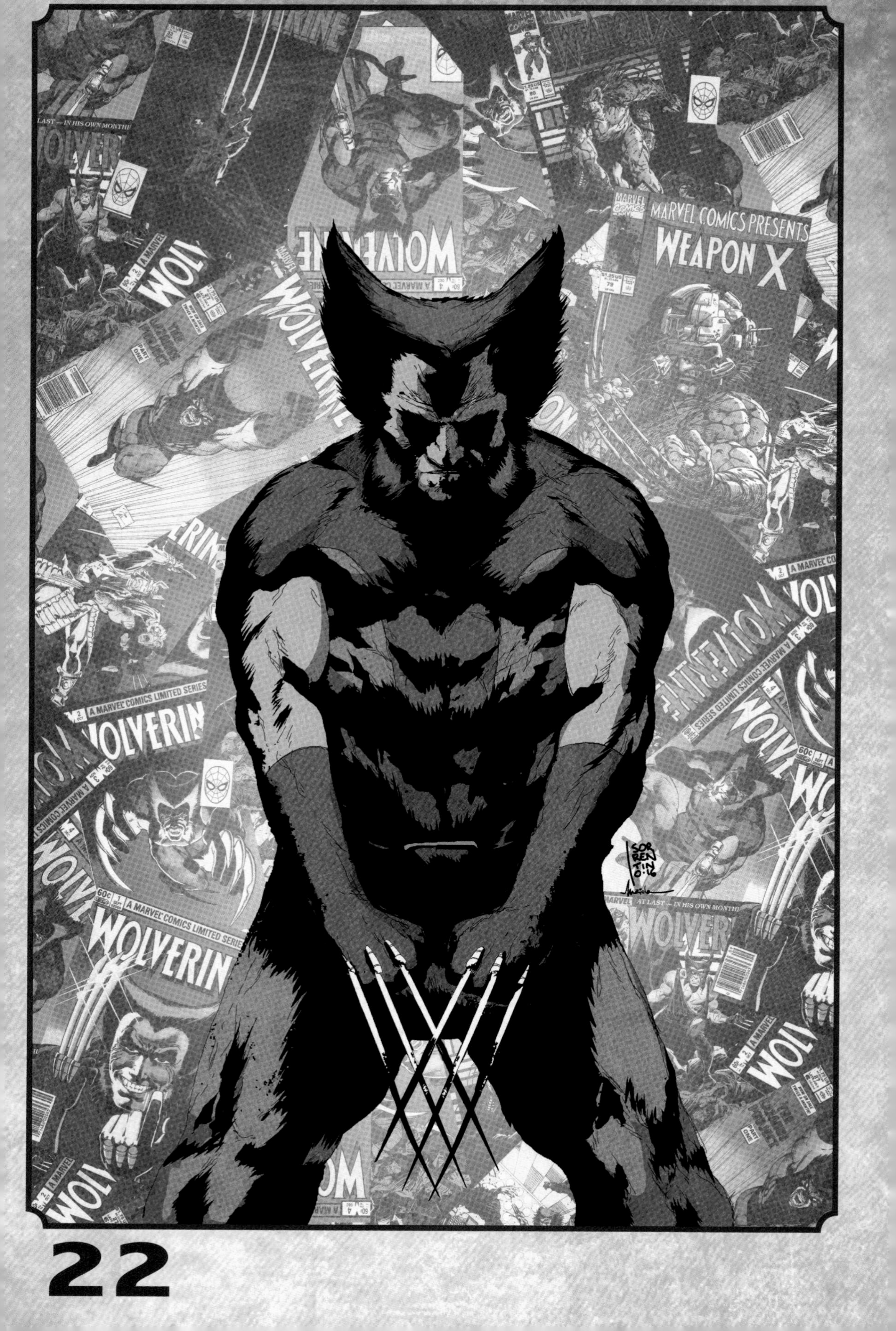
MARVEL COMICS PRESENTS
WEAPON X
WOLVERINE
A MARVEL COMICS LIMITED SERIES
WOLVERIN
A MARVEL COMICS LIMITED SERIES
WOLVERIN
AT LAST — IN HIS OWN MONTHL
WOLVER

22

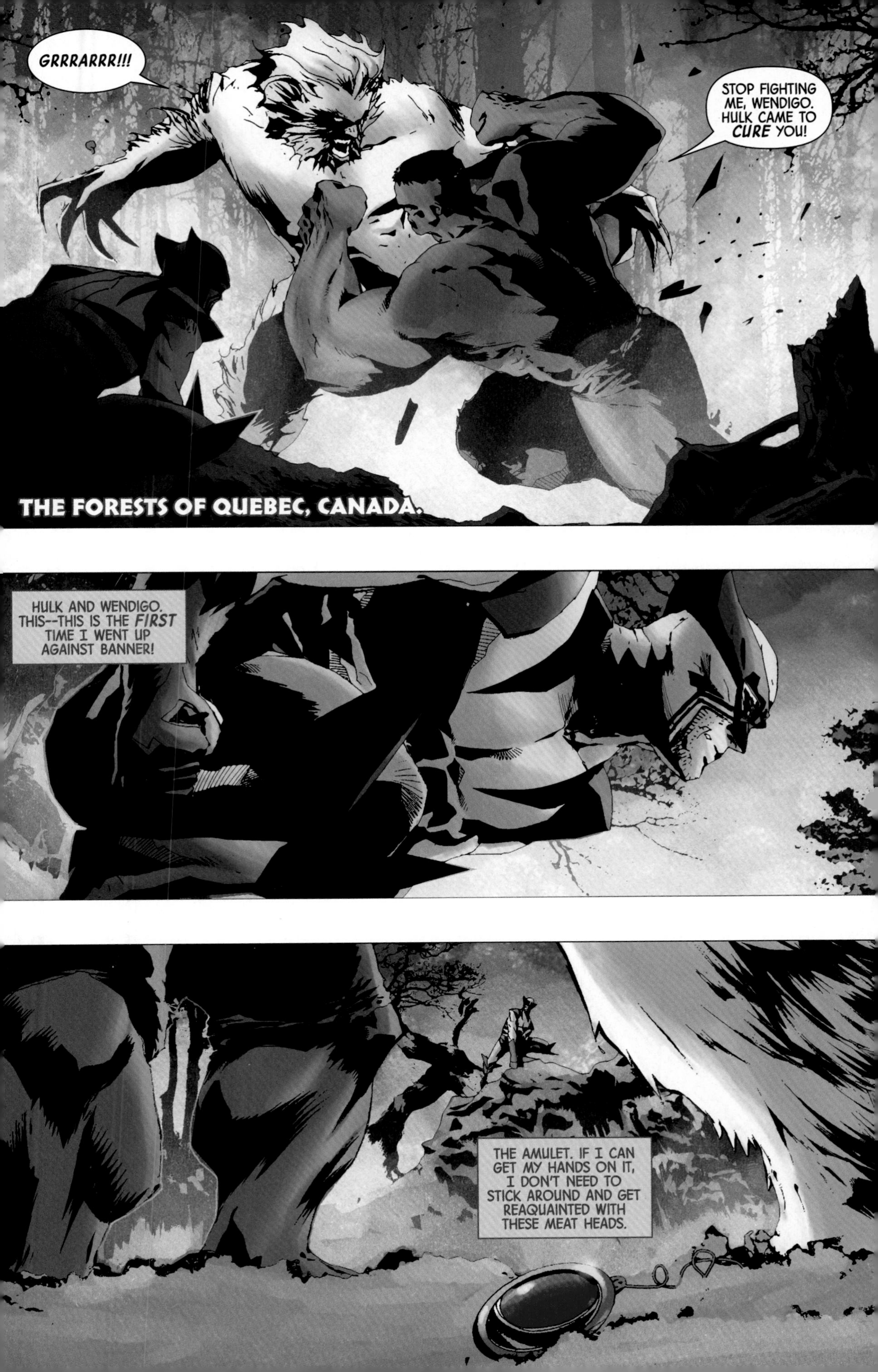
GRRRARRR!!!
STOP FIGHTING ME, WENDIGO. HULK CAME TO CURE YOU!
THE FORESTS OF QUEBEC, CANADA.
HULK AND WENDIGO. THIS--THIS IS THE FIRST TIME I WENT UP AGAINST BANNER!
THE AMULET. IF I CAN GET MY HANDS ON IT, I DON'T NEED TO STICK AROUND AND GET REAQUAINTED WITH THESE MEAT HEADS.

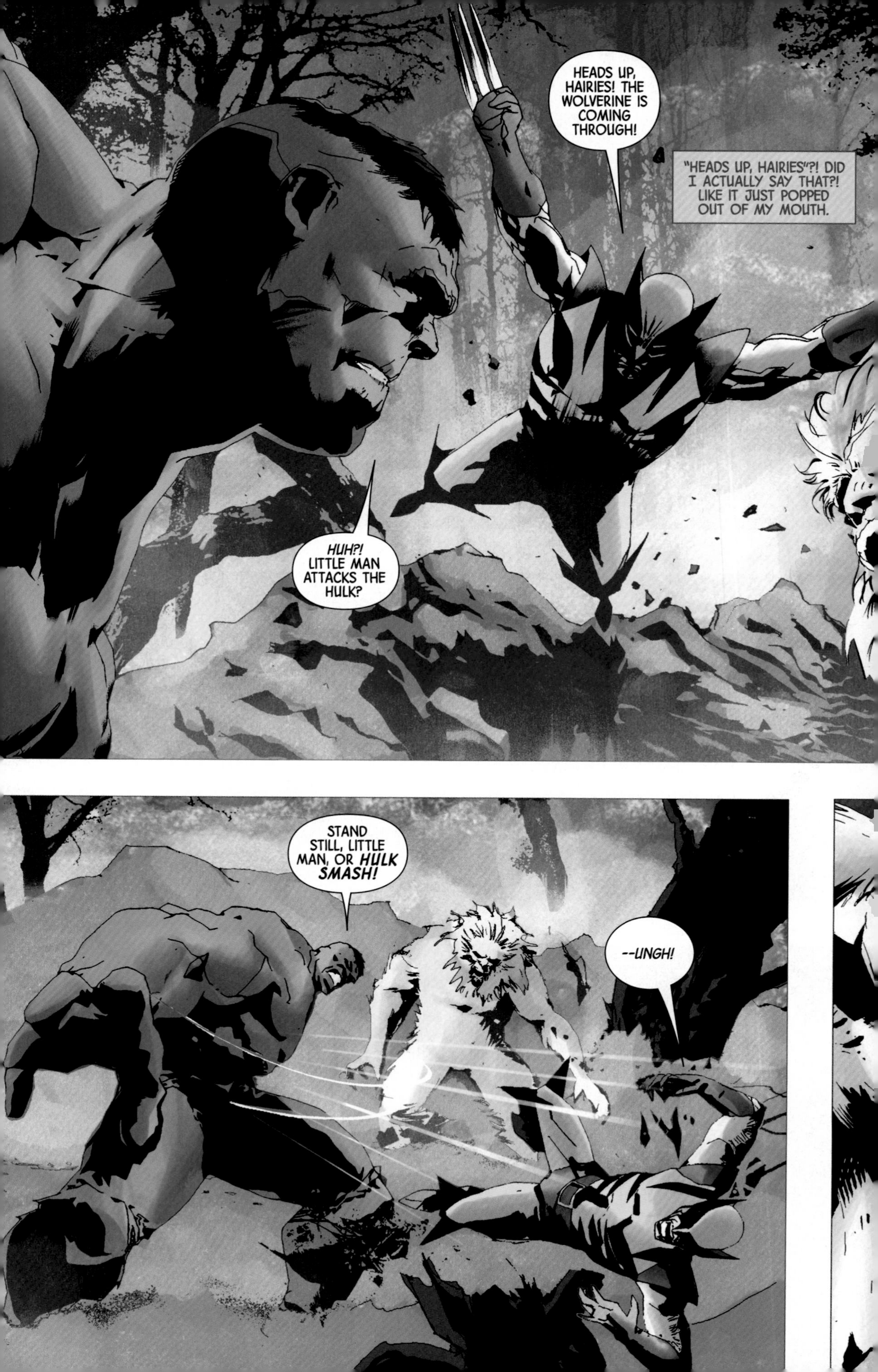
HEADS UP, HAIRIES! THE WOLVERINE IS COMING THROUGH!
"HEADS UP, HAIRIES"?! DID I ACTUALLY SAY THAT?! LIKE IT JUST POPPED OUT OF MY MOUTH.
HUH?! LITTLE MAN ATTACKS THE HULK?
STAND STILL, LITTLE MAN, OR ***HULK SMASH!***
--UNGH!

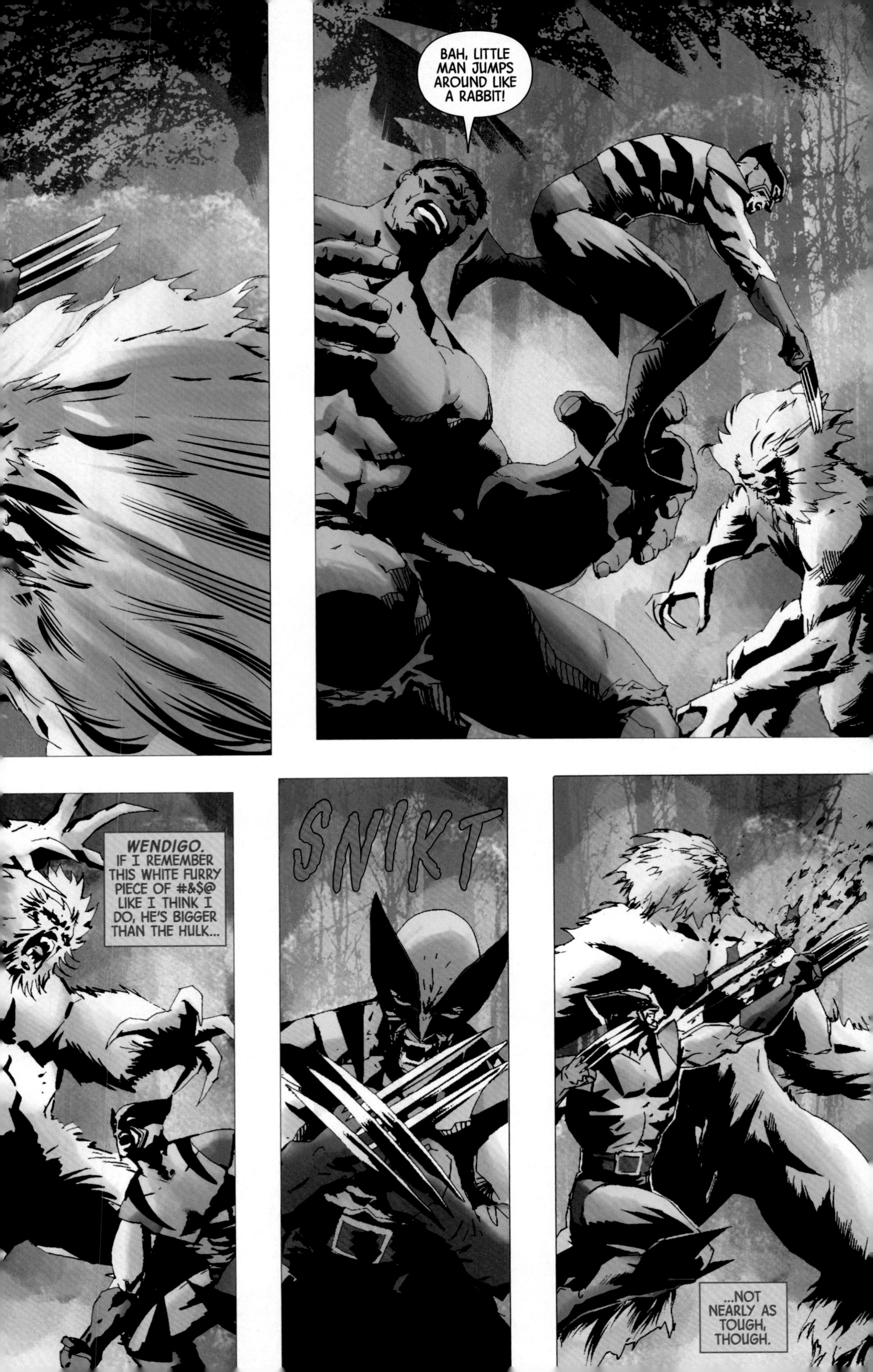
BAH, LITTLE MAN JUMPS AROUND LIKE A RABBIT!
WENDIGO. IF I REMEMBER THIS WHITE FURRY PIECE OF #&$@ LIKE I THINK I DO, HE'S BIGGER THAN THE HULK...
SNIKT
...NOT NEARLY AS TOUGH, THOUGH.

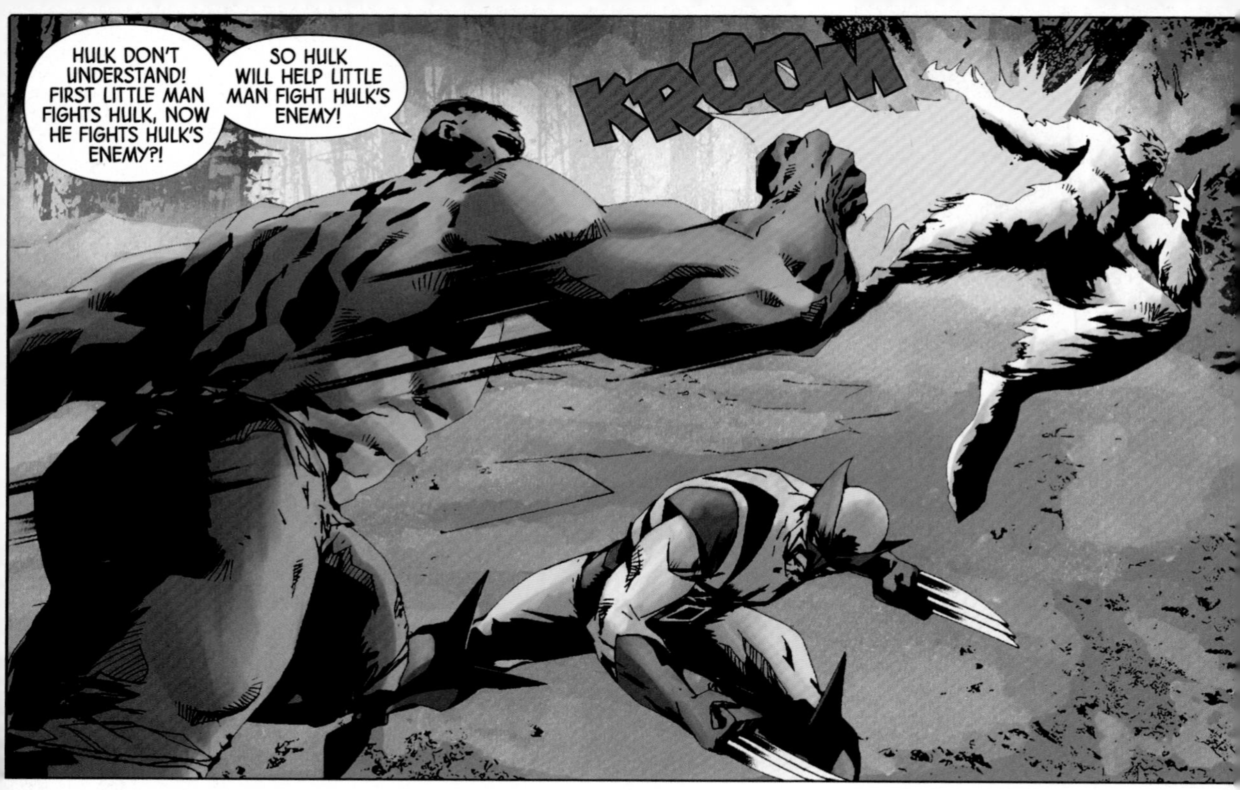
HULK DON'T UNDERSTAND! FIRST LITTLE MAN FIGHTS HULK, NOW HE FIGHTS HULK'S ENEMY?!
SO HULK WILL HELP LITTLE MAN FIGHT HULK'S ENEMY!
KROOM

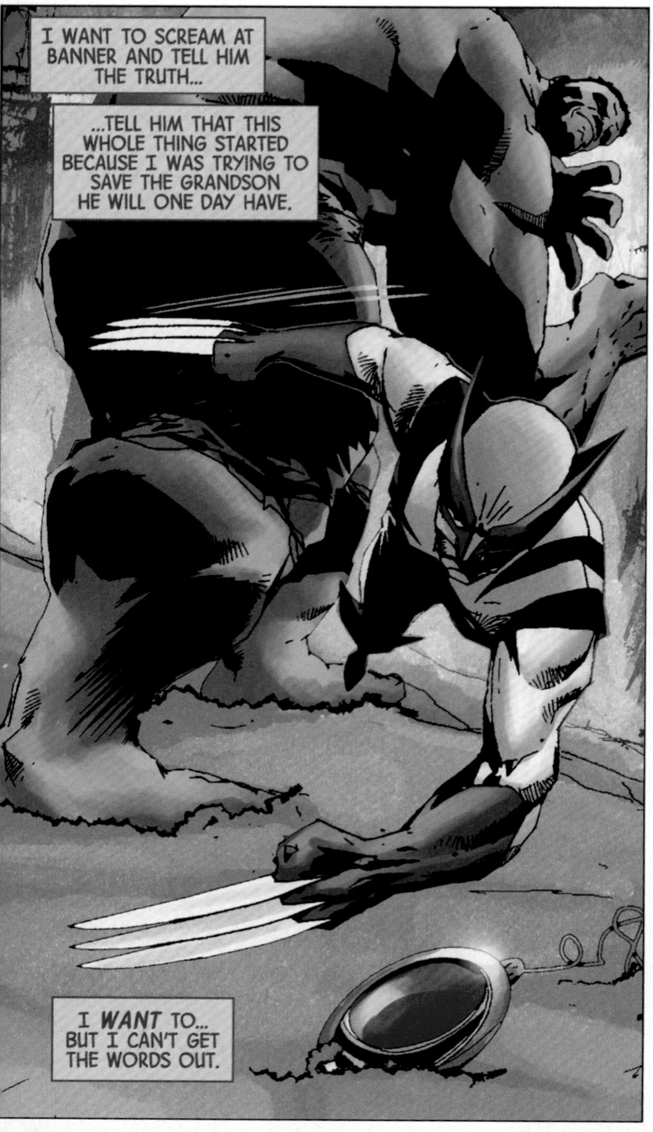
I WANT TO SCREAM AT BANNER AND TELL HIM THE TRUTH...
...TELL HIM THAT THIS WHOLE THING STARTED BECAUSE I WAS TRYING TO SAVE THE GRANDSON HE WILL ONE DAY HAVE.
I *WANT* TO... BUT I CAN'T GET THE WORDS OUT.

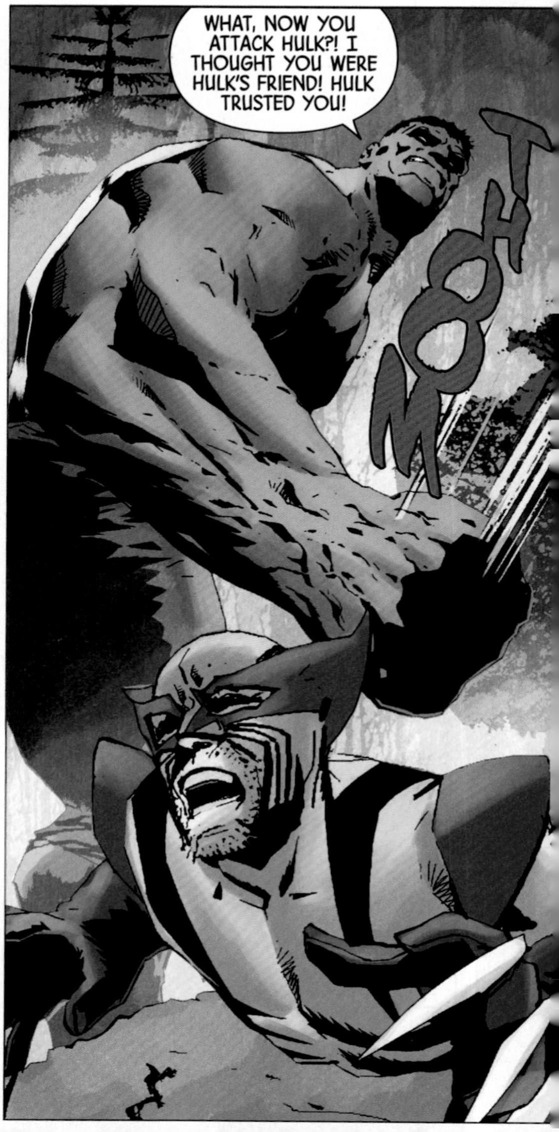
WHAT, NOW YOU ATTACK HULK?! I THOUGHT YOU WERE HULK'S FRIEND! HULK TRUSTED YOU!
THOOM

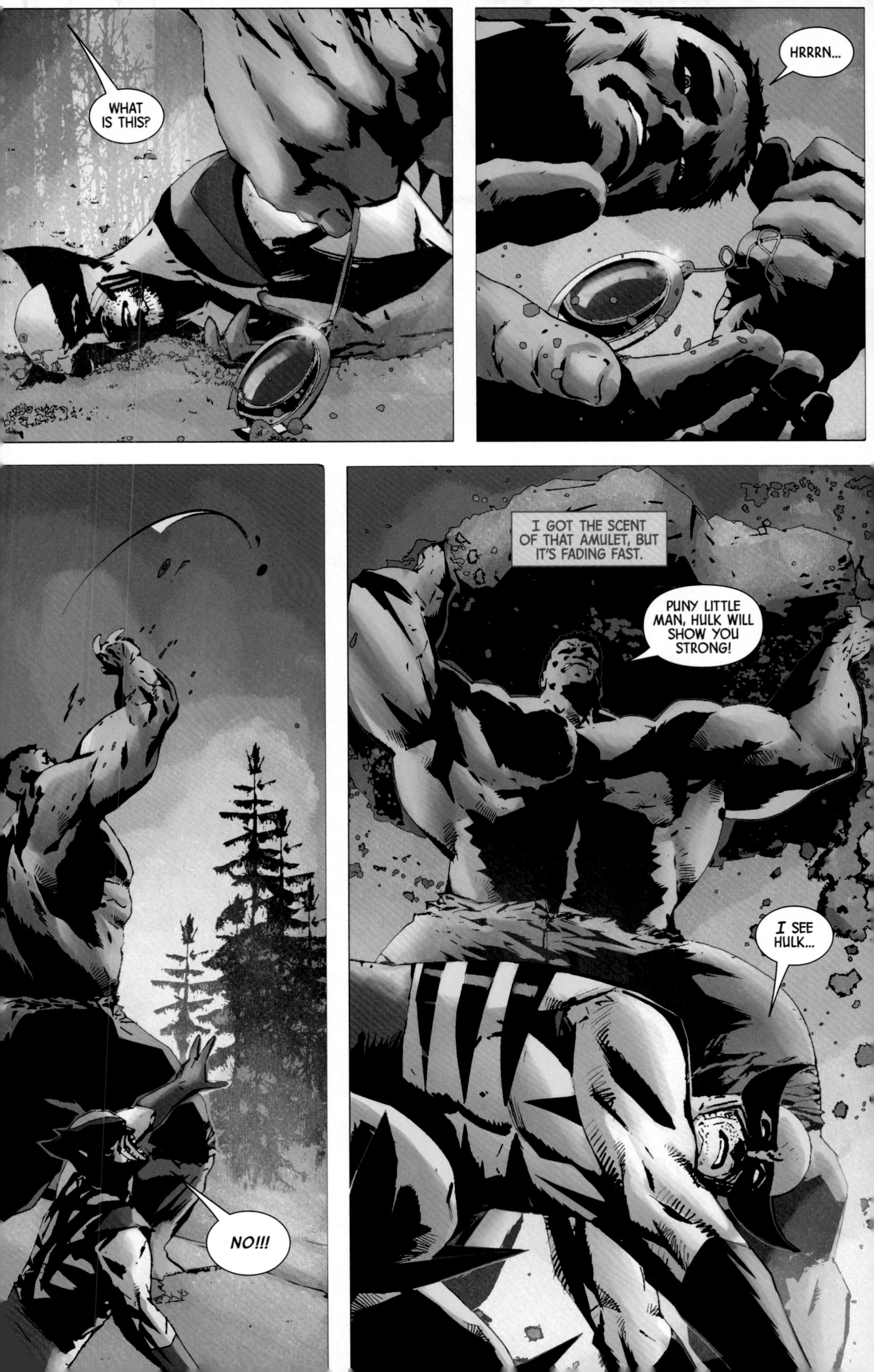
WHAT IS THIS?
HRRRN...
NO!!!
I GOT THE SCENT OF THAT AMULET, BUT IT'S FADING FAST.
PUNY LITTLE MAN, HULK WILL SHOW YOU STRONG!
I SEE HULK...

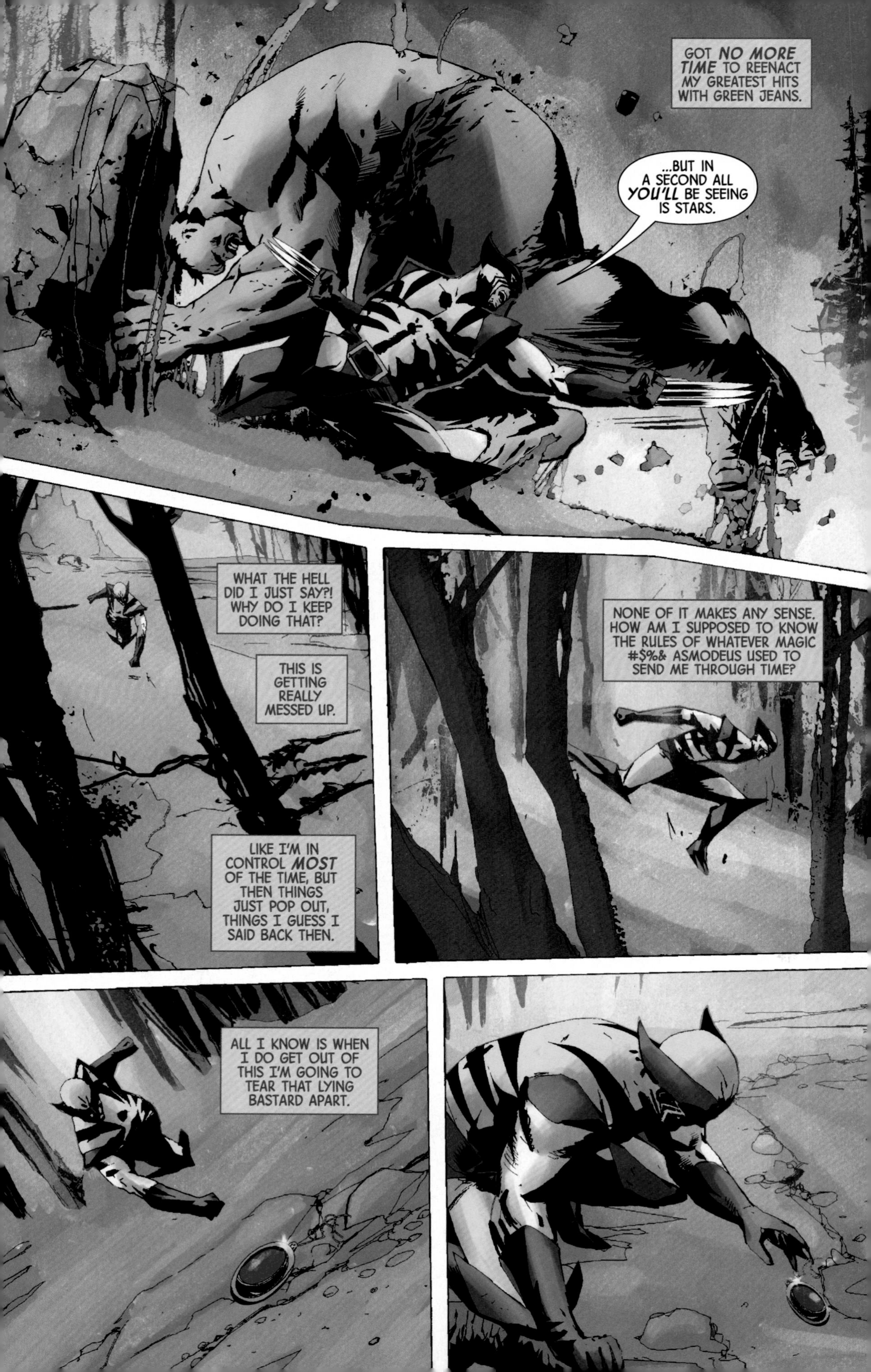
GOT NO MORE TIME TO REENACT MY GREATEST HITS WITH GREEN JEANS.
...BUT IN A SECOND ALL YOU'LL BE SEEING IS STARS.
WHAT THE HELL DID I JUST SAY?! WHY DO I KEEP DOING THAT?
THIS IS GETTING REALLY MESSED UP.
LIKE I'M IN CONTROL MOST OF THE TIME, BUT THEN THINGS JUST POP OUT, THINGS I GUESS I SAID BACK THEN.
NONE OF IT MAKES ANY SENSE. HOW AM I SUPPOSED TO KNOW THE RULES OF WHATEVER MAGIC #$%& ASMODEUS USED TO SEND ME THROUGH TIME?
ALL I KNOW IS WHEN I DO GET OUT OF THIS I'M GOING TO TEAR THAT LYING BASTARD APART.

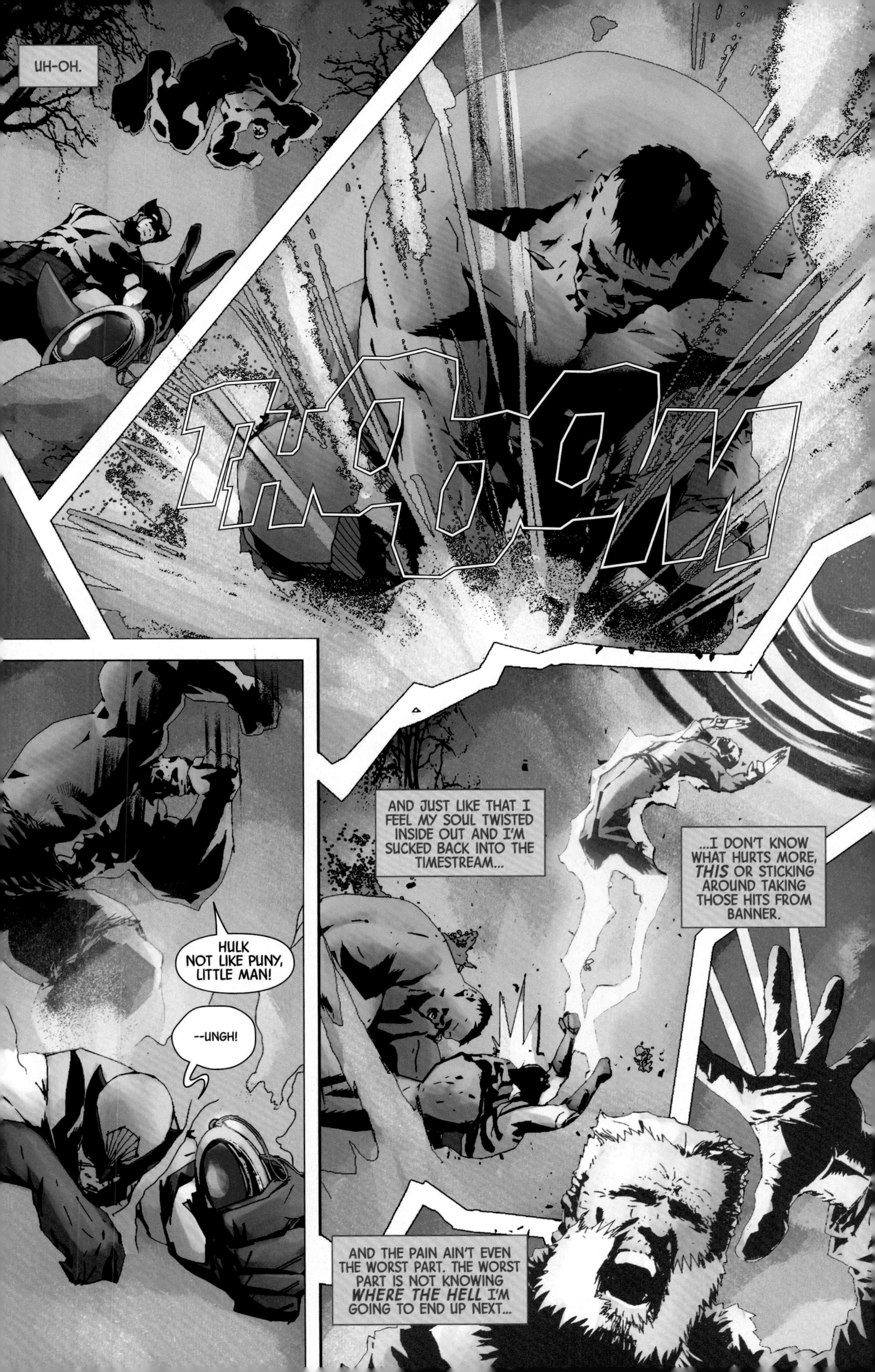
UH-OH.
THOOOM
HULK NOT LIKE PUNY, LITTLE MAN!
--UNGH!
AND JUST LIKE THAT I FEEL MY SOUL TWISTED INSIDE OUT AND I'M SUCKED BACK INTO THE TIMESTREAM...
...I DON'T KNOW WHAT HURTS MORE, THIS OR STICKING AROUND TAKING THOSE HITS FROM BANNER.
AND THE PAIN AIN'T EVEN THE WORST PART. THE WORST PART IS NOT KNOWING WHERE THE HELL I'M GOING TO END UP NEXT...

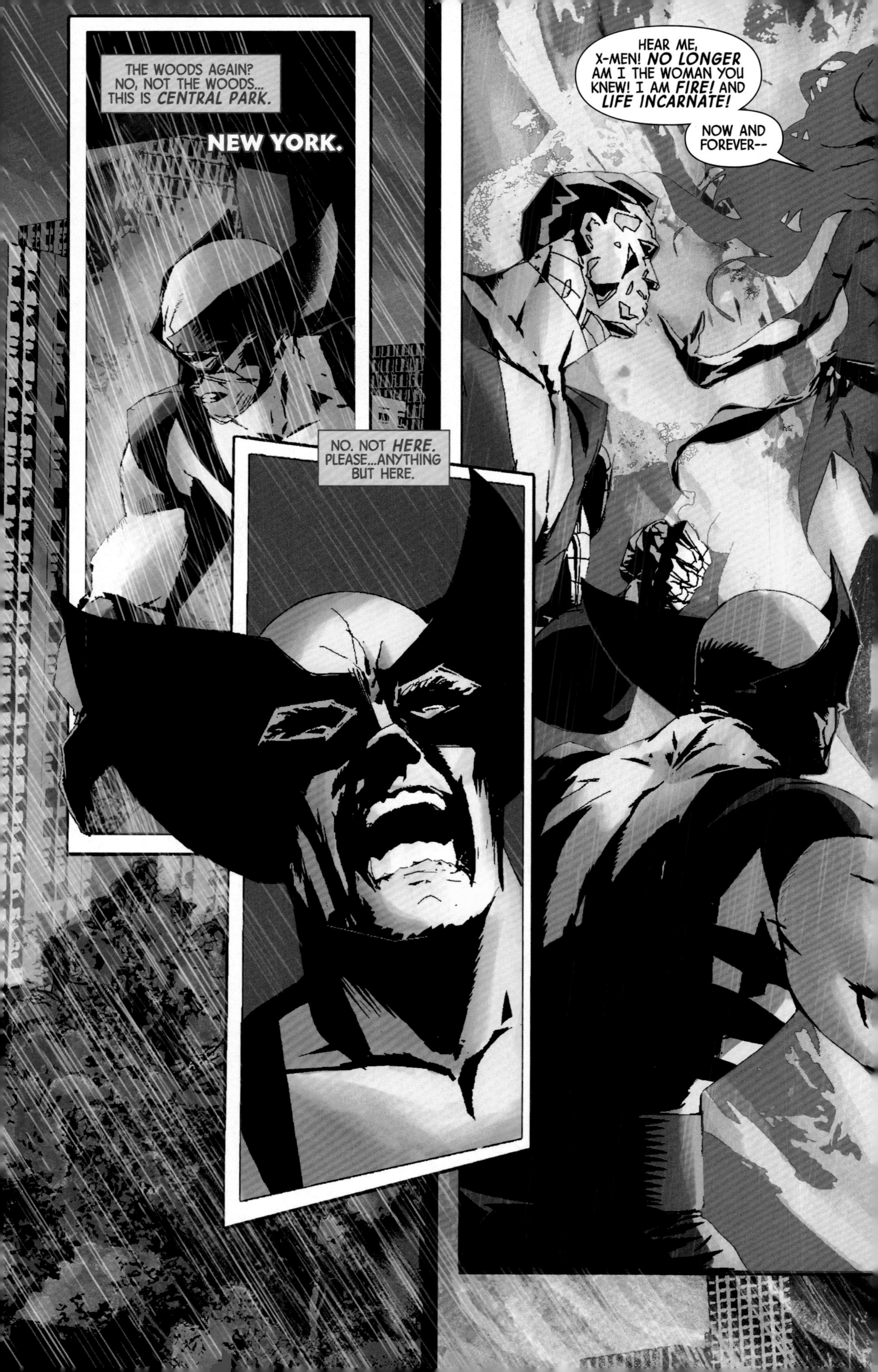
THE WOODS AGAIN? NO, NOT THE WOODS... THIS IS CENTRAL PARK.
NEW YORK.
HEAR ME, X-MEN! NO LONGER AM I THE WOMAN YOU KNEW! I AM FIRE! AND LIFE INCARNATE!
NOW AND FOREVER--
NO. NOT HERE. PLEASE...ANYTHING BUT HERE.

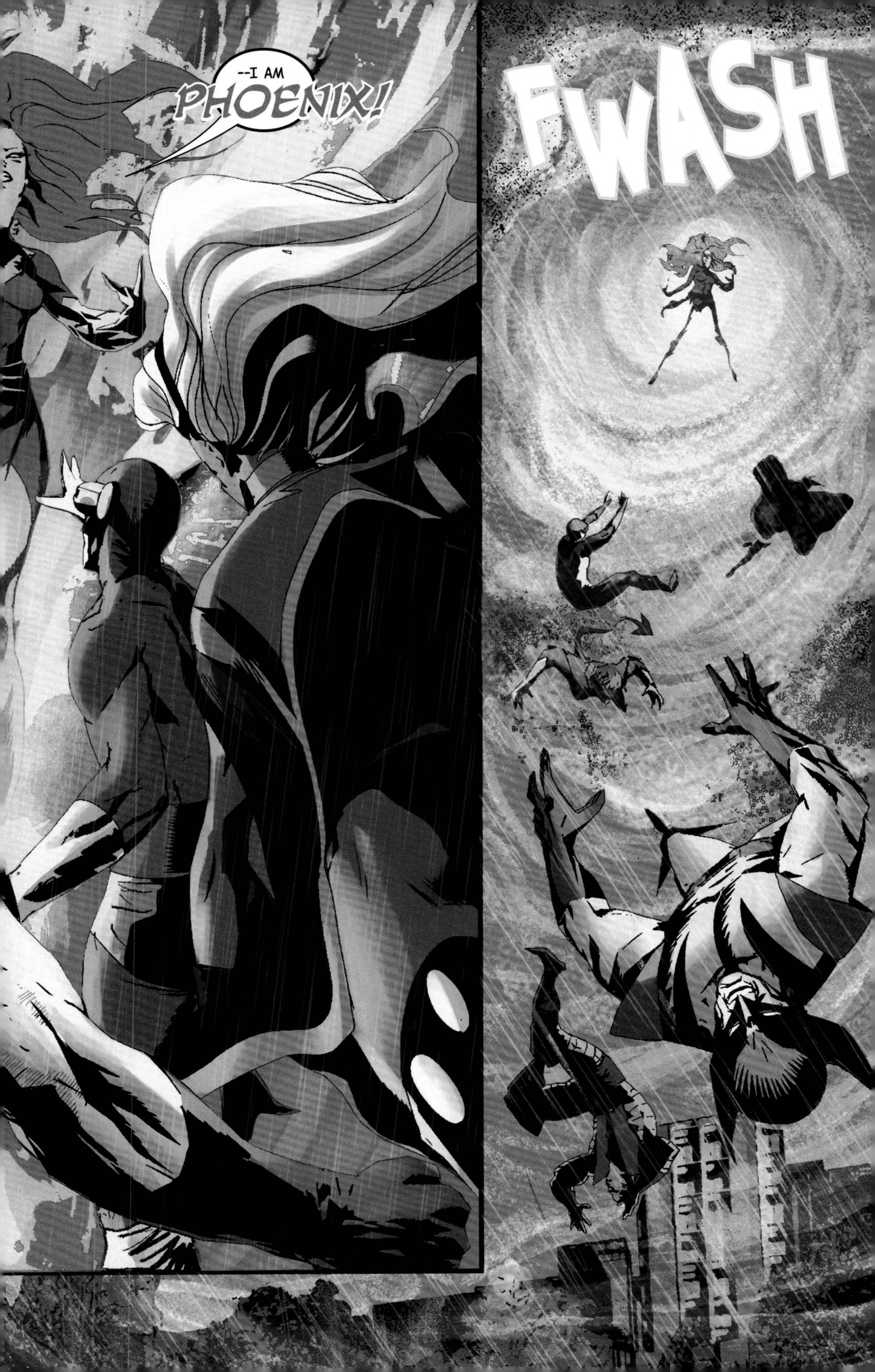
--I AM PHOENIX!
FWASH

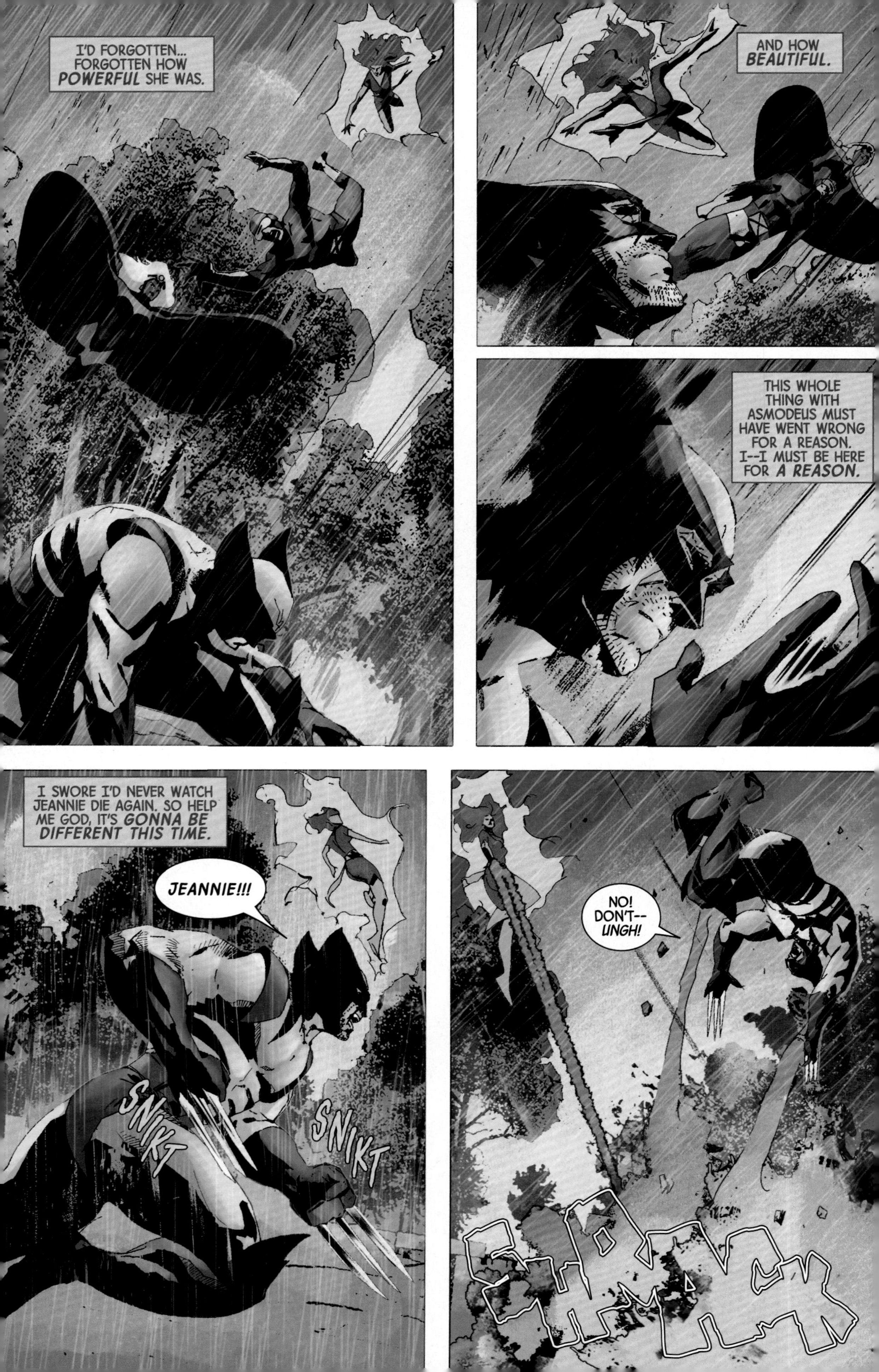

I'D FORGOTTEN... FORGOTTEN HOW POWERFUL SHE WAS.
AND HOW BEAUTIFUL.
THIS WHOLE THING WITH ASMODEUS MUST HAVE WENT WRONG FOR A REASON. I--I MUST BE HERE FOR A REASON.
I SWORE I'D NEVER WATCH JEANNIE DIE AGAIN. SO HELP ME GOD, IT'S GONNA BE DIFFERENT THIS TIME.
JEANNIE!!!
SNIKT
SNIKT
NO! DON'T-- UNGH!

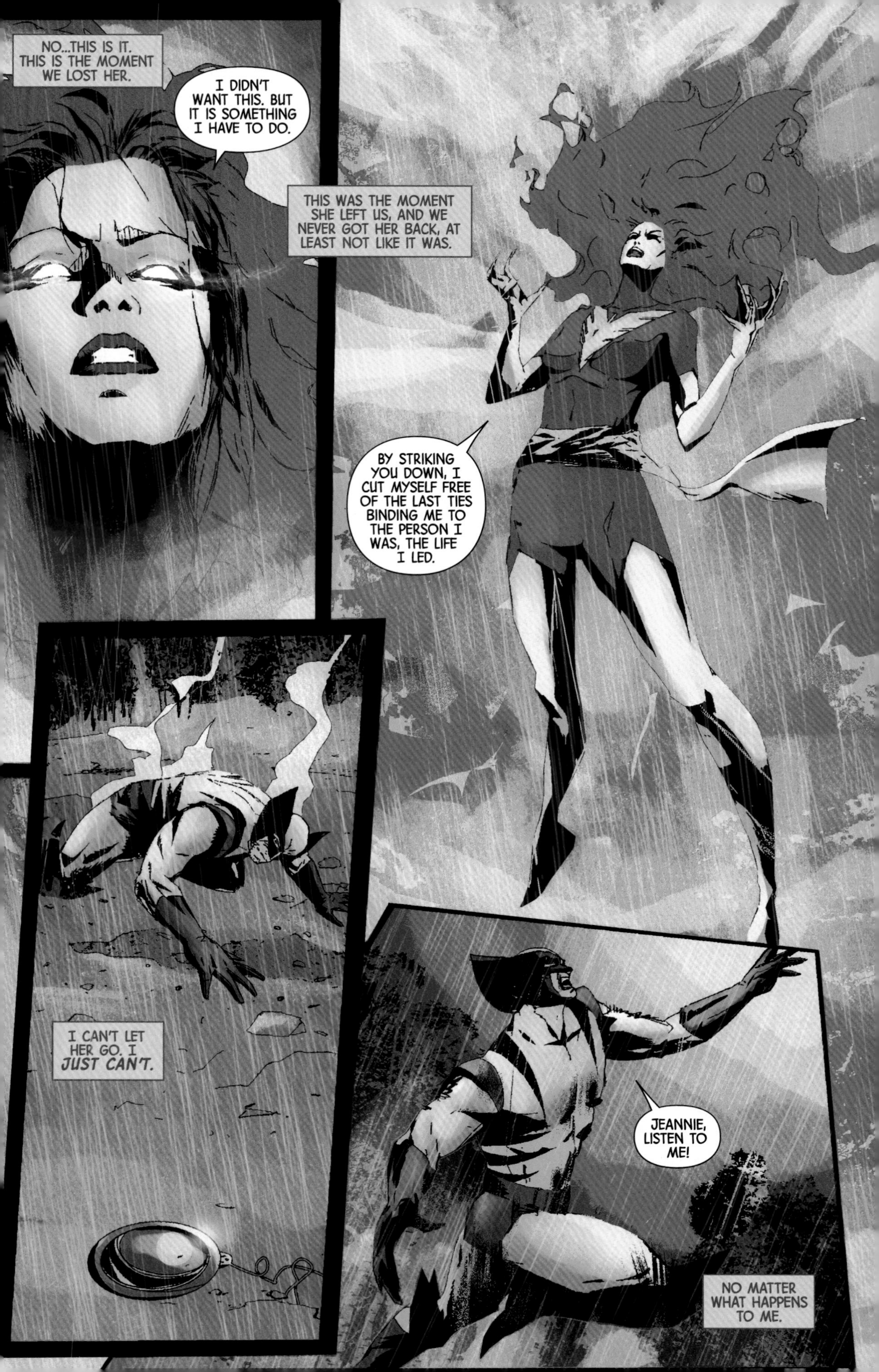
NO...THIS IS IT. THIS IS THE MOMENT WE LOST HER.
I DIDN'T WANT THIS. BUT IT IS SOMETHING I HAVE TO DO.
THIS WAS THE MOMENT SHE LEFT US, AND WE NEVER GOT HER BACK, AT LEAST NOT LIKE IT WAS.
BY STRIKING YOU DOWN, I CUT MYSELF FREE OF THE LAST TIES BINDING ME TO THE PERSON I WAS, THE LIFE I LED.
I CAN'T LET HER GO. I *JUST CAN'T.*
JEANNIE, LISTEN TO ME!
NO MATTER WHAT HAPPENS TO ME.

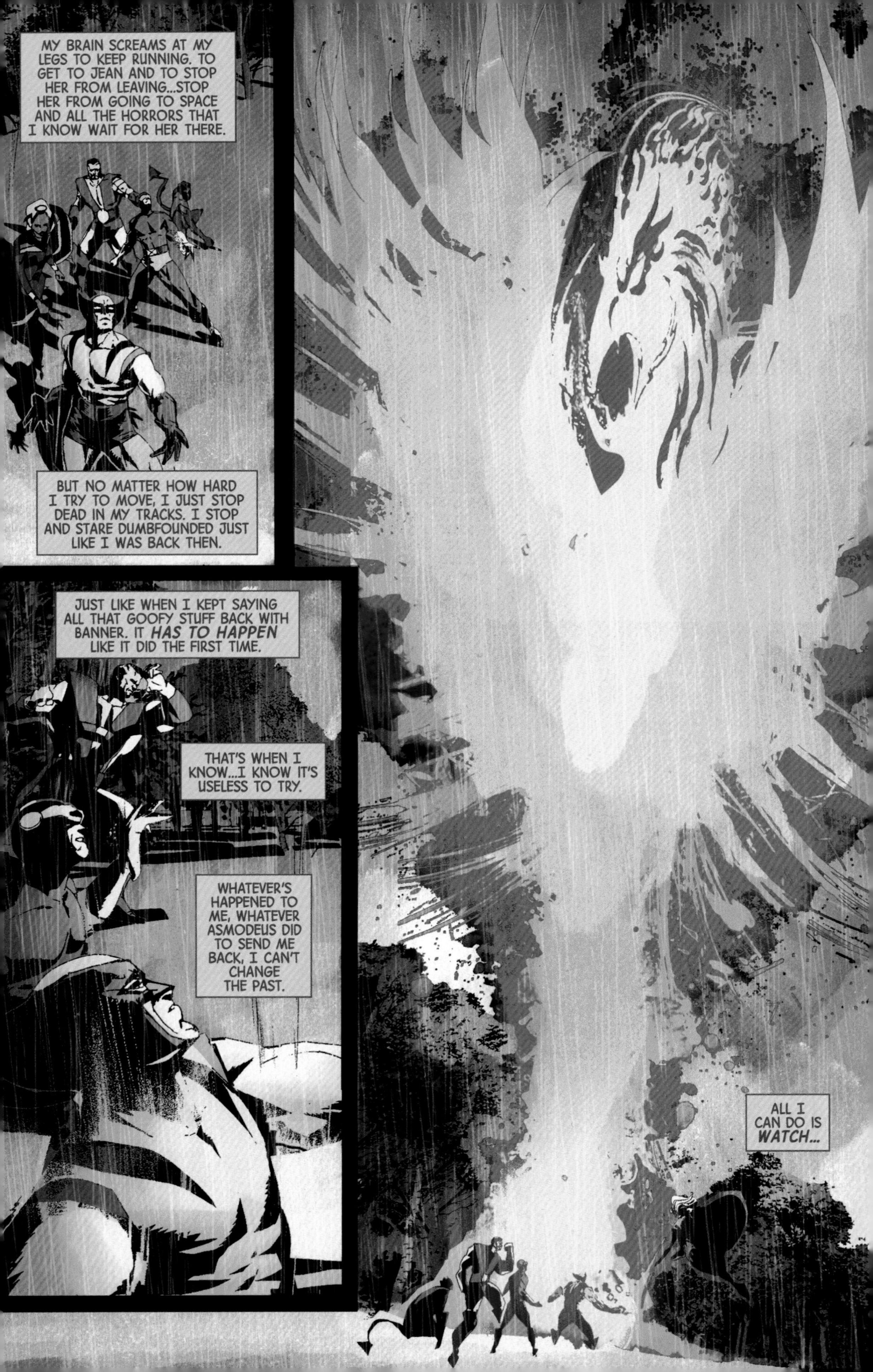
MY BRAIN SCREAMS AT MY LEGS TO KEEP RUNNING. TO GET TO JEAN AND TO STOP HER FROM LEAVING...STOP HER FROM GOING TO SPACE AND ALL THE HORRORS THAT I KNOW WAIT FOR HER THERE.
BUT NO MATTER HOW HARD I TRY TO MOVE, I JUST STOP DEAD IN MY TRACKS. I STOP AND STARE DUMBFOUNDED JUST LIKE I WAS BACK THEN.
JUST LIKE WHEN I KEPT SAYING ALL THAT GOOFY STUFF BACK WITH BANNER. IT *HAS TO HAPPEN* LIKE IT DID THE FIRST TIME.
THAT'S WHEN I KNOW...I KNOW IT'S USELESS TO TRY.
WHATEVER'S HAPPENED TO ME, WHATEVER ASMODEUS DID TO SEND ME BACK, I CAN'T CHANGE THE PAST.
ALL I CAN DO IS *WATCH...*

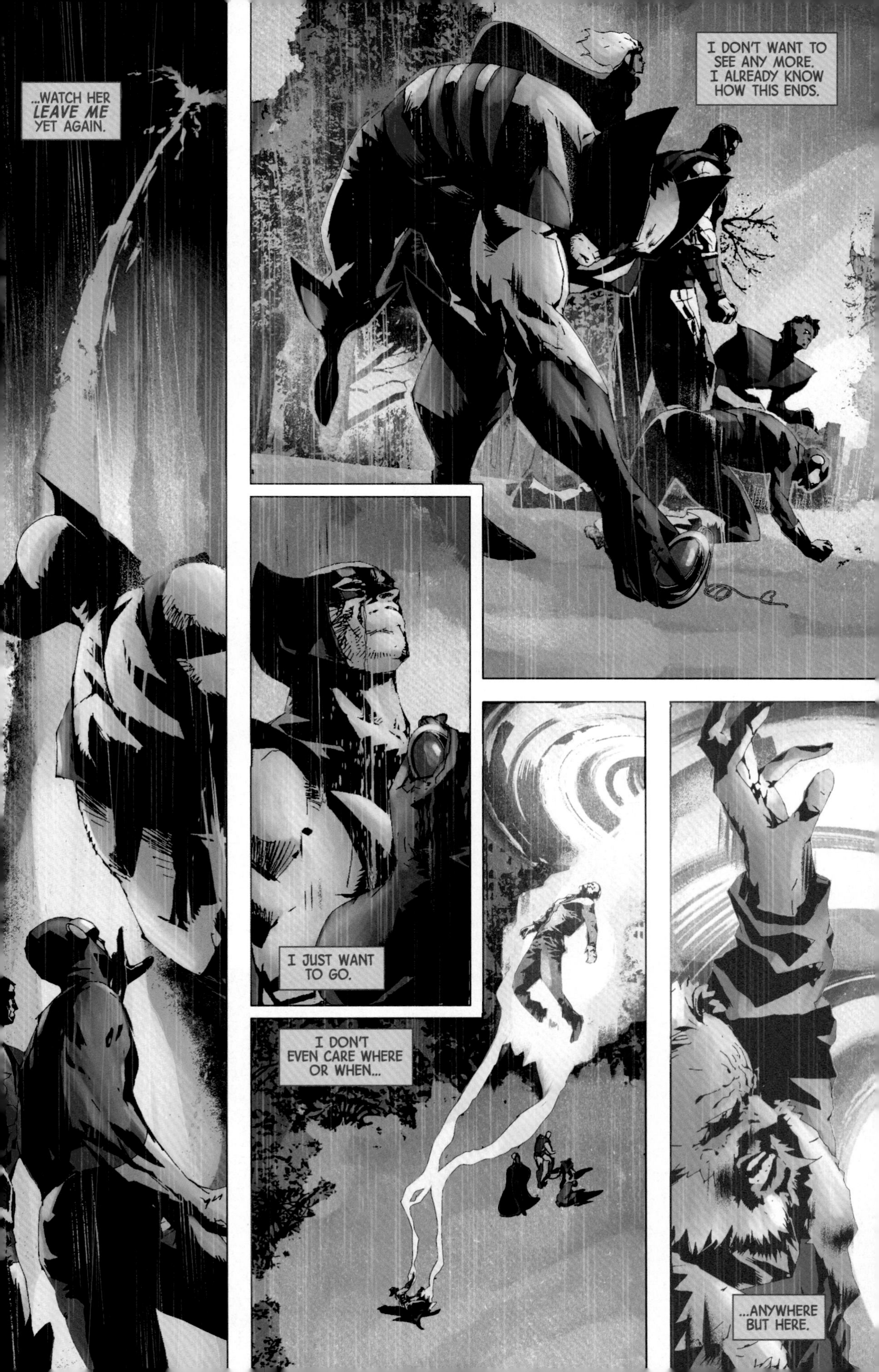
...WATCH HER LEAVE ME YET AGAIN.
I DON'T WANT TO SEE ANY MORE. I ALREADY KNOW HOW THIS ENDS.
I JUST WANT TO GO.
I DON'T EVEN CARE WHERE OR WHEN...
...ANYWHERE BUT HERE.

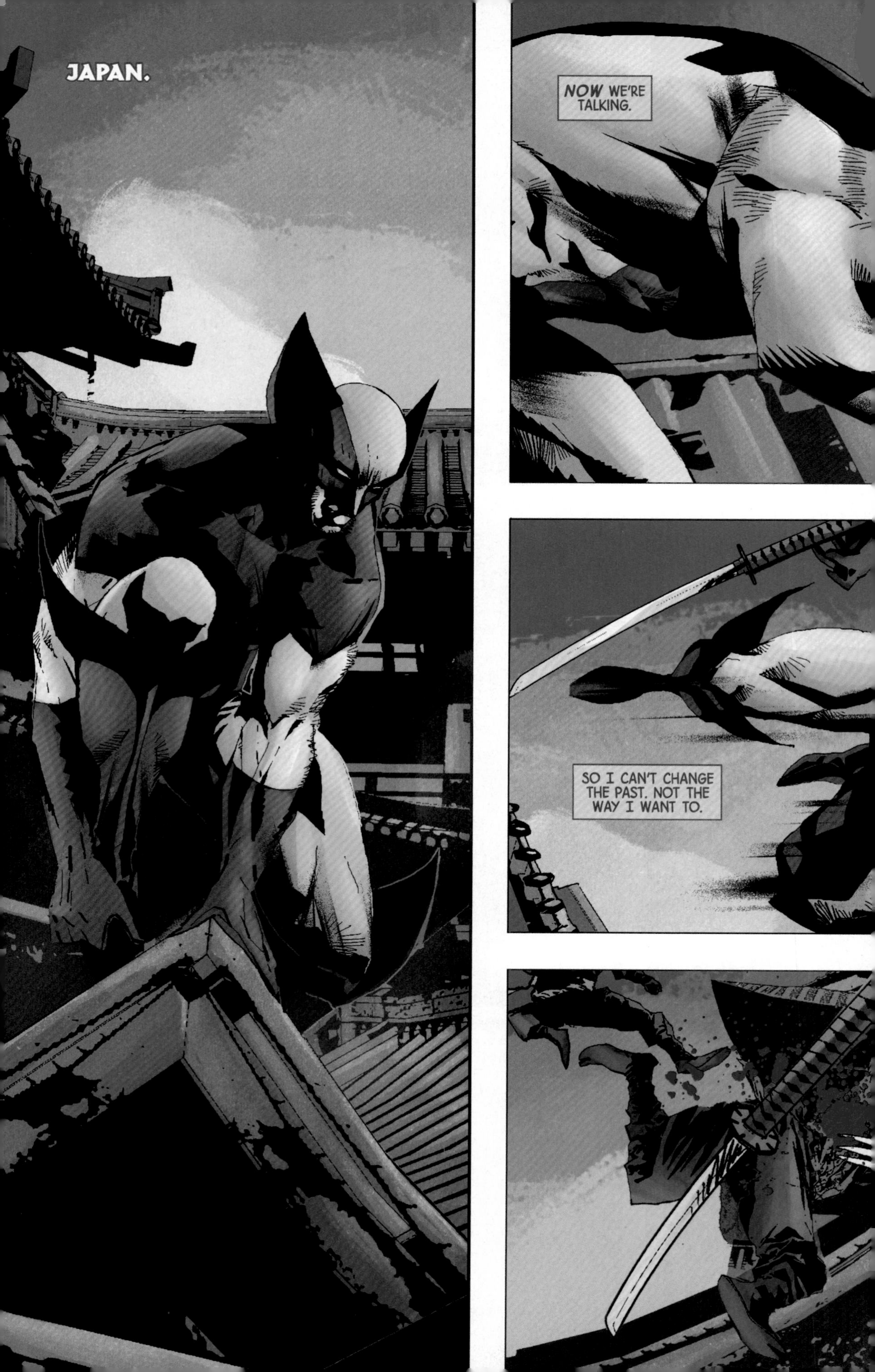
JAPAN.
NOW WE'RE TALKING.
SO I CAN'T CHANGE THE PAST. NOT THE WAY I WANT TO.

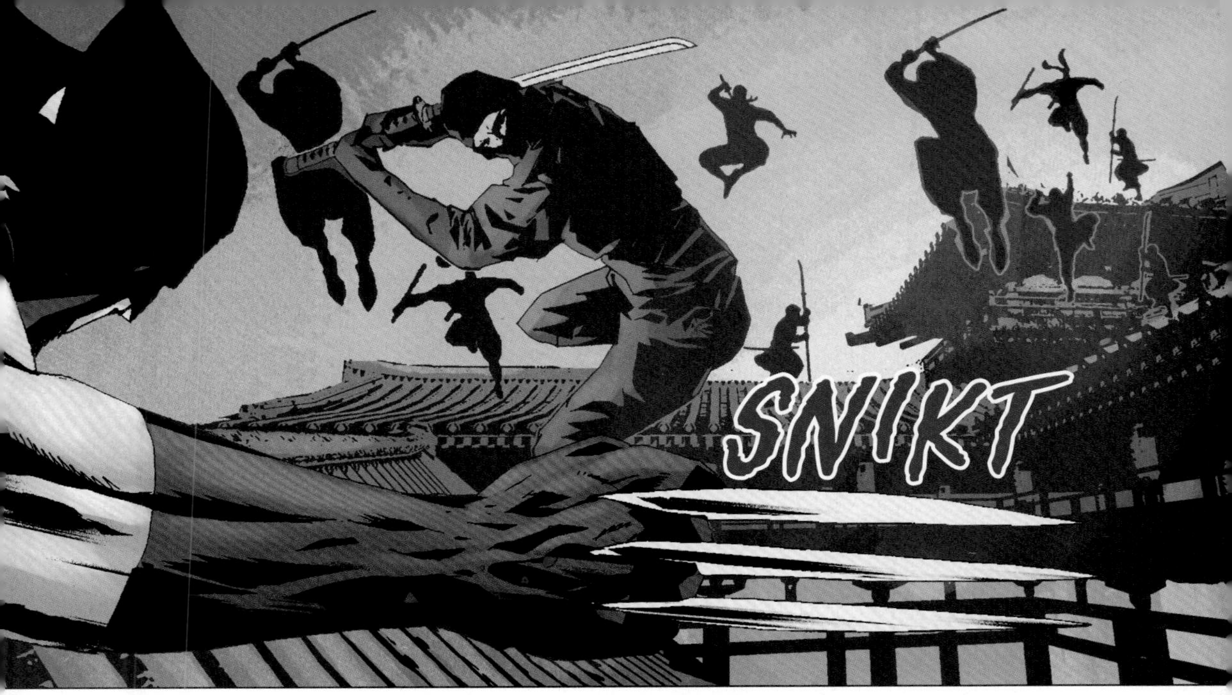
SNIKT

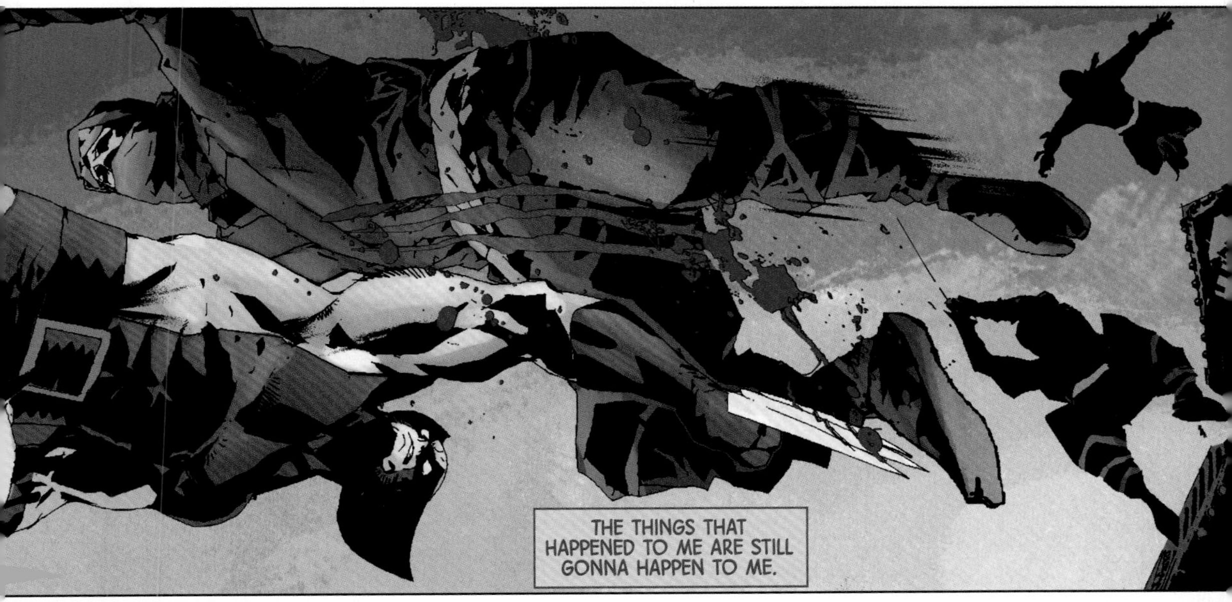
THE THINGS THAT HAPPENED TO ME ARE STILL GONNA HAPPEN TO ME.

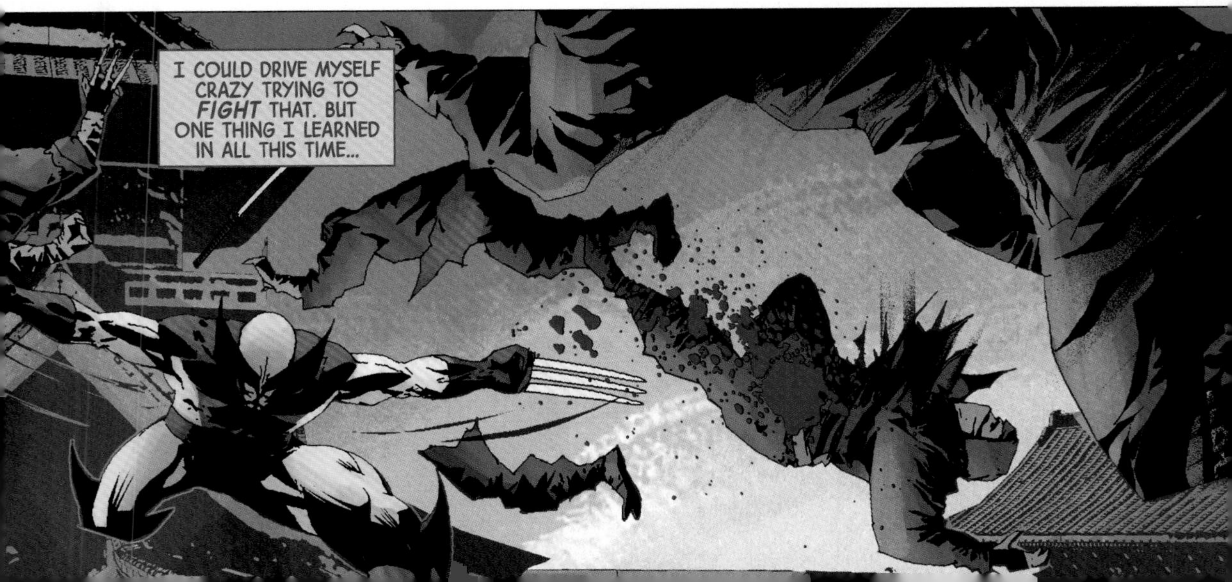
I COULD DRIVE MYSELF CRAZY TRYING TO FIGHT THAT. BUT ONE THING I LEARNED IN ALL THIS TIME...

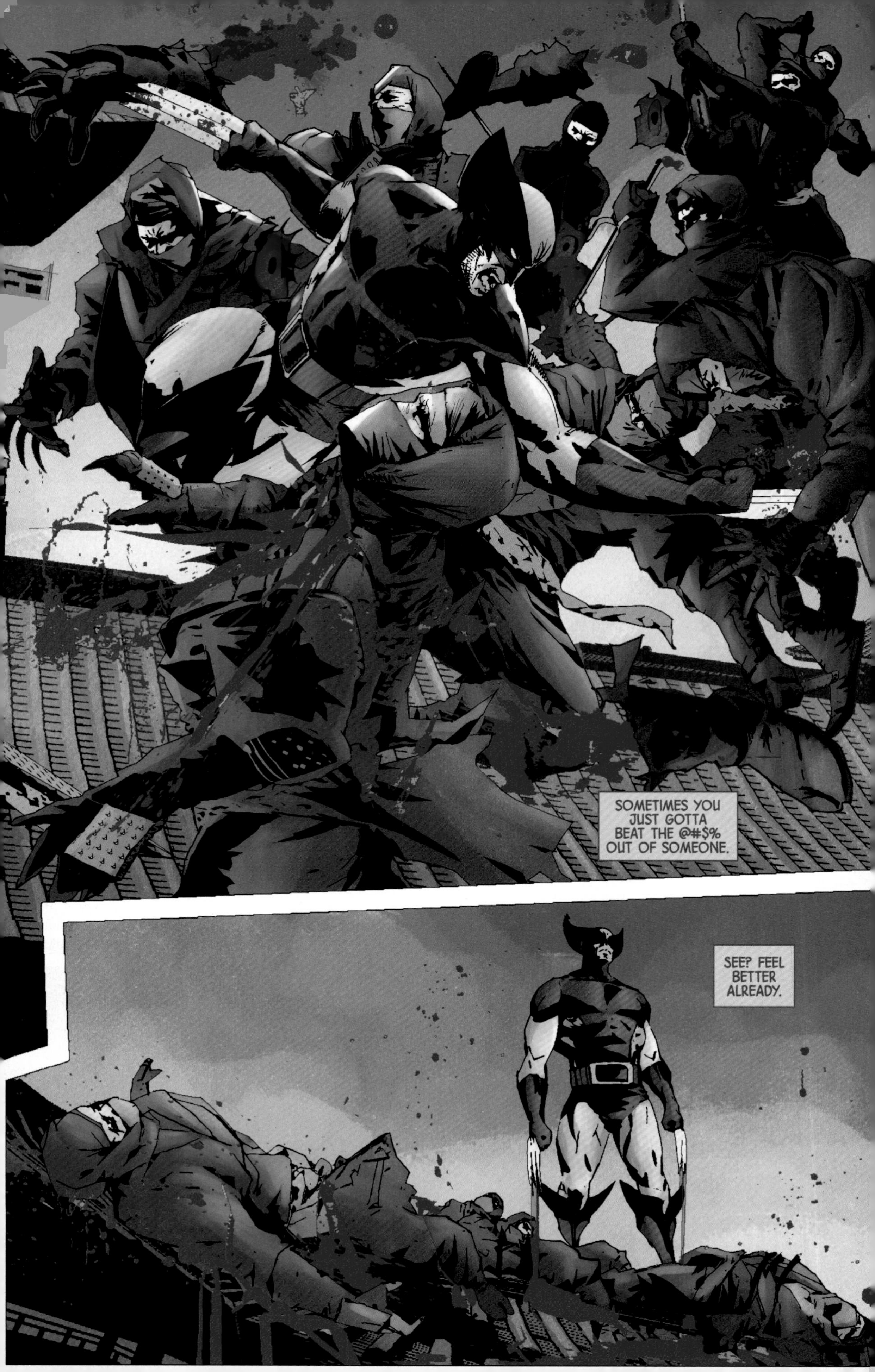
SOMETIMES YOU JUST GOTTA BEAT THE @#$% OUT OF SOMEONE.
SEE? FEEL BETTER ALREADY.

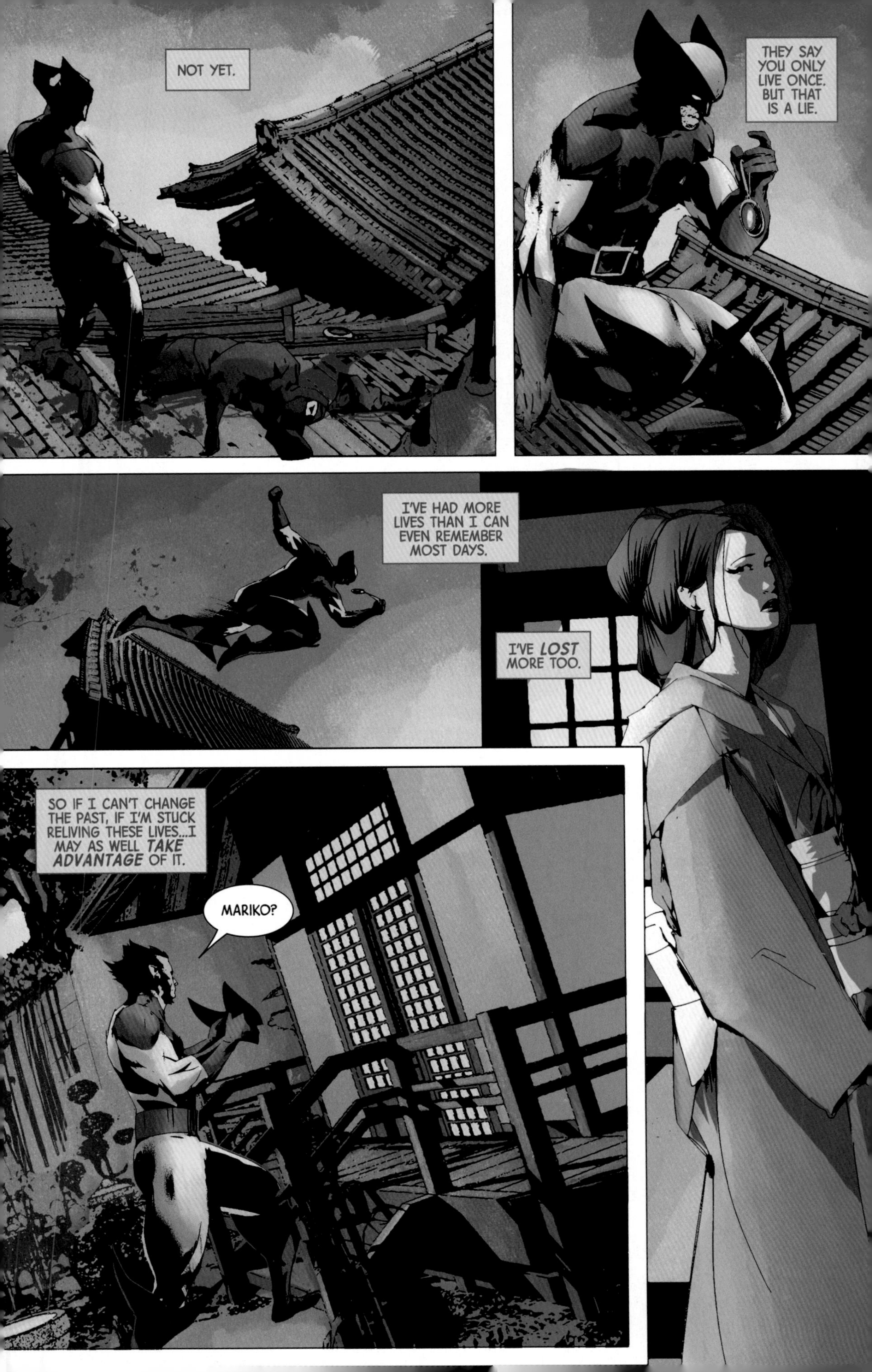
NOT YET.
THEY SAY YOU ONLY LIVE ONCE. BUT THAT IS A LIE.
I'VE HAD MORE LIVES THAN I CAN EVEN REMEMBER MOST DAYS.
I'VE *LOST* MORE TOO.
SO IF I CAN'T CHANGE THE PAST, IF I'M STUCK RELIVING THESE LIVES...I MAY AS WELL *TAKE ADVANTAGE* OF IT.
MARIKO?

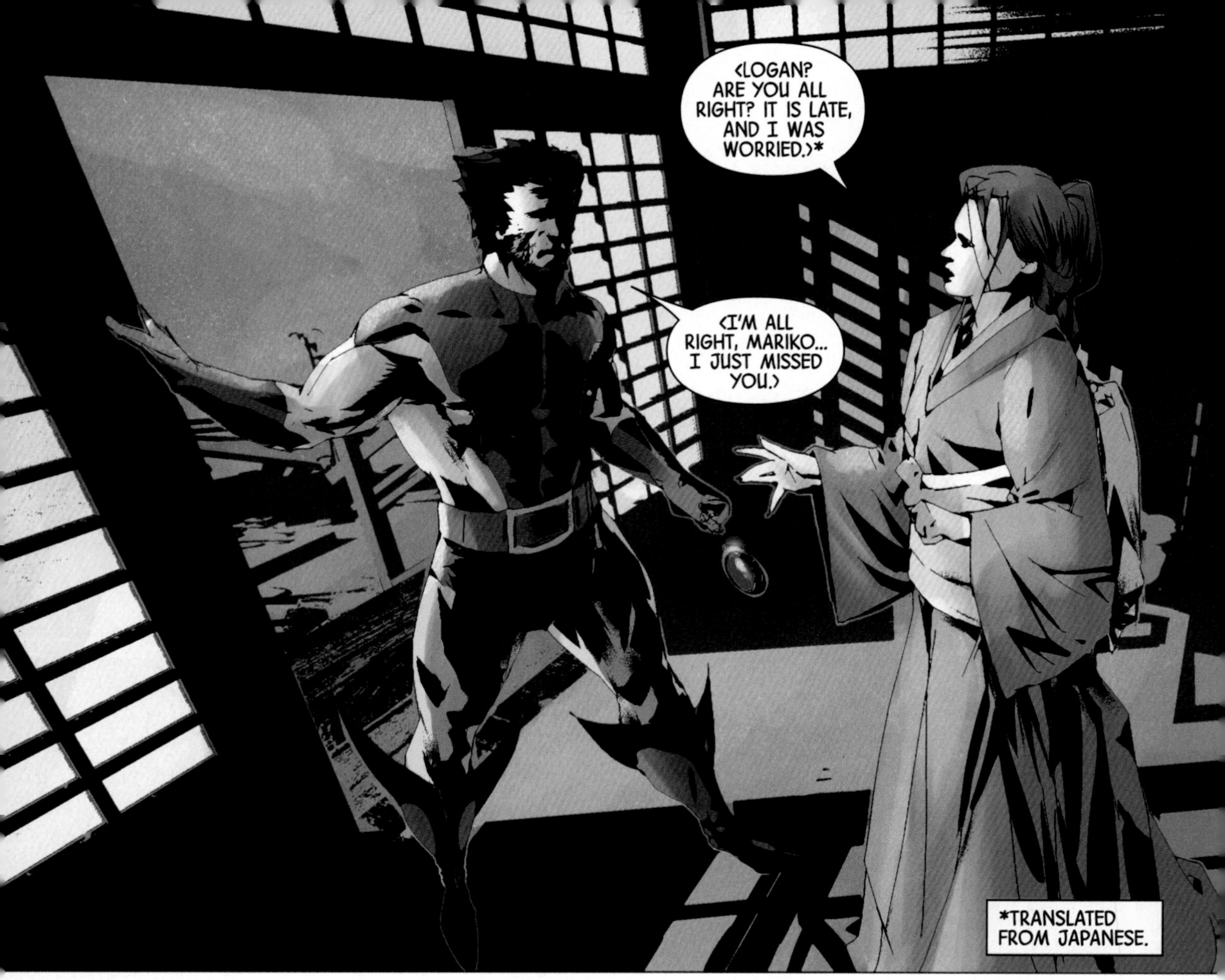
<LOGAN? ARE YOU ALL RIGHT? IT IS LATE, AND I WAS WORRIED.>*
<I'M ALL RIGHT, MARIKO... I JUST MISSED YOU.>
*TRANSLATED FROM JAPANESE.

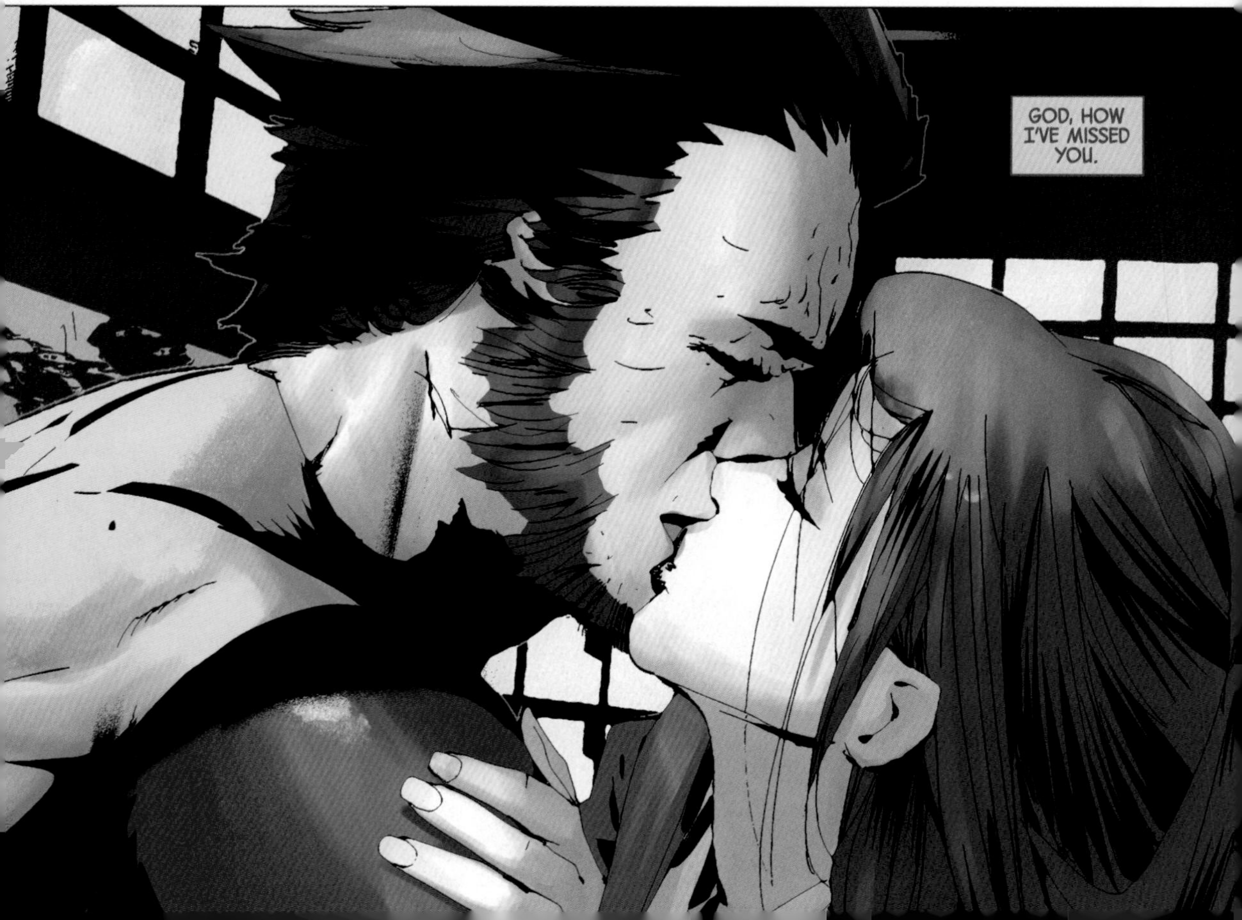
GOD, HOW I'VE MISSED YOU.

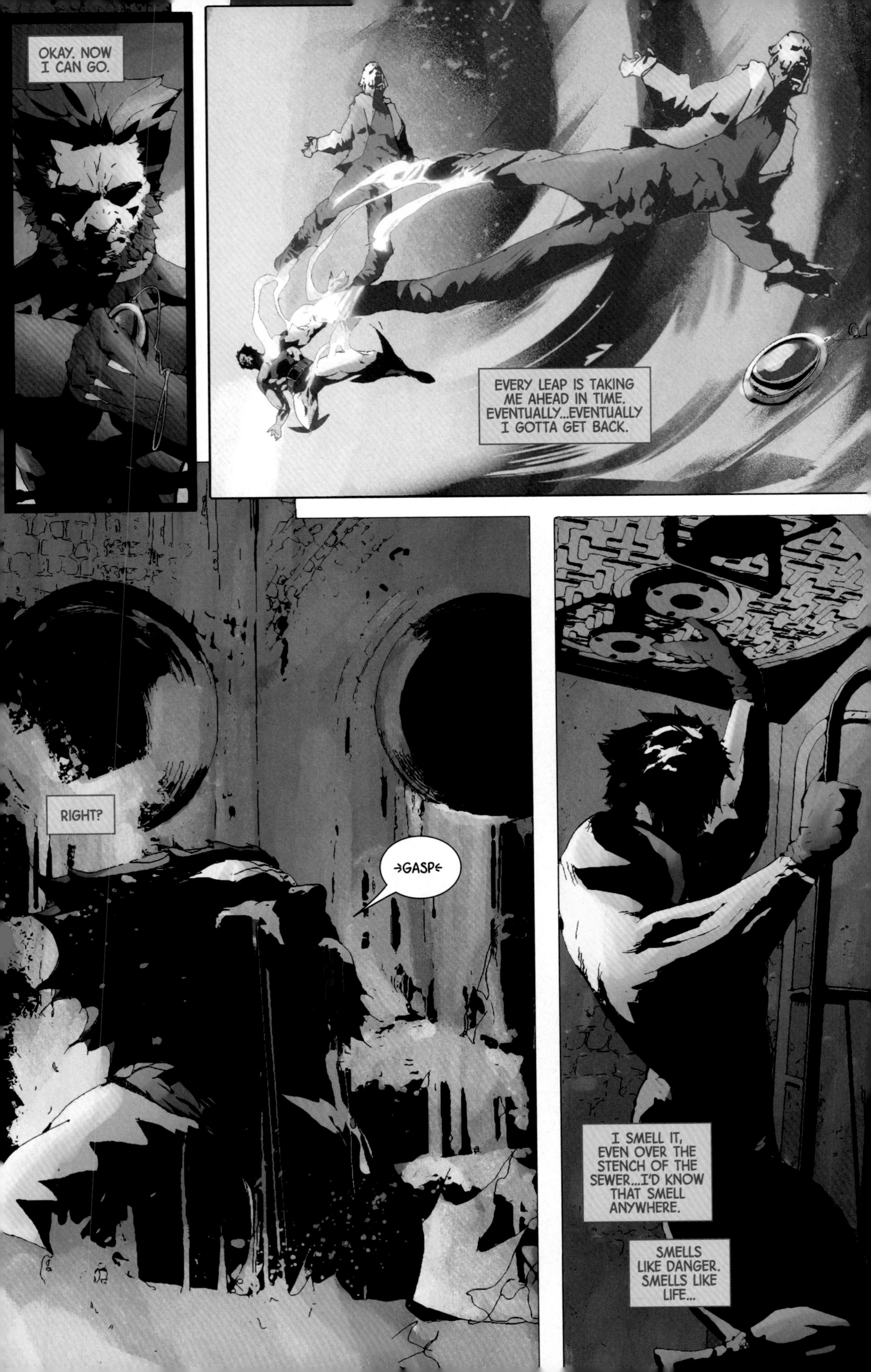

OKAY. NOW I CAN GO.
EVERY LEAP IS TAKING ME AHEAD IN TIME. EVENTUALLY...EVENTUALLY I GOTTA GET BACK.
RIGHT?
GASP
I SMELL IT, EVEN OVER THE STENCH OF THE SEWER...I'D KNOW THAT SMELL ANYWHERE.
SMELLS LIKE DANGER. SMELLS LIKE LIFE...

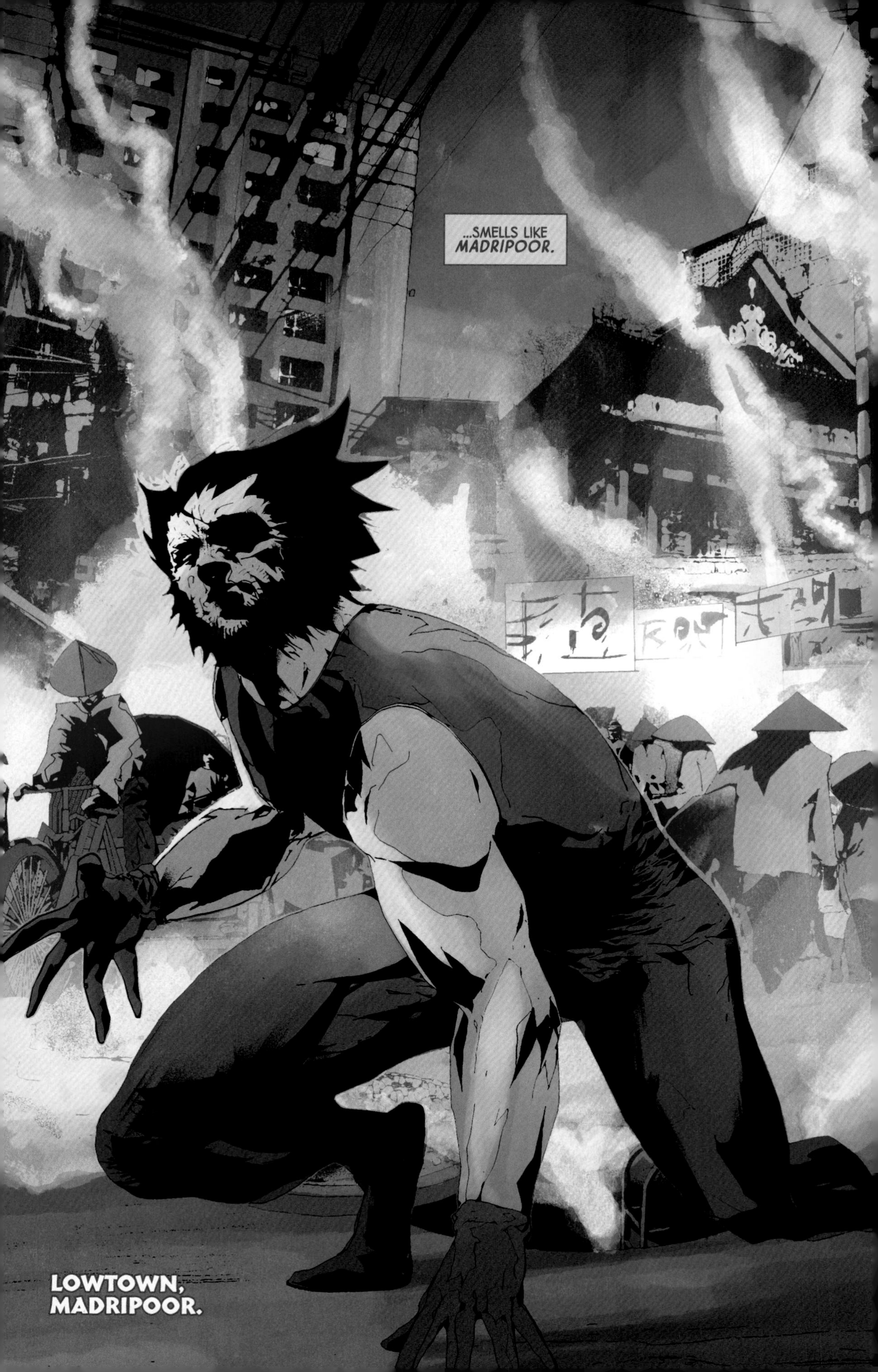
...SMELLS LIKE MADRIPOOR.
LOWTOWN, MADRIPOOR.

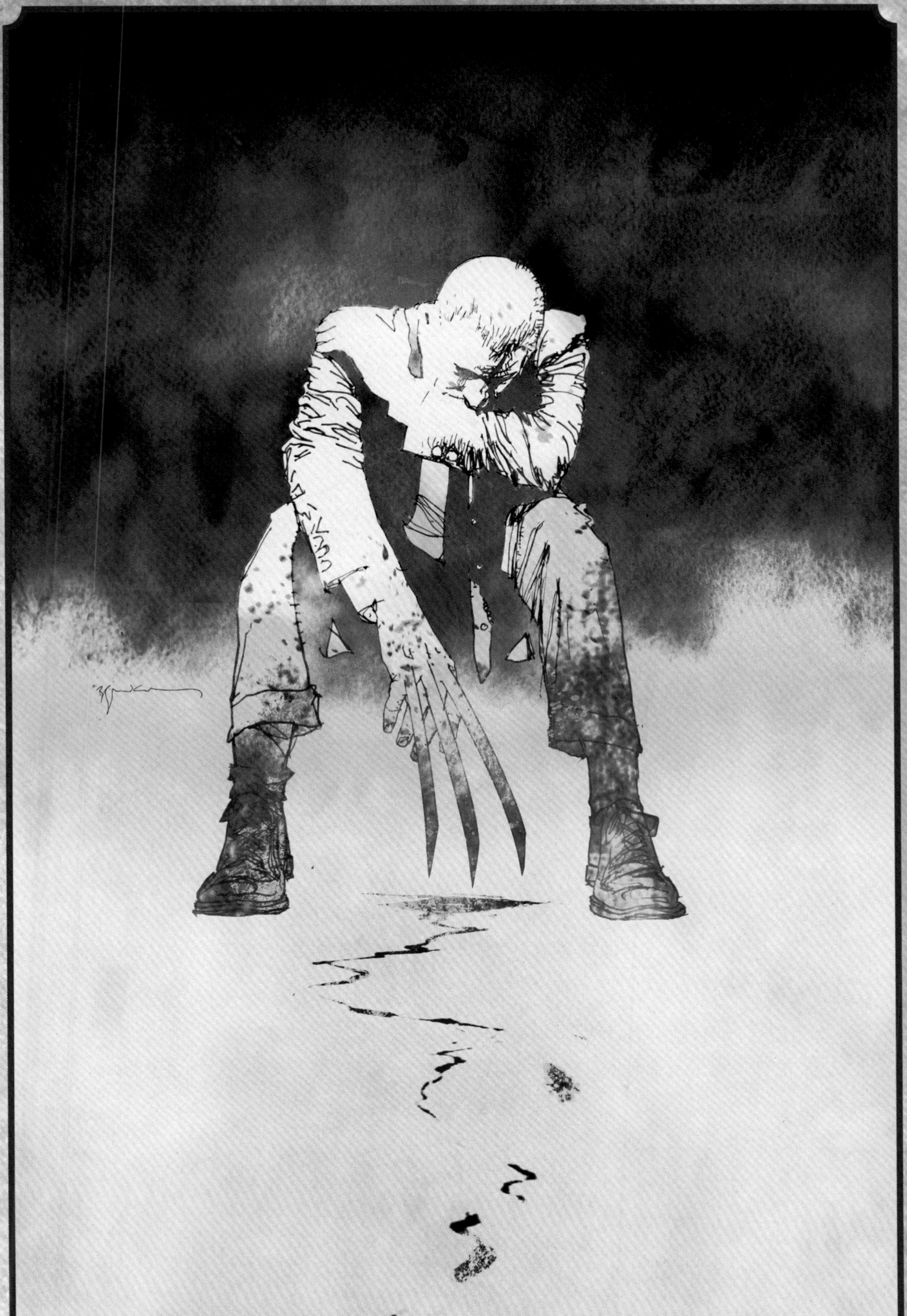

#23 VARIANT
BY BILL SIENKIEWICZ

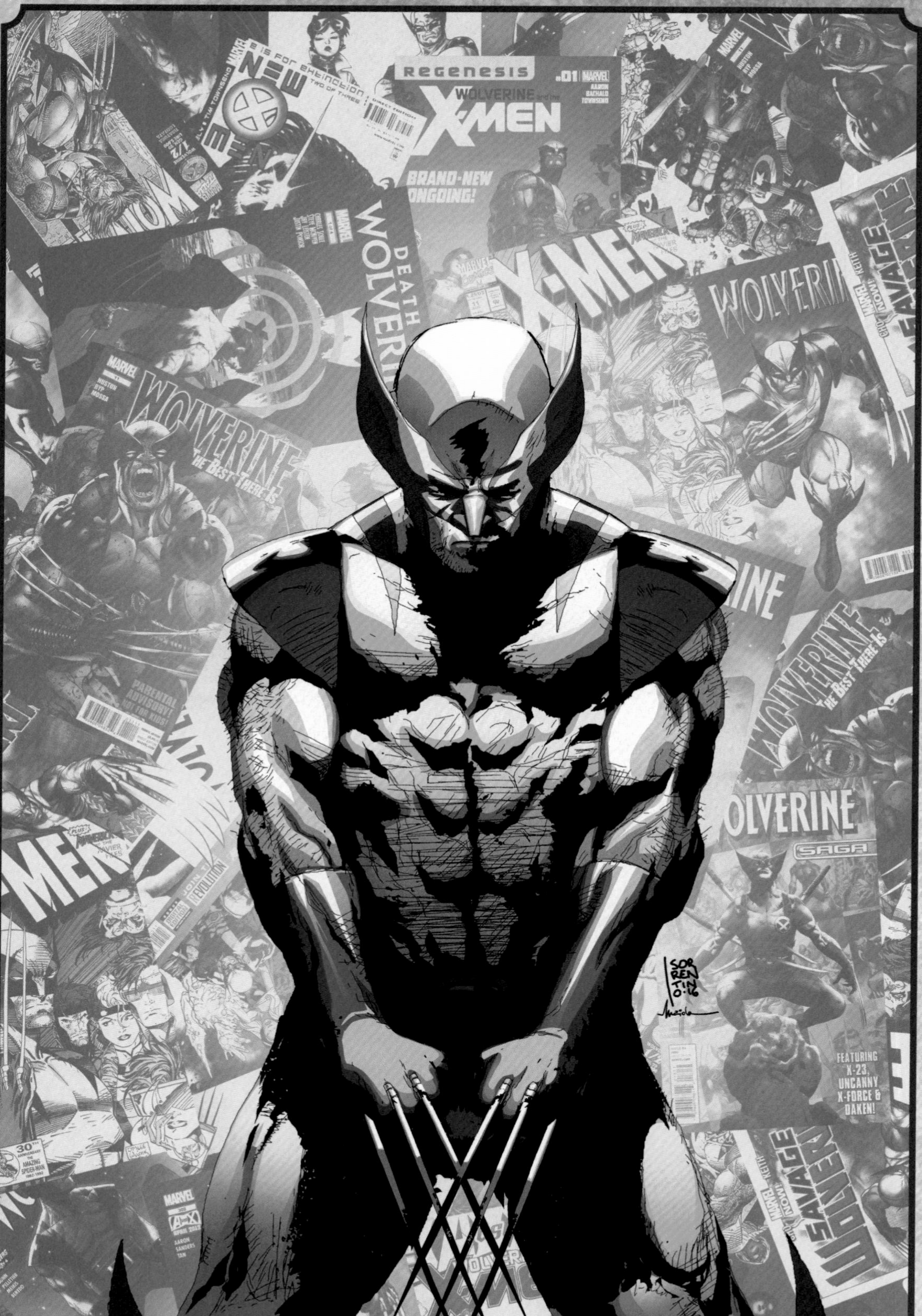
Regenesis
#01 MARVEL
WOLVERINE and the X-MEN
AARON BACHALO TOWNSEND
BRAND-NEW ONGOING!
DEATH OF WOLVERINE
X-MEN
WOLVERINE
WOLVERINE THE BEST THERE IS
PARENTAL ADVISORY! NOT FOR KIDS!
WOLVERINE
SAGA
FEATURING X-23, UNCANNY X-FORCE & DAKEN!
SAVAGE WOLVERINE
SORRENTINO 0·16

23

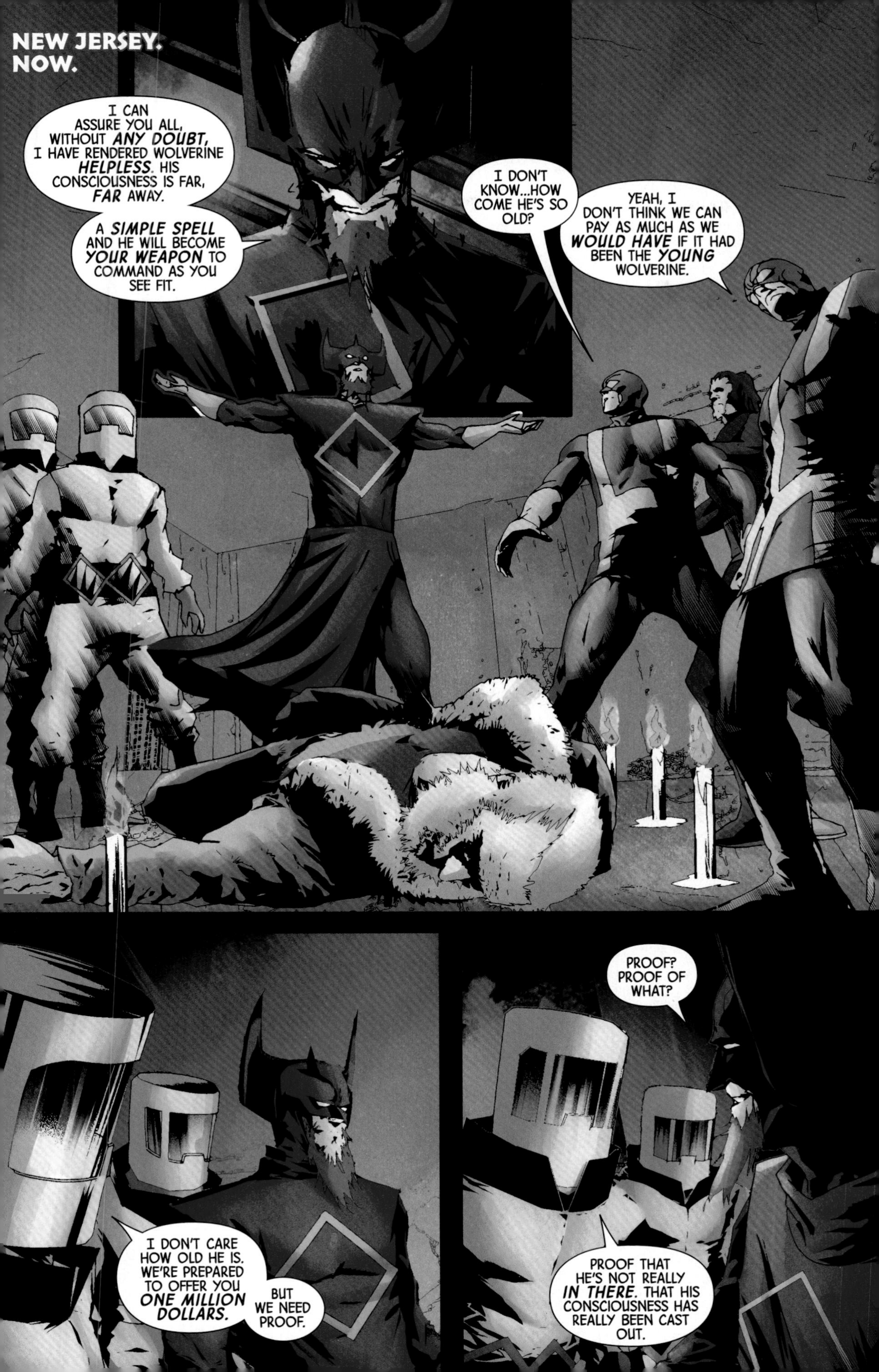
NEW JERSEY. NOW.
I CAN ASSURE YOU ALL, WITHOUT ANY DOUBT, I HAVE RENDERED WOLVERINE HELPLESS. HIS CONSCIOUSNESS IS FAR, FAR AWAY.
A SIMPLE SPELL AND HE WILL BECOME YOUR WEAPON TO COMMAND AS YOU SEE FIT.
I DON'T KNOW...HOW COME HE'S SO OLD?
YEAH, I DON'T THINK WE CAN PAY AS MUCH AS WE WOULD HAVE IF IT HAD BEEN THE YOUNG WOLVERINE.
I DON'T CARE HOW OLD HE IS. WE'RE PREPARED TO OFFER YOU ONE MILLION DOLLARS.
BUT WE NEED PROOF.
PROOF? PROOF OF WHAT?
PROOF THAT HE'S NOT REALLY IN THERE. THAT HIS CONSCIOUSNESS HAS REALLY BEEN CAST OUT.

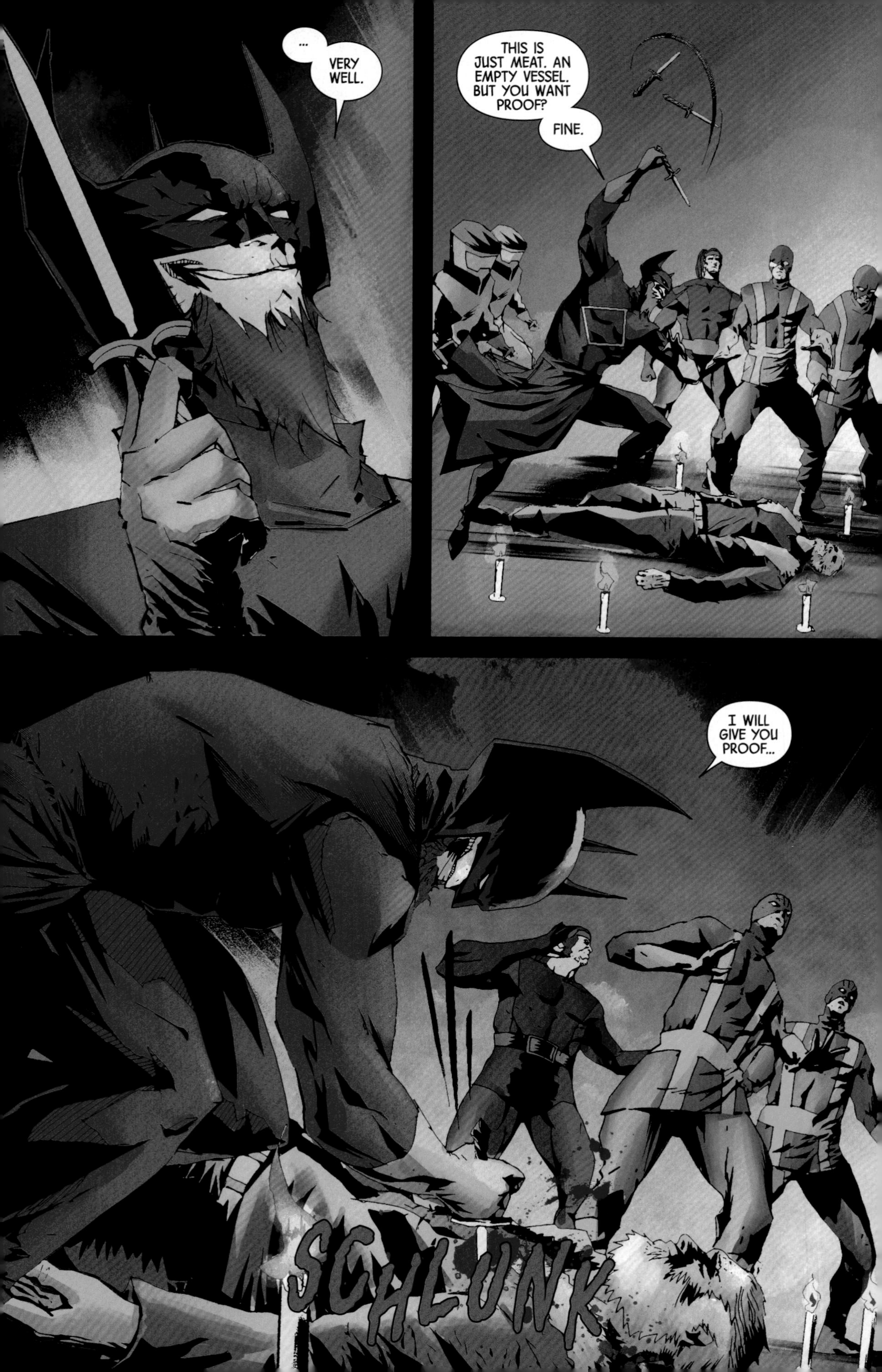
...
VERY WELL.
THIS IS JUST MEAT. AN EMPTY VESSEL. BUT YOU WANT PROOF?
FINE.
I WILL GIVE YOU PROOF...
SCHLUNK

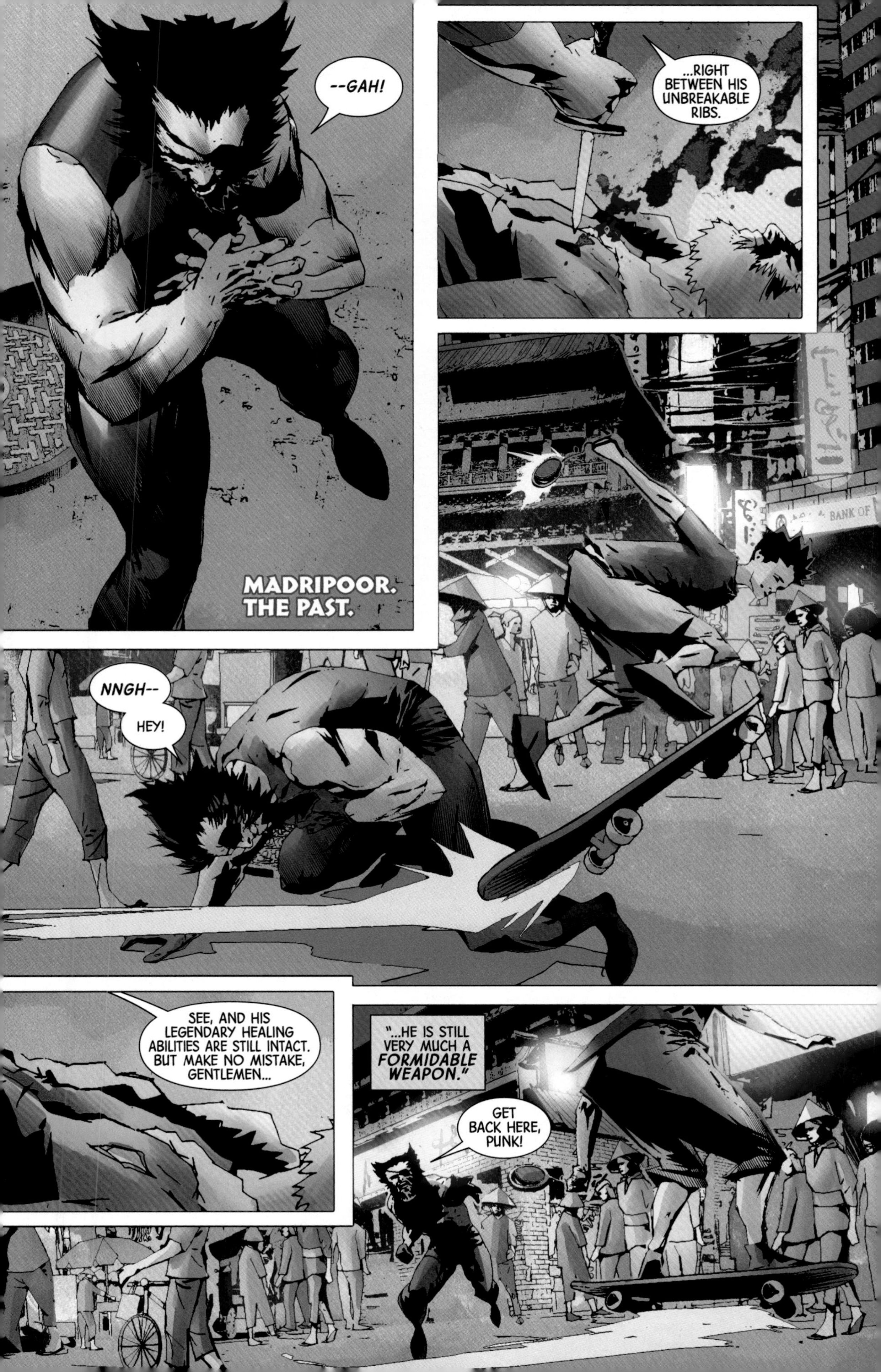
--GAH!
...RIGHT BETWEEN HIS UNBREAKABLE RIBS.
MADRIPOOR. THE PAST.
BANK OF
NNGH--
HEY!
SEE, AND HIS LEGENDARY HEALING ABILITIES ARE STILL INTACT. BUT MAKE NO MISTAKE, GENTLEMEN...
"...HE IS STILL VERY MUCH A FORMIDABLE WEAPON."
GET BACK HERE, PUNK!

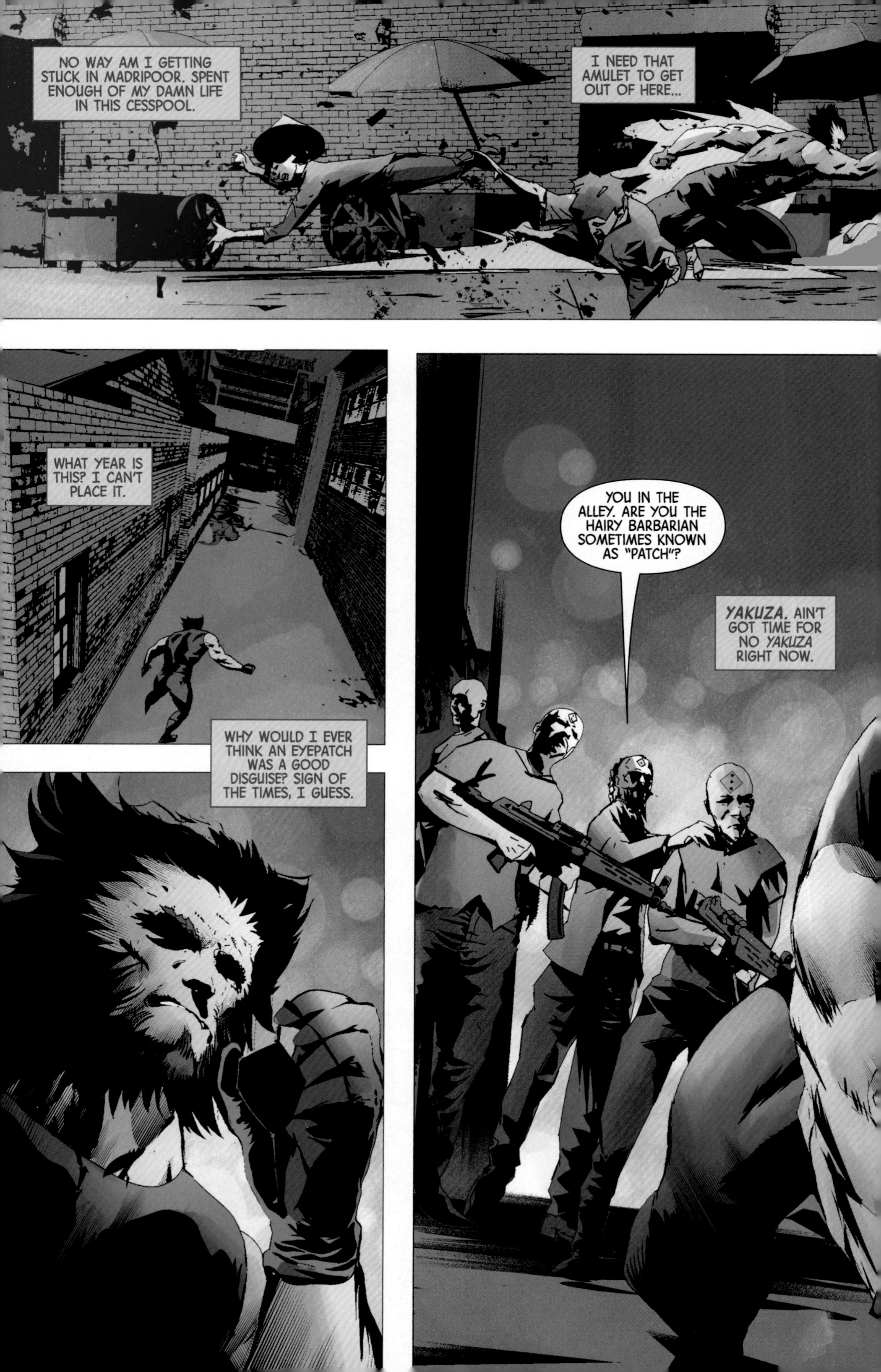
NO WAY AM I GETTING STUCK IN MADRIPOOR. SPENT ENOUGH OF MY DAMN LIFE IN THIS CESSPOOL.
I NEED THAT AMULET TO GET OUT OF HERE...
WHAT YEAR IS THIS? I CAN'T PLACE IT.
WHY WOULD I EVER THINK AN EYEPATCH WAS A GOOD DISGUISE? SIGN OF THE TIMES, I GUESS.
YOU IN THE ALLEY. ARE YOU THE HAIRY BARBARIAN SOMETIMES KNOWN AS "PATCH"?
YAKUZA. AIN'T GOT TIME FOR NO YAKUZA RIGHT NOW.

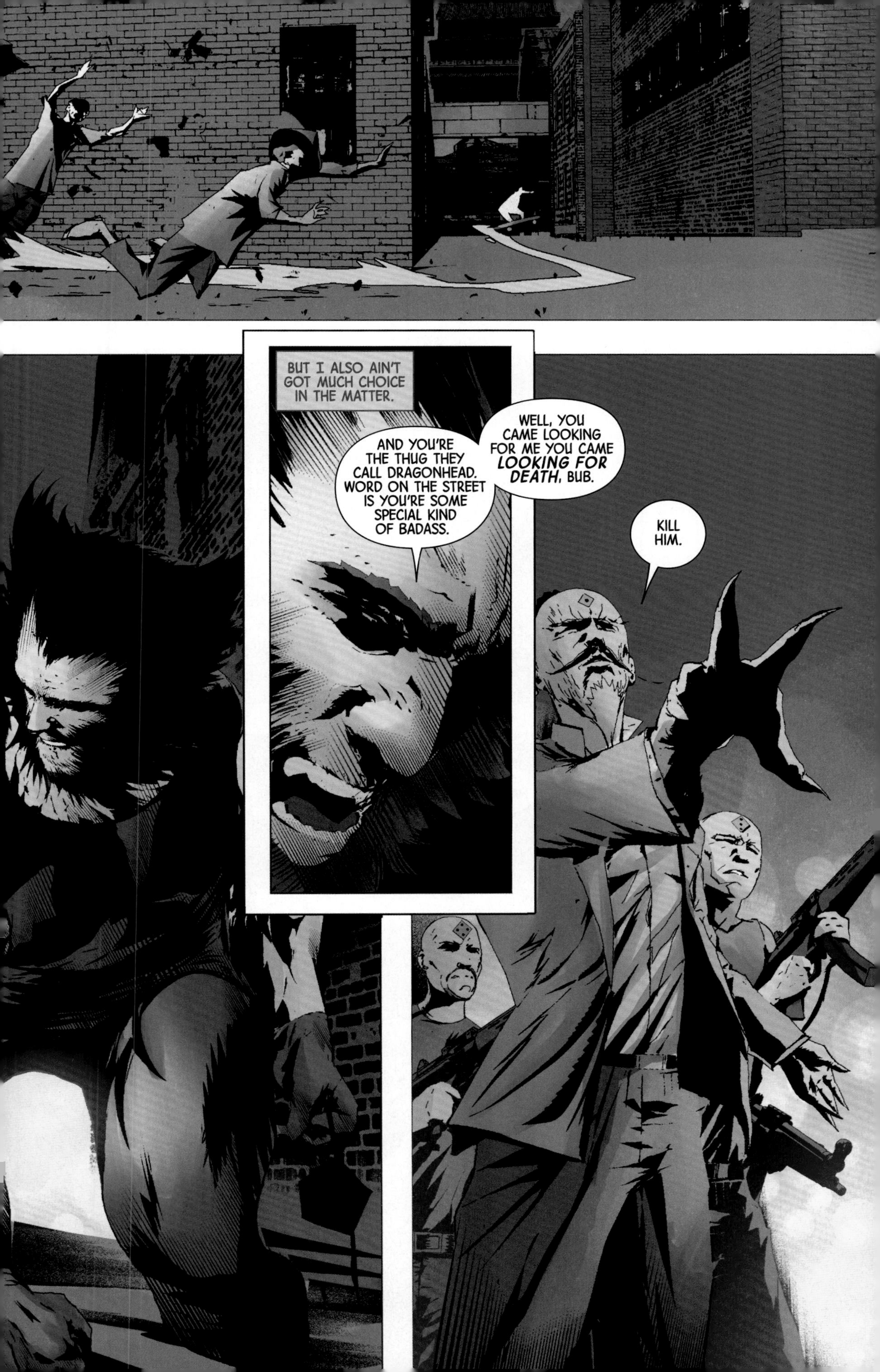
BUT I ALSO AIN'T GOT MUCH CHOICE IN THE MATTER.
AND YOU'RE THE THUG THEY CALL DRAGONHEAD. WORD ON THE STREET IS YOU'RE SOME SPECIAL KIND OF BADASS.
WELL, YOU CAME LOOKING FOR ME YOU CAME LOOKING FOR DEATH, BUB.
KILL HIM.

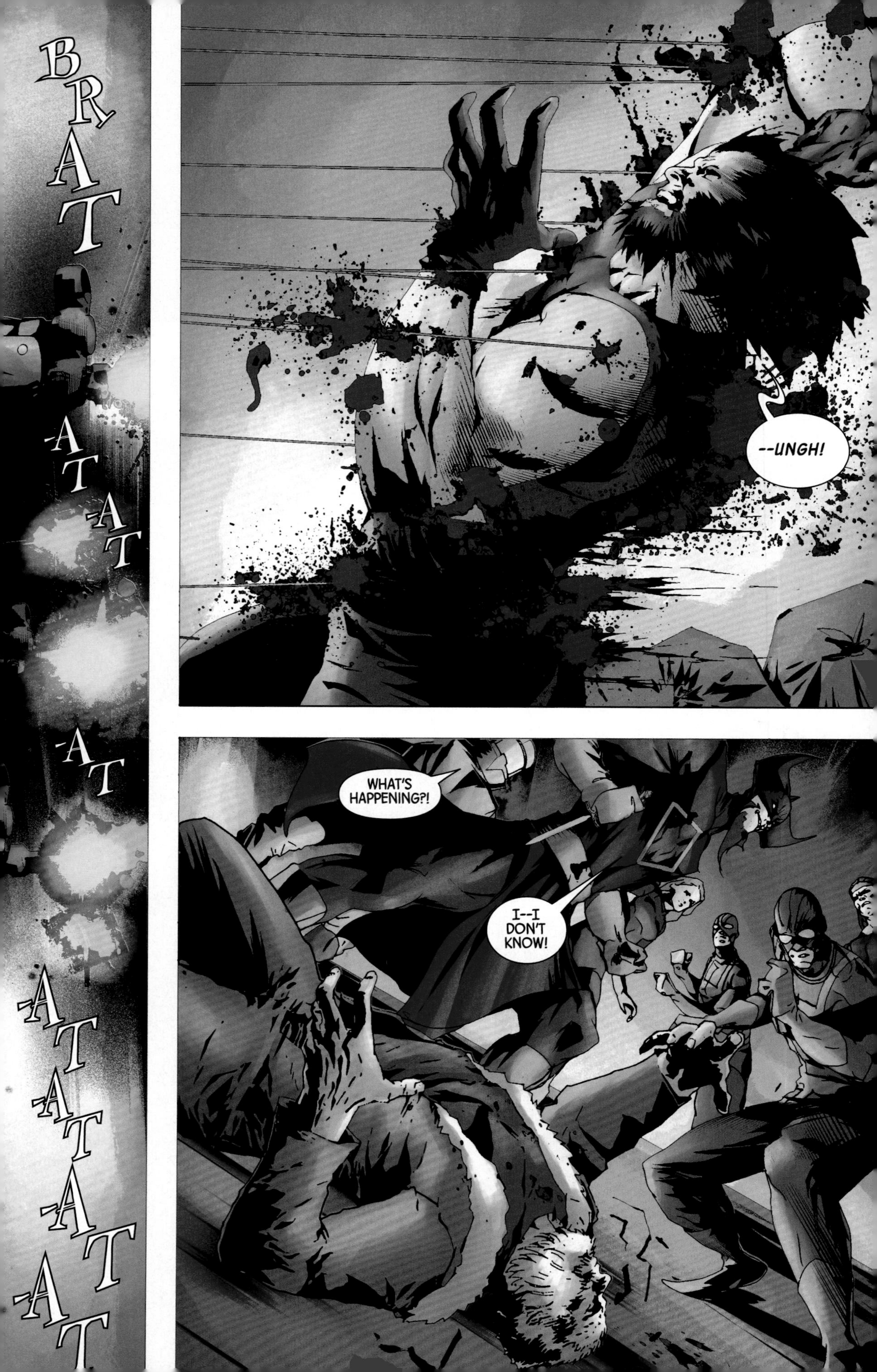
BRAT
-AT-AT
-AT
-A-TAT-AT-AT-AT
--UNGH!
WHAT'S HAPPENING?!
I--I DON'T KNOW!

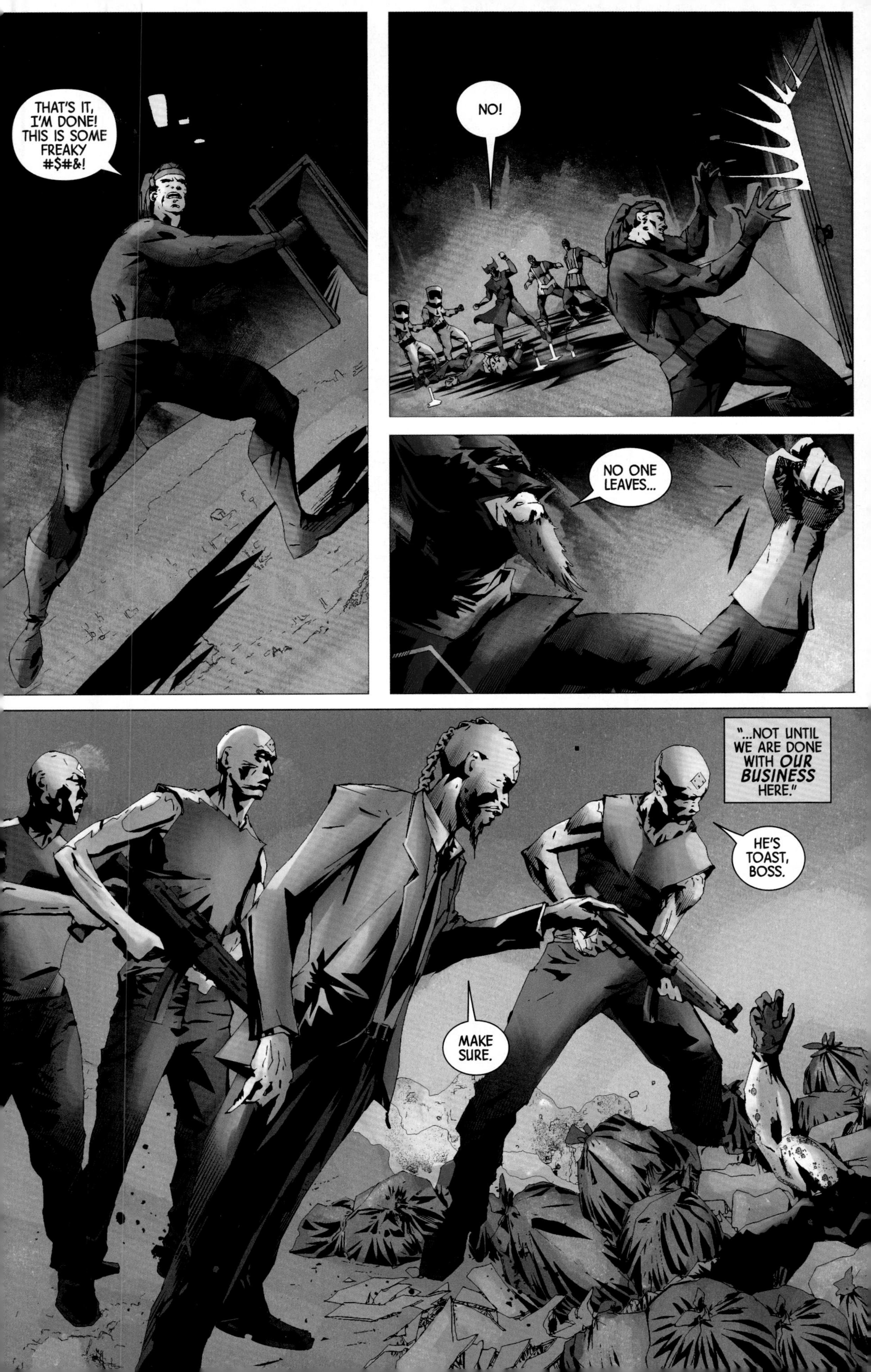
THAT'S IT, I'M DONE! THIS IS SOME FREAKY #$#&!
NO!
NO ONE LEAVES...
"...NOT UNTIL WE ARE DONE WITH *OUR BUSINESS* HERE."
HE'S TOAST, BOSS.
MAKE SURE.

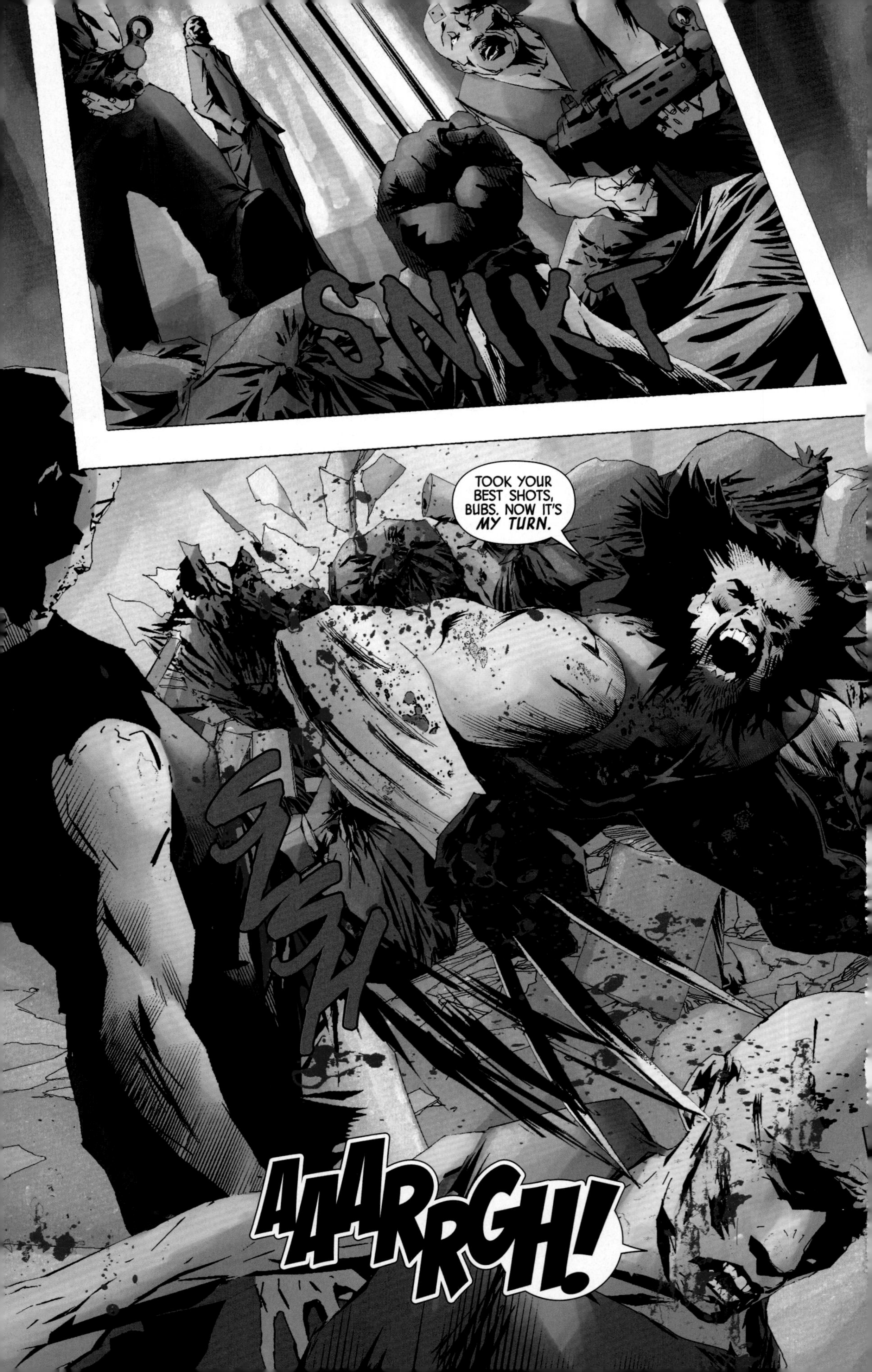
SNIKT
TOOK YOUR BEST SHOTS, BUBS. NOW IT'S *MY TURN.*
SNSH
AAARRGH!

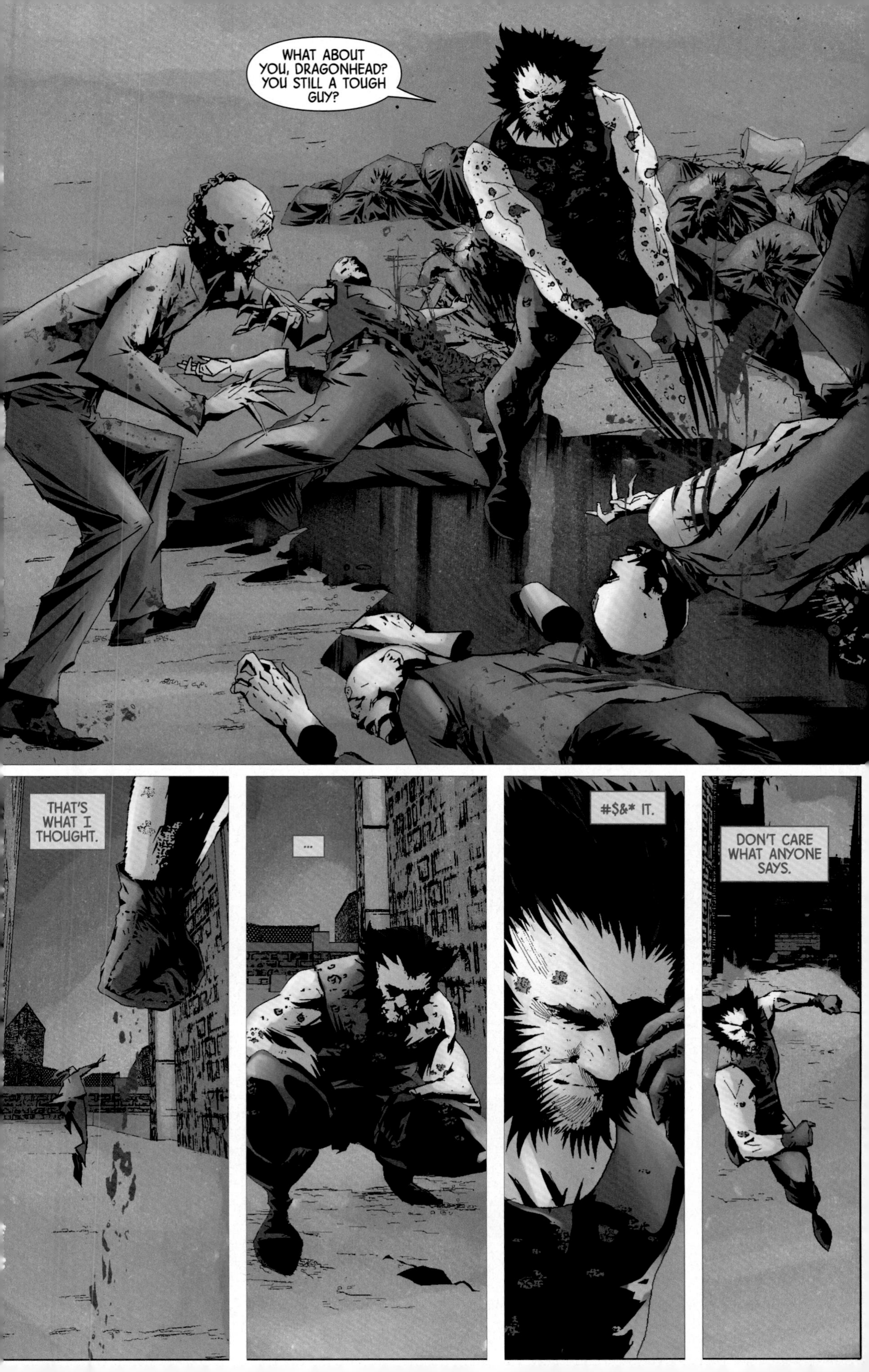
WHAT ABOUT YOU, DRAGONHEAD? YOU STILL A TOUGH GUY?
THAT'S WHAT I THOUGHT.
...
#$&* IT.
DON'T CARE WHAT ANYONE SAYS.

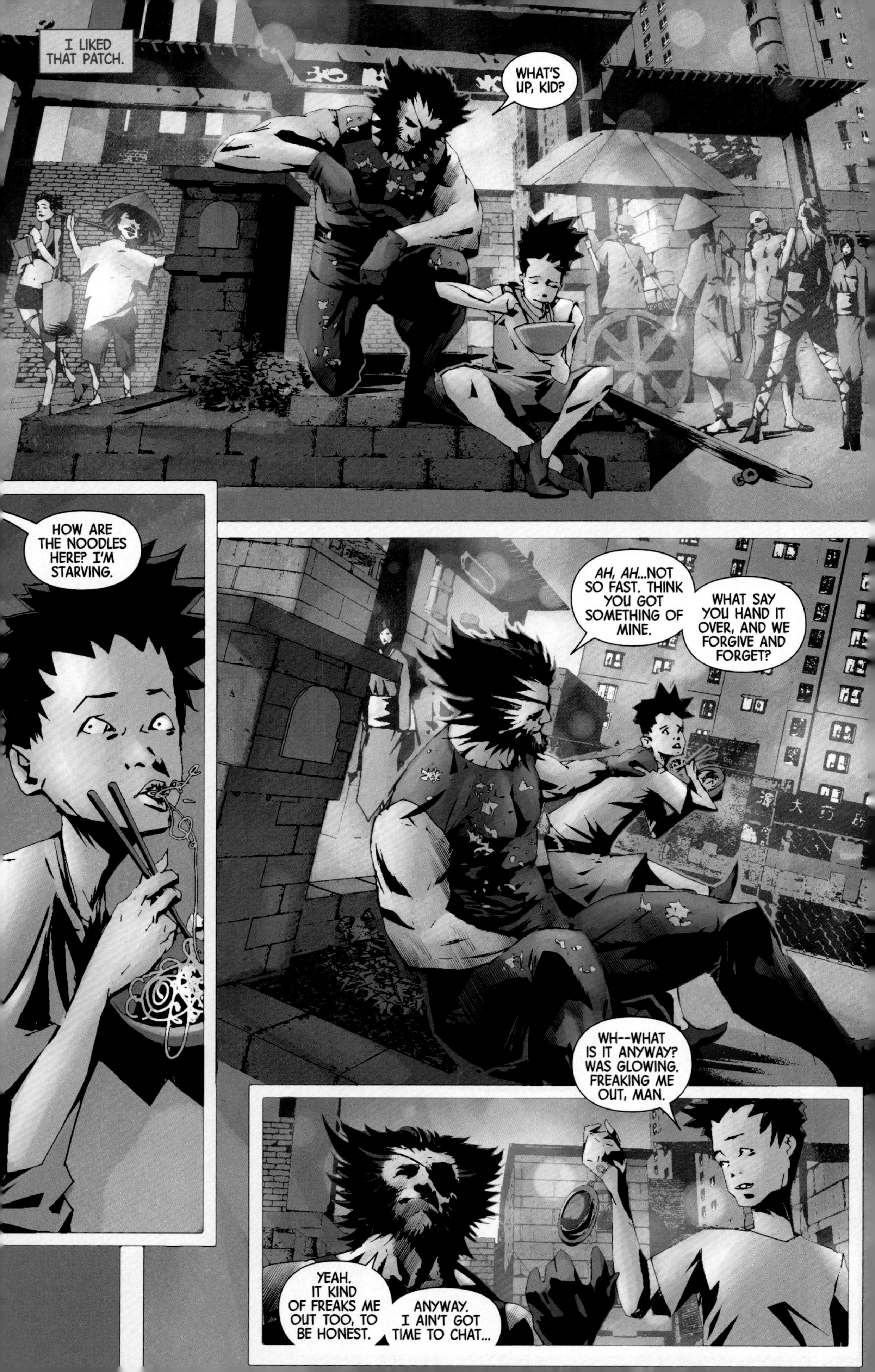
I LIKED THAT PATCH.
WHAT'S UP, KID?
HOW ARE THE NOODLES HERE? I'M STARVING.
AH, AH...NOT SO FAST. THINK YOU GOT SOMETHING OF MINE.
WHAT SAY YOU HAND IT OVER, AND WE FORGIVE AND FORGET?
WH--WHAT IS IT ANYWAY? WAS GLOWING. FREAKING ME OUT, MAN.
YEAH. IT KIND OF FREAKS ME OUT TOO, TO BE HONEST.
ANYWAY. I AIN'T GOT TIME TO CHAT...

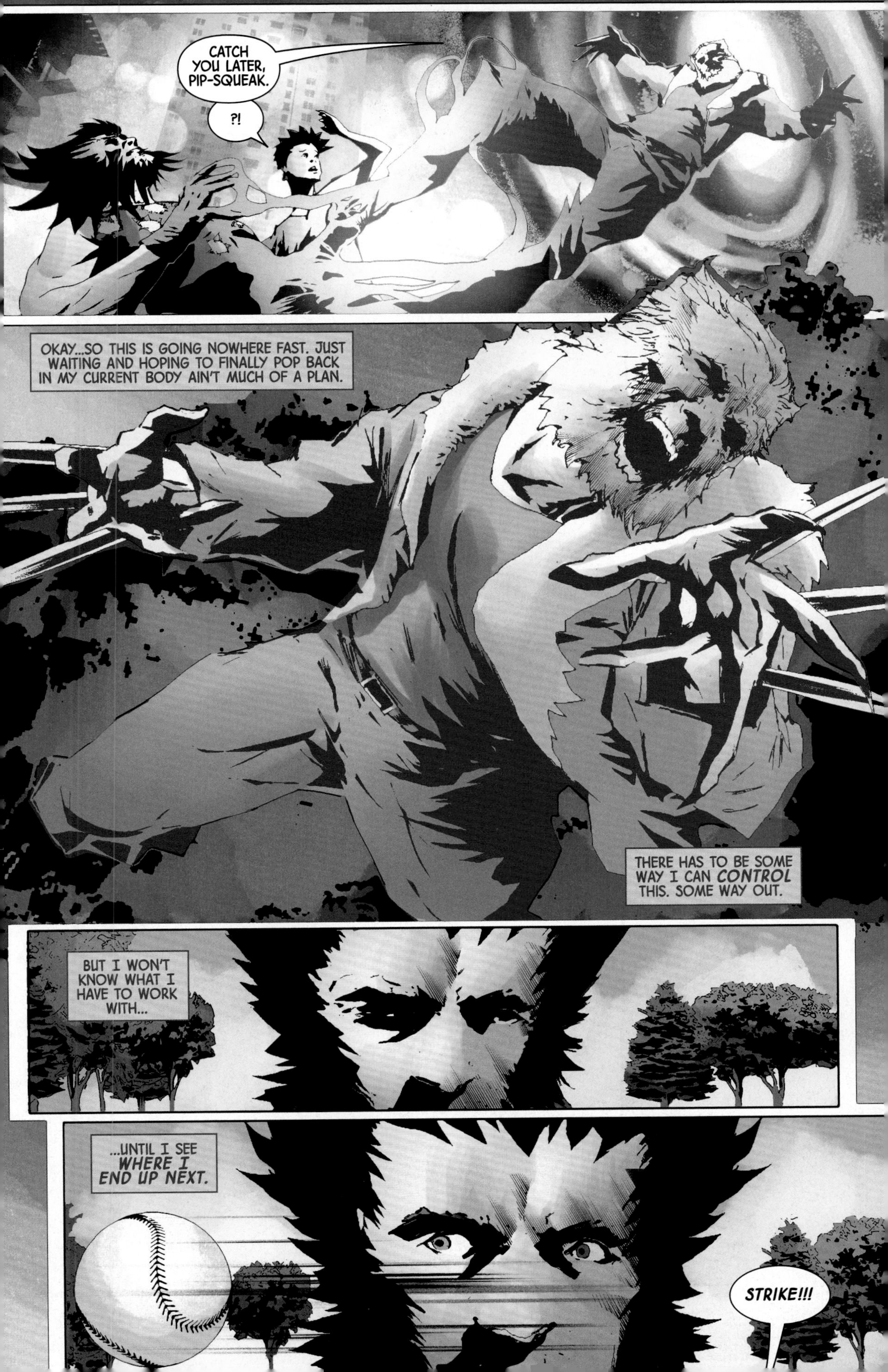
CATCH YOU LATER, PIP-SQUEAK.
?!
OKAY...SO THIS IS GOING NOWHERE FAST. JUST WAITING AND HOPING TO FINALLY POP BACK IN MY CURRENT BODY AIN'T MUCH OF A PLAN.
THERE HAS TO BE SOME WAY I CAN *CONTROL* THIS. SOME WAY OUT.
BUT I WON'T KNOW WHAT I HAVE TO WORK WITH...
...UNTIL I SEE *WHERE I END UP NEXT.*
STRIKE!!!

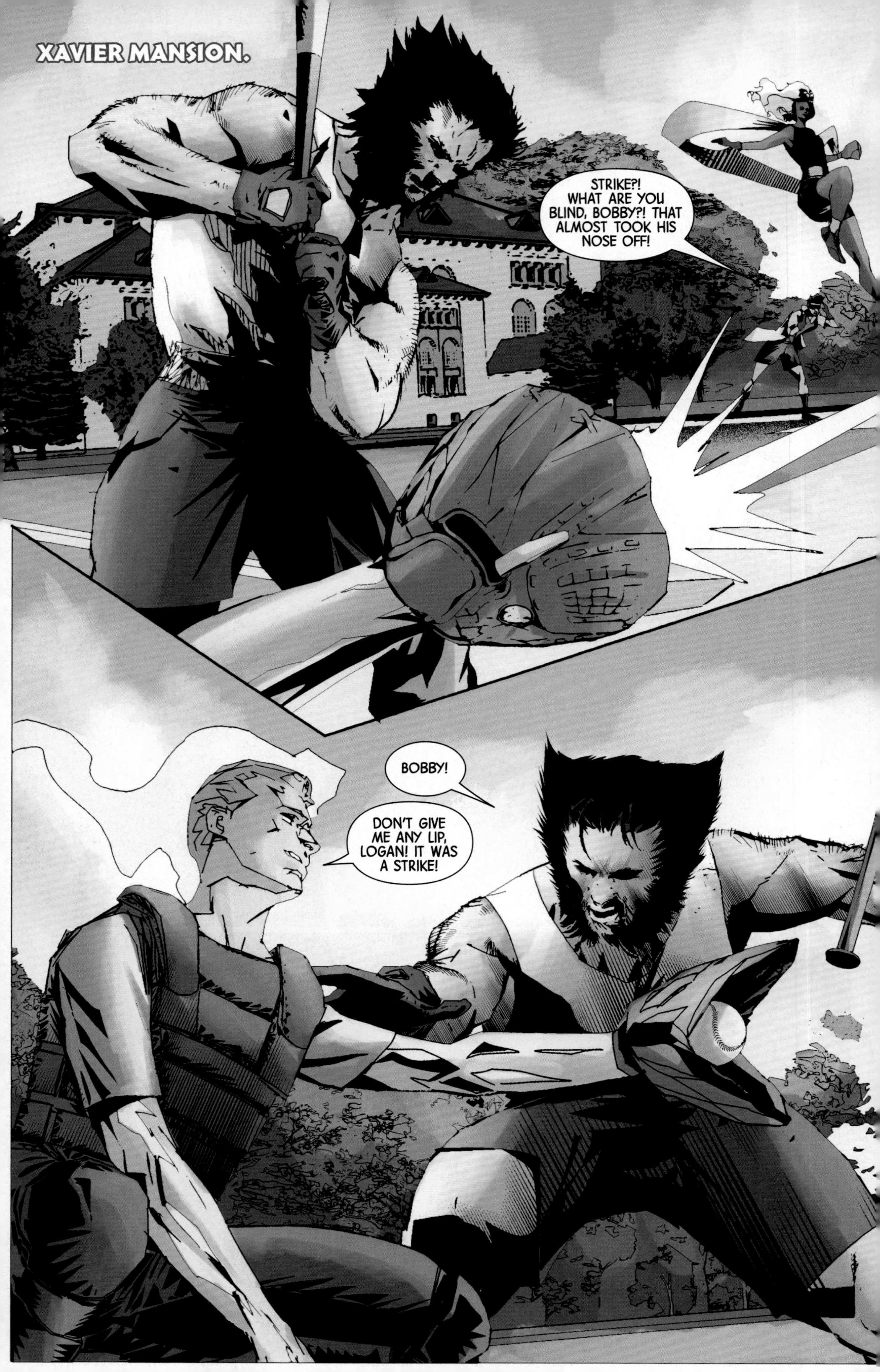
XAVIER MANSION.
STRIKE?! WHAT ARE YOU BLIND, BOBBY?! THAT ALMOST TOOK HIS NOSE OFF!
BOBBY!
DON'T GIVE ME ANY LIP, LOGAN! IT WAS A STRIKE!

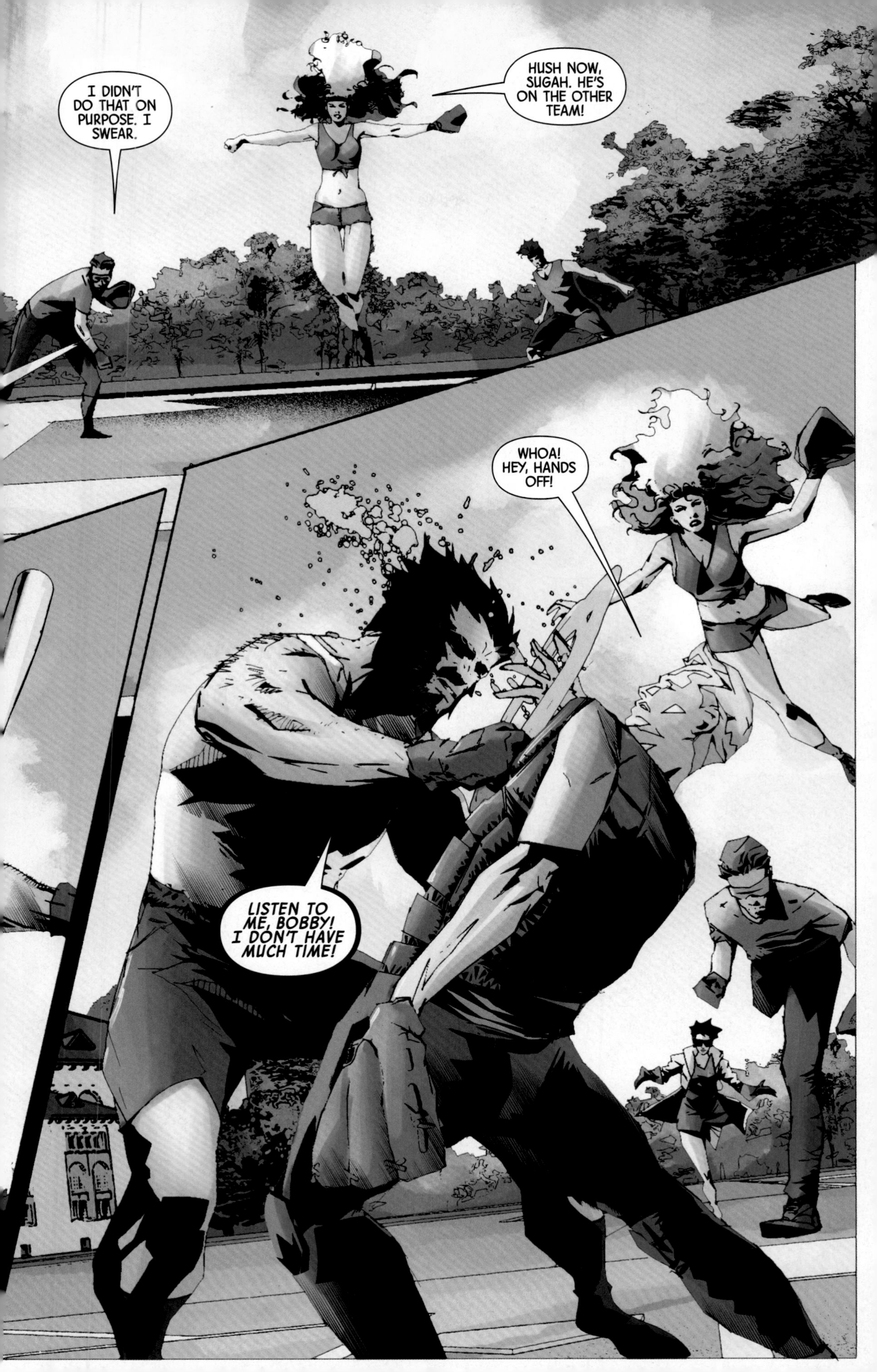
I DIDN'T DO THAT ON PURPOSE. I SWEAR.
HUSH NOW, SUGAH. HE'S ON THE OTHER TEAM!
WHOA! HEY, HANDS OFF!
LISTEN TO ME, BOBBY! I DON'T HAVE MUCH TIME!

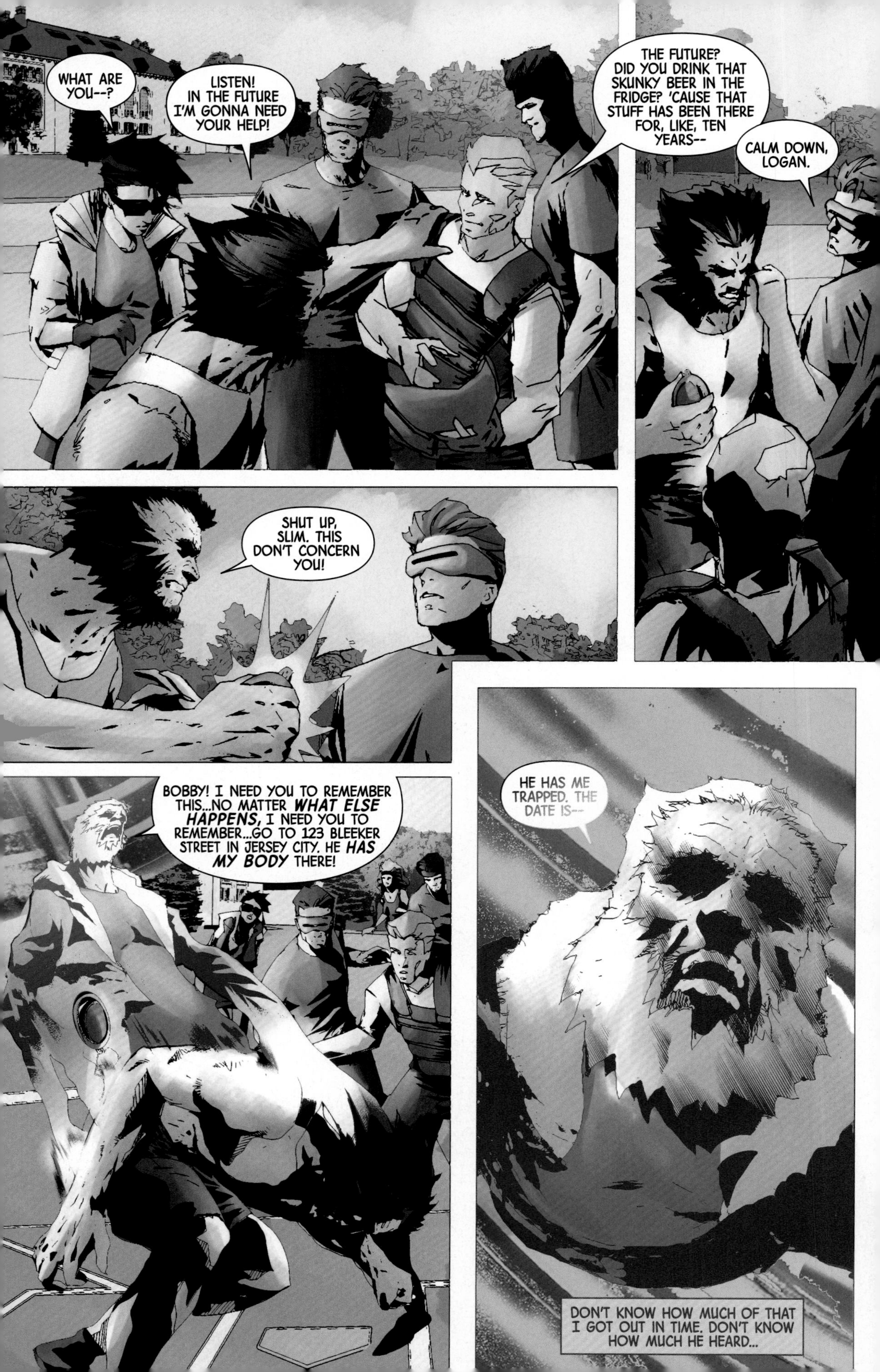
WHAT ARE YOU--?
LISTEN! IN THE FUTURE I'M GONNA NEED YOUR HELP!
THE FUTURE? DID YOU DRINK THAT SKUNKY BEER IN THE FRIDGE? 'CAUSE THAT STUFF HAS BEEN THERE FOR, LIKE, TEN YEARS--
CALM DOWN, LOGAN.
SHUT UP, SLIM. THIS DON'T CONCERN YOU!
BOBBY! I NEED YOU TO REMEMBER THIS...NO MATTER WHAT ELSE HAPPENS, I NEED YOU TO REMEMBER...GO TO 123 BLEEKER STREET IN JERSEY CITY. HE HAS MY BODY THERE!
HE HAS ME TRAPPED. THE DATE IS--
DON'T KNOW HOW MUCH OF THAT I GOT OUT IN TIME. DON'T KNOW HOW MUCH HE HEARD...

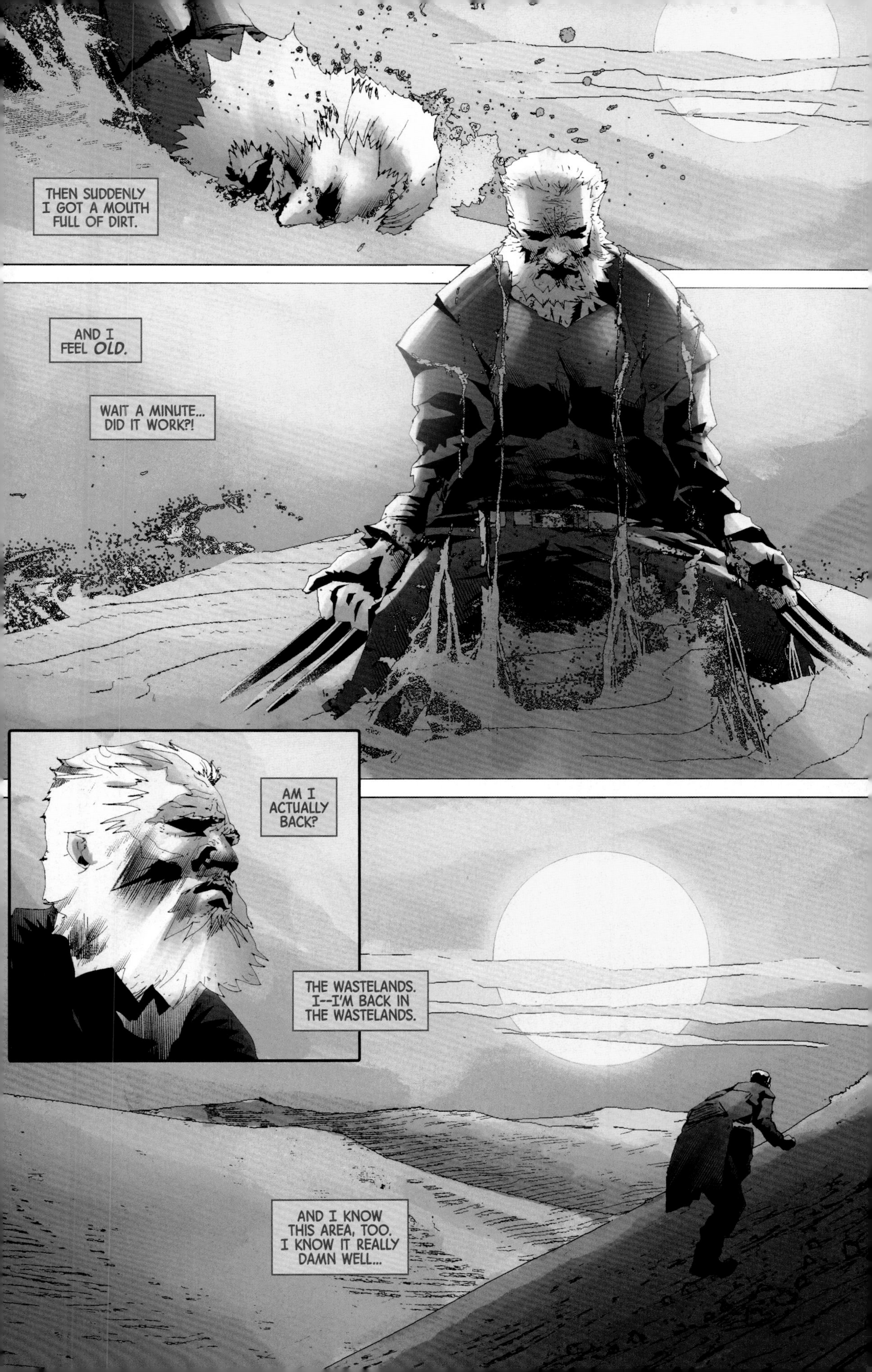
THEN SUDDENLY I GOT A MOUTH FULL OF DIRT.
AND I FEEL OLD.
WAIT A MINUTE... DID IT WORK?!
AM I ACTUALLY BACK?
THE WASTELANDS. I--I'M BACK IN THE WASTELANDS.
AND I KNOW THIS AREA, TOO. I KNOW IT REALLY DAMN WELL...

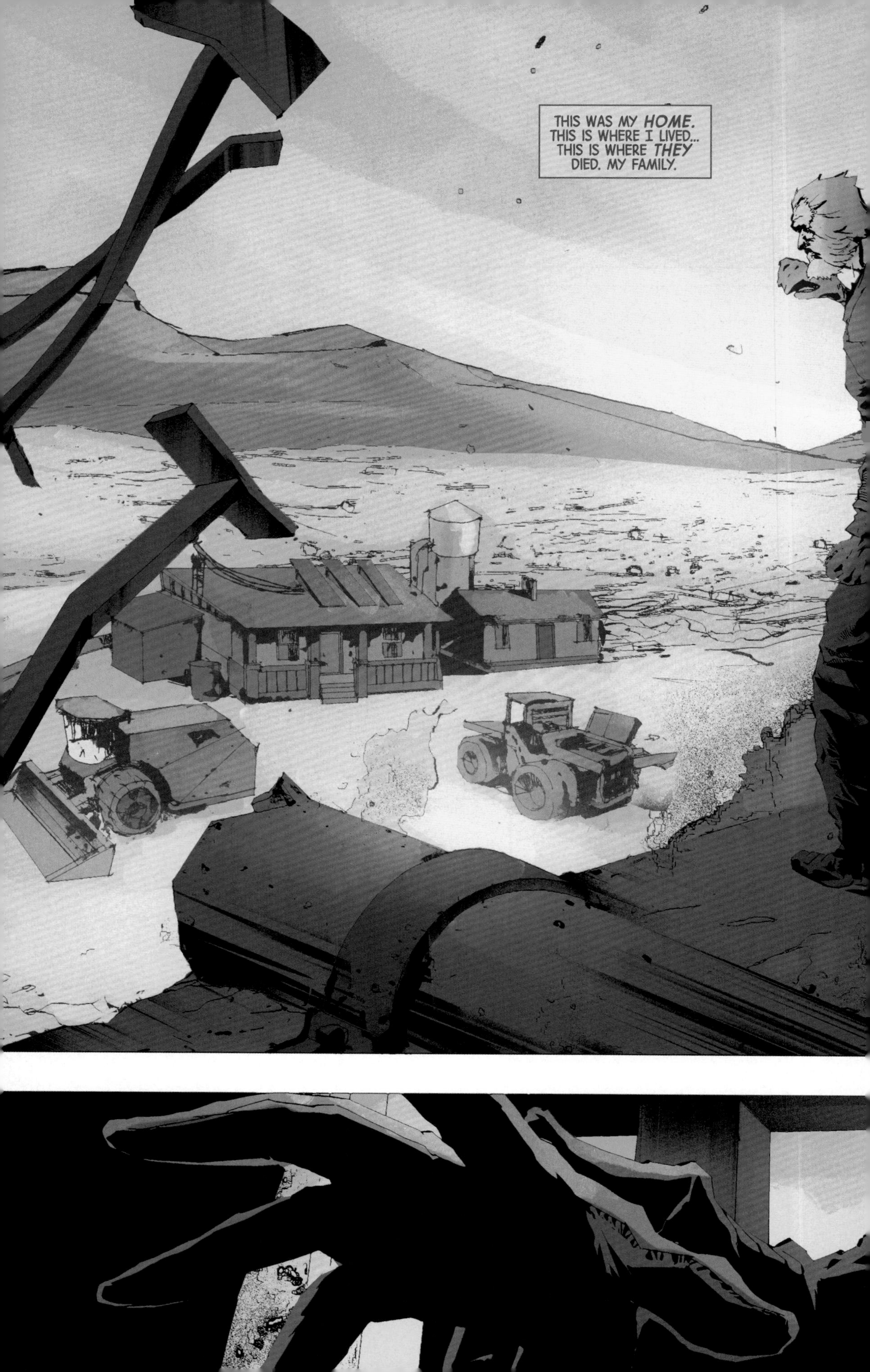
THIS WAS MY *HOME.* THIS IS WHERE I LIVED... THIS IS WHERE *THEY* DIED. MY FAMILY.

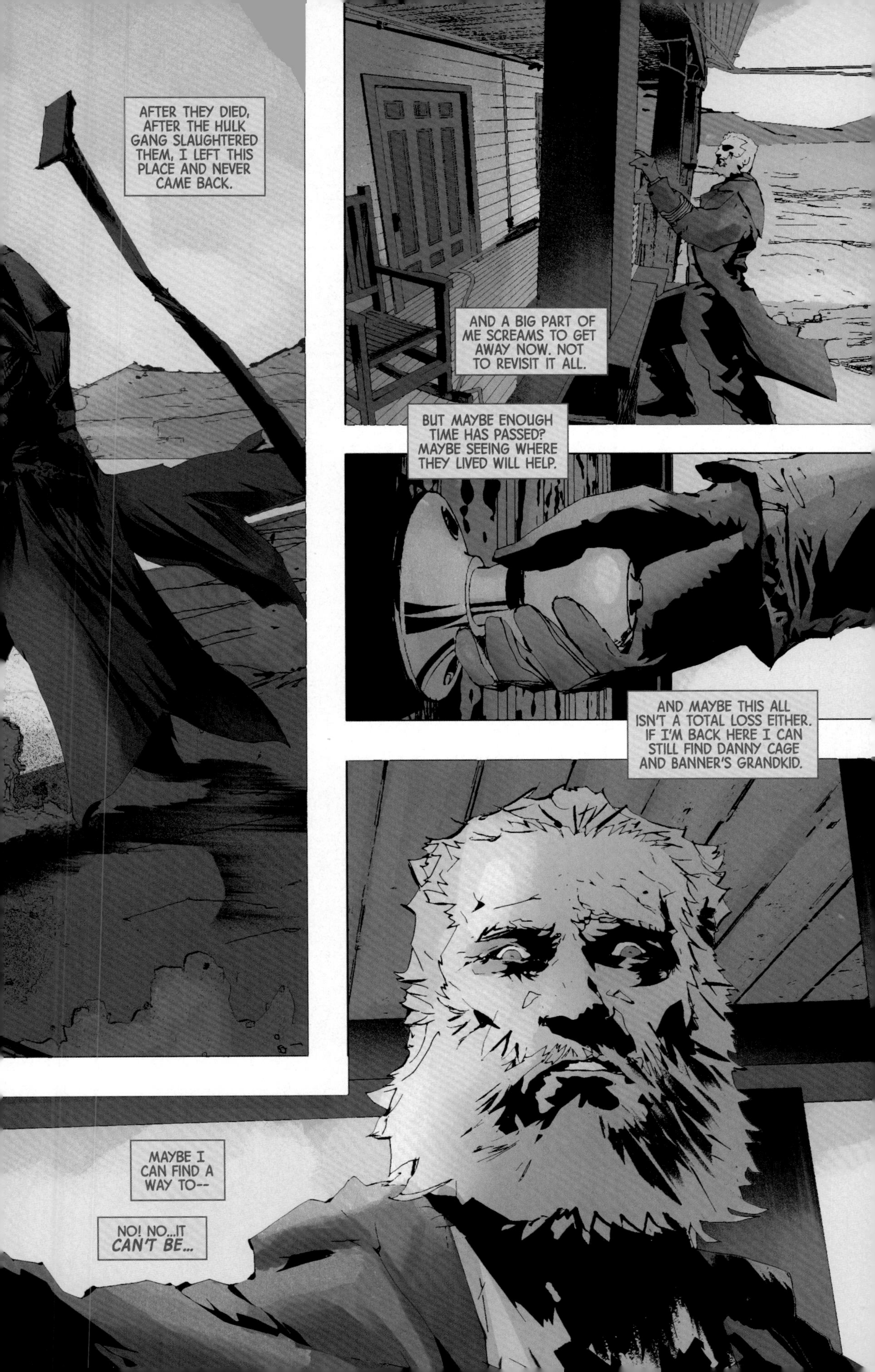
AFTER THEY DIED, AFTER THE HULK GANG SLAUGHTERED THEM, I LEFT THIS PLACE AND NEVER CAME BACK.
AND A BIG PART OF ME SCREAMS TO GET AWAY NOW. NOT TO REVISIT IT ALL.
BUT MAYBE ENOUGH TIME HAS PASSED? MAYBE SEEING WHERE THEY LIVED WILL HELP.
AND MAYBE THIS ALL ISN'T A TOTAL LOSS EITHER. IF I'M BACK HERE I CAN STILL FIND DANNY CAGE AND BANNER'S GRANDKID.
MAYBE I CAN FIND A WAY TO--
NO! NO...IT CAN'T BE...

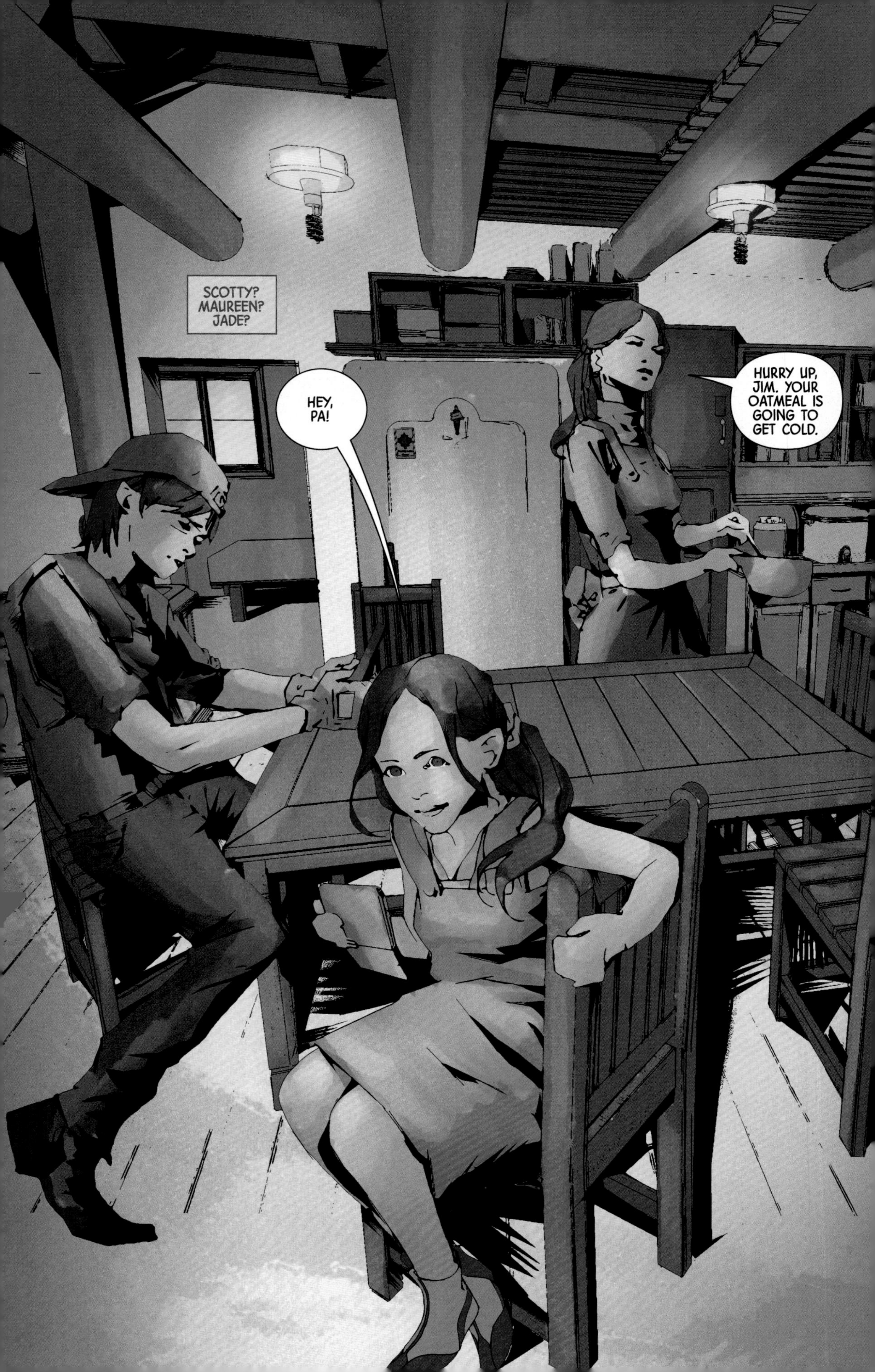
SCOTTY? MAUREEN? JADE?
HEY, PA!
HURRY UP, JIM. YOUR OATMEAL IS GOING TO GET COLD.

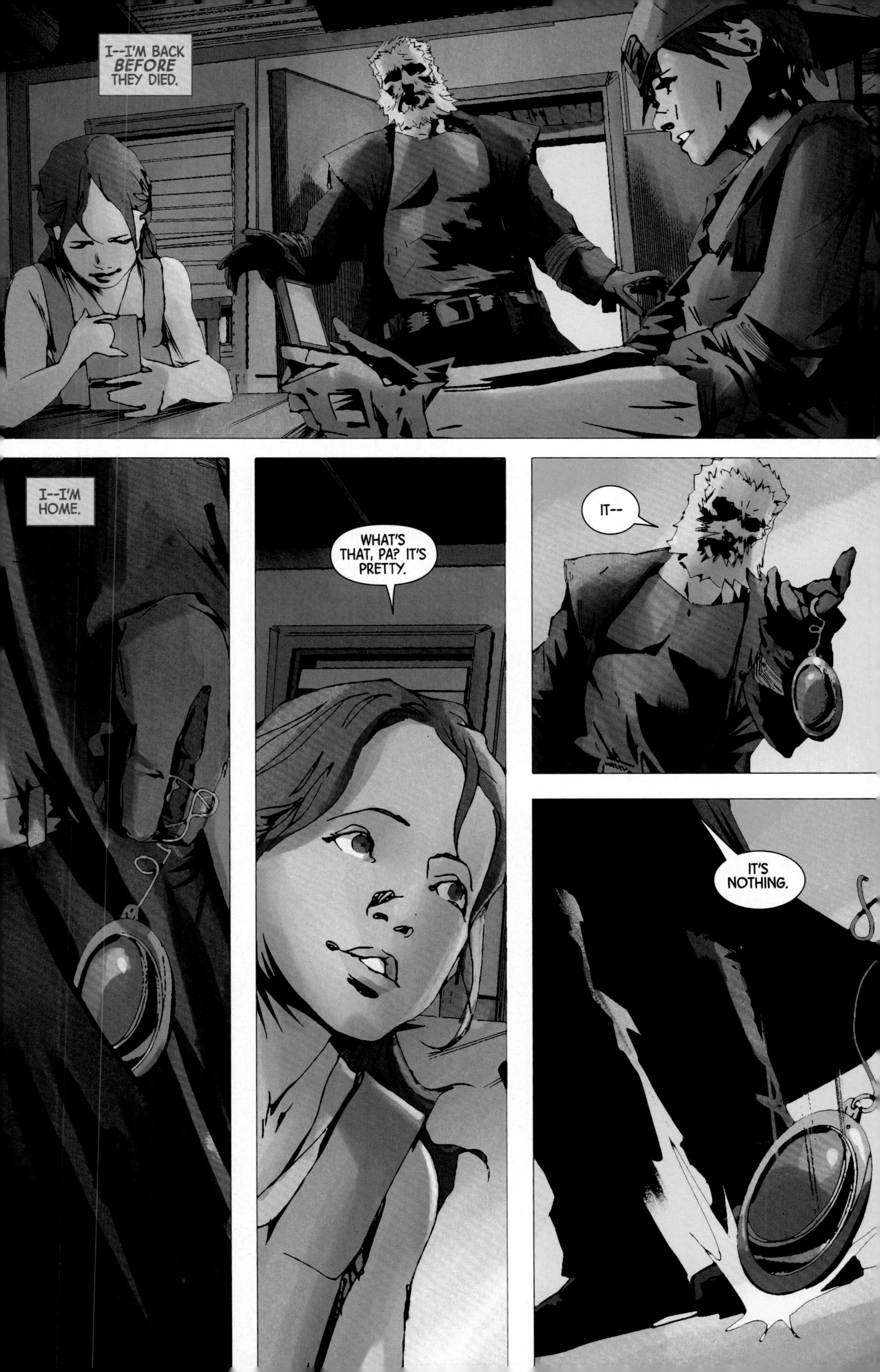
I--I'M BACK BEFORE THEY DIED.
I--I'M HOME.
WHAT'S THAT, PA? IT'S PRETTY.
IT--
IT'S NOTHING.

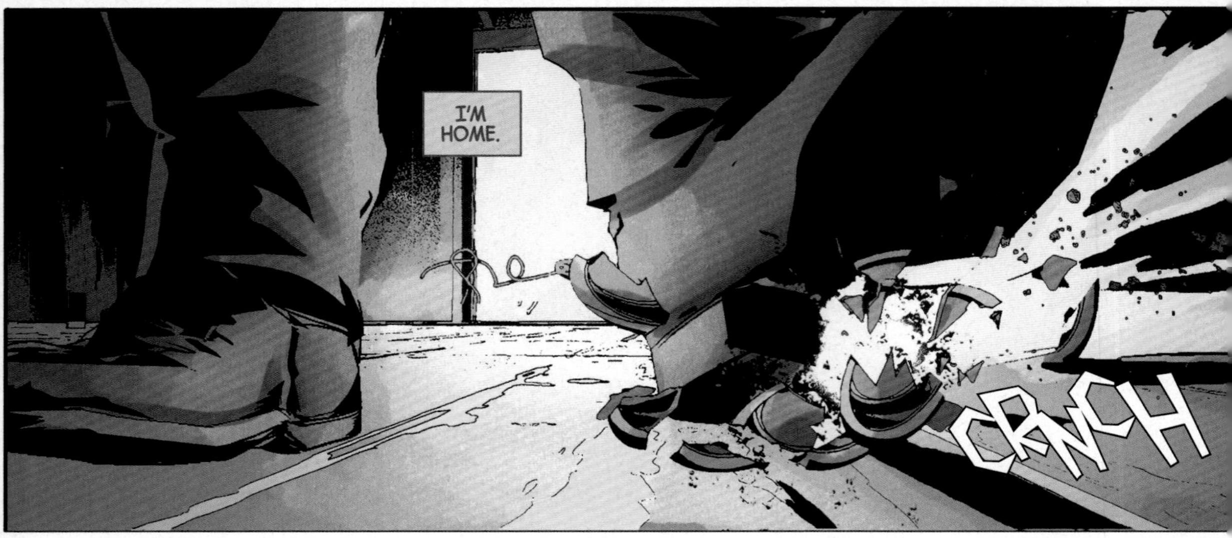
I'M HOME.
CRNCH

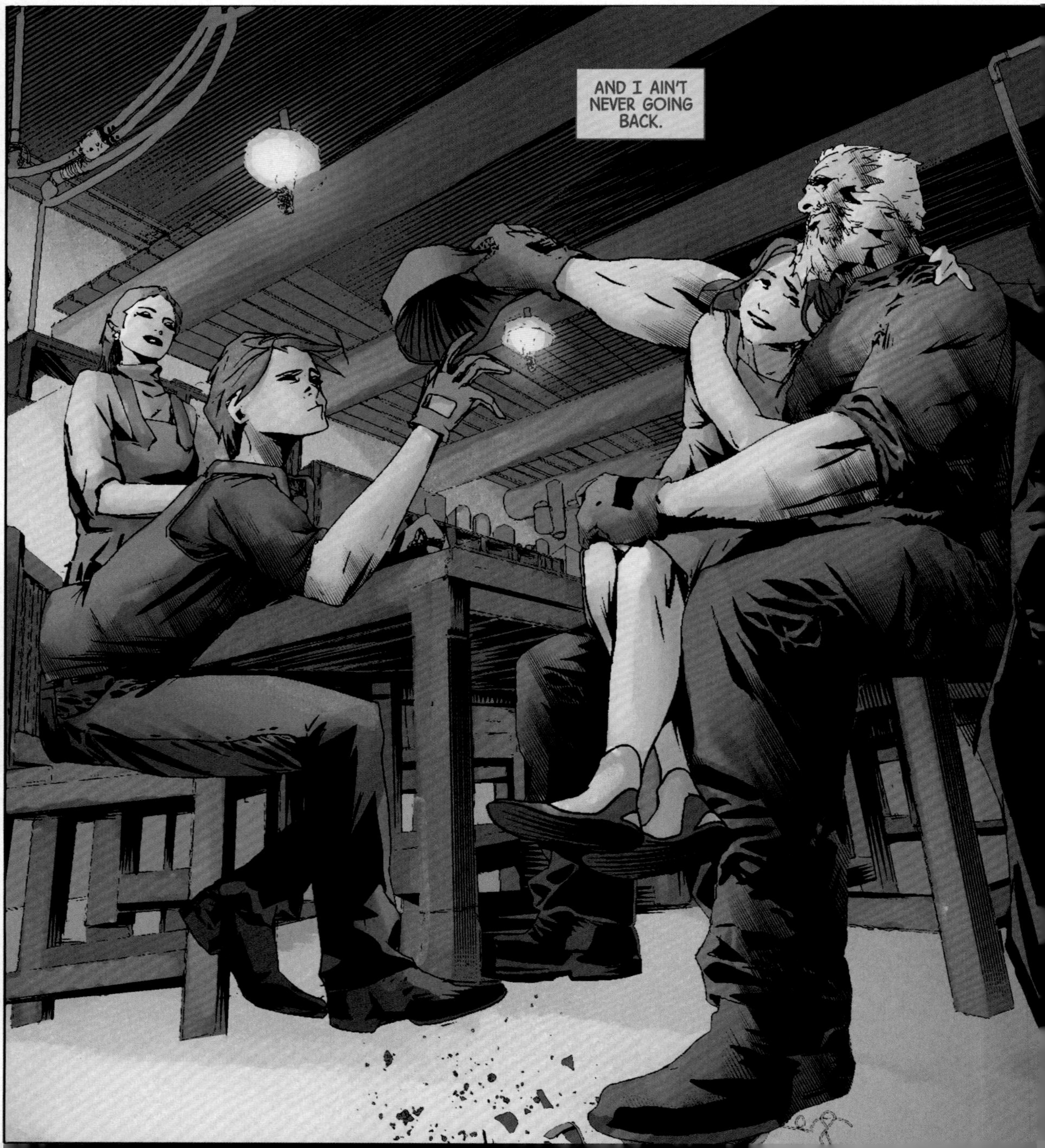
AND I AIN'T NEVER GOING BACK.

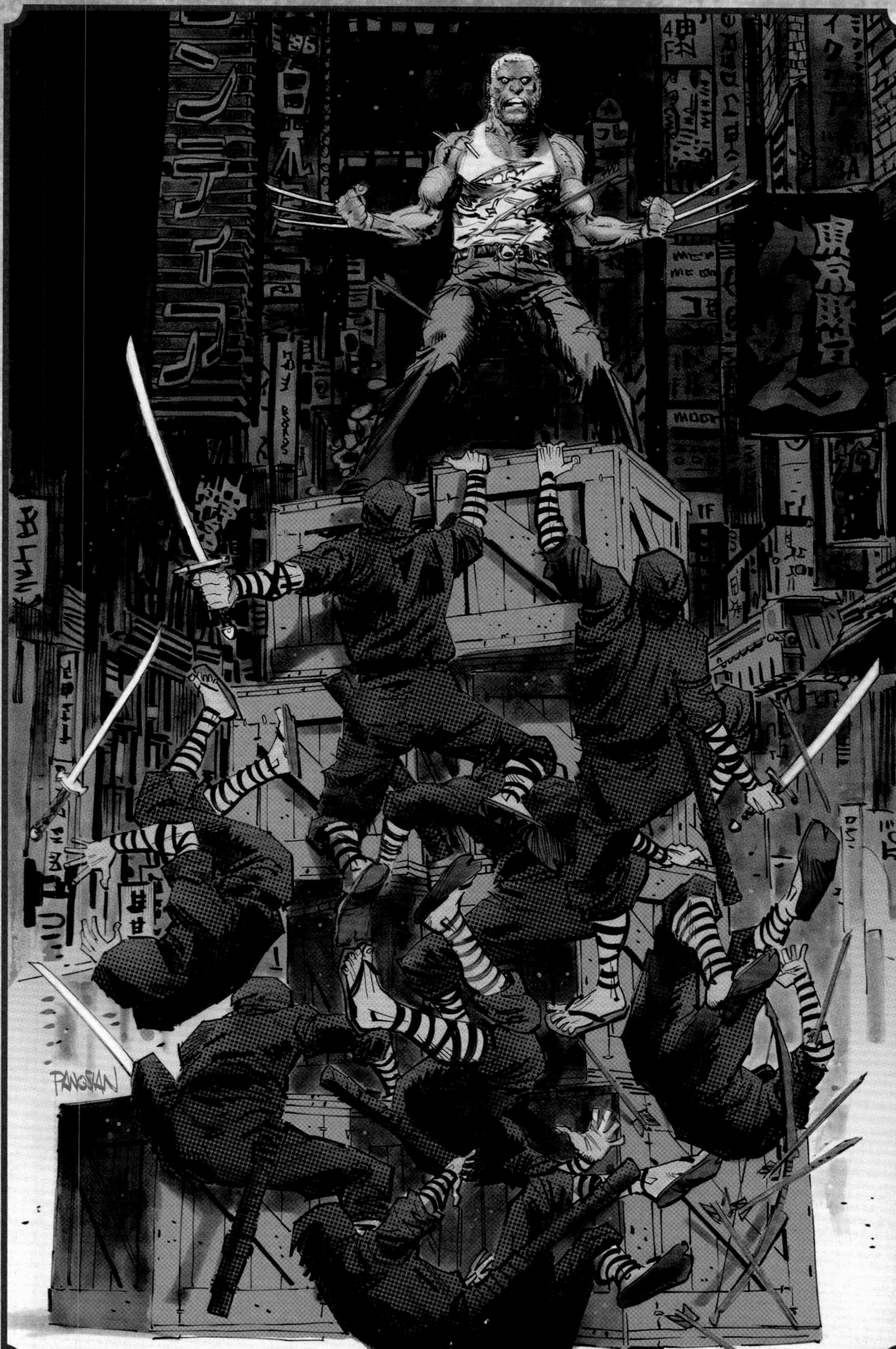
PANOSIAN

#23 VARIANT
BY DAN PANOSIAN

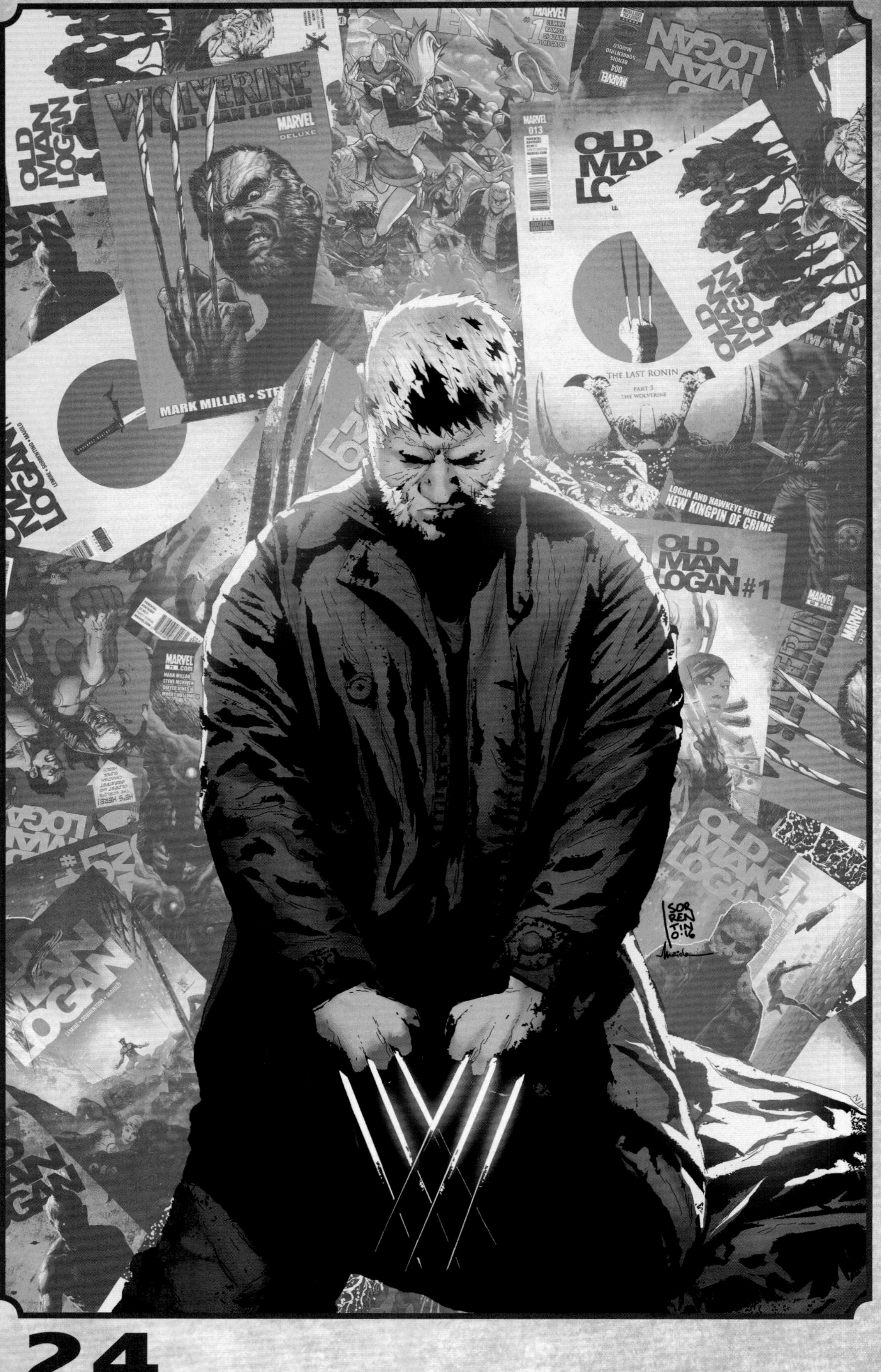
WOLVERINE
OLD MAN LOGAN
MARVEL
DELUXE
MARK MILLAR • STE
OLD MAN LOGAN
MARVEL
013
OLD MAN LOG
THE LAST RONIN
PART 5
THE WOLVERINE
LOGAN AND HAWKEYE MEET THE
NEW KINGPIN OF CRIME
OLD MAN LOGAN #1
MARVEL
MARK MILLAR
STEVE MCNIVEN
DEXTER VINES
MORRY HOLLOWELL
OLD MAN LOGAN

24

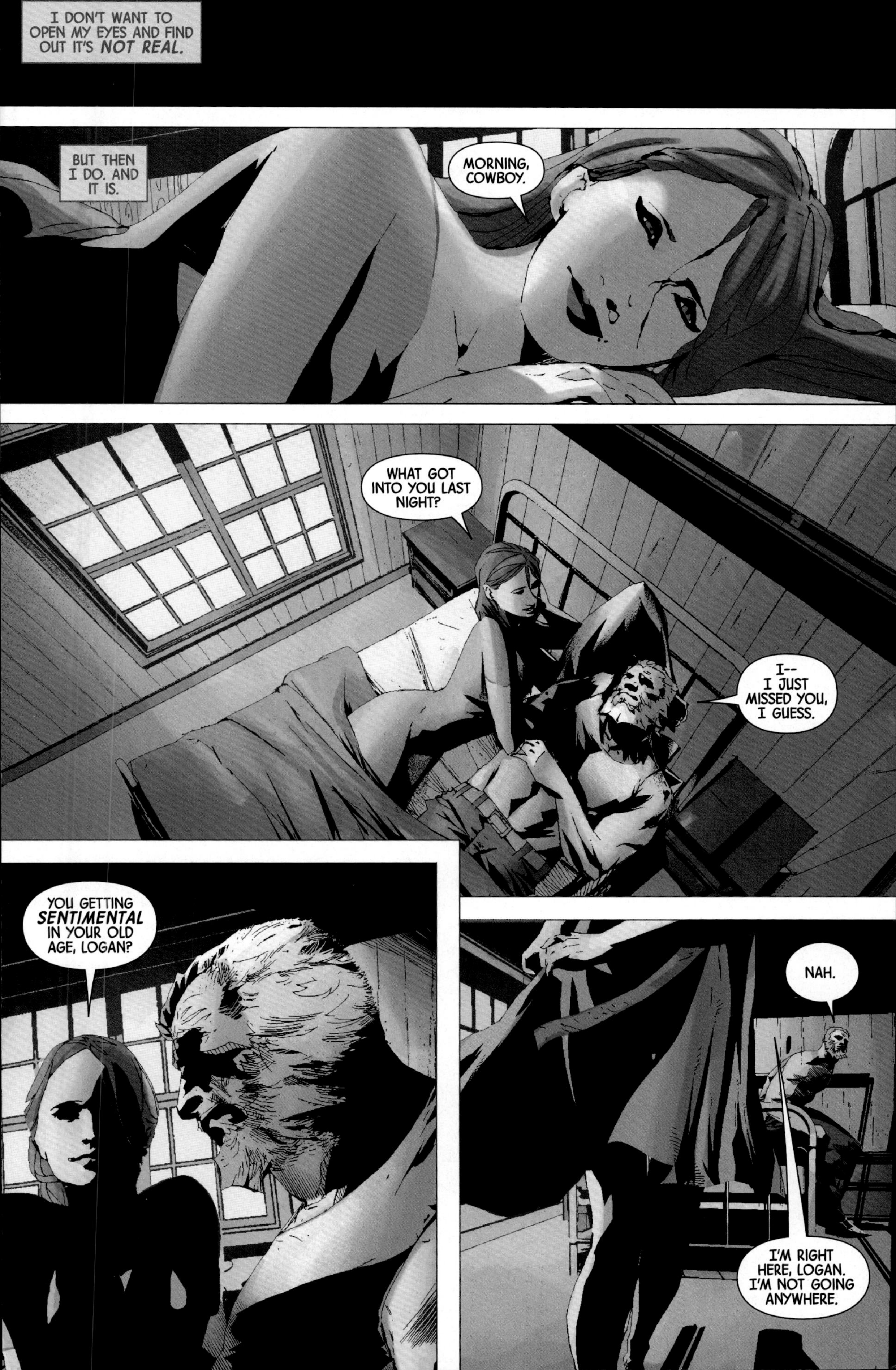
I DON'T WANT TO OPEN MY EYES AND FIND OUT IT'S NOT REAL.
BUT THEN I DO. AND IT IS.
MORNING, COWBOY.
WHAT GOT INTO YOU LAST NIGHT?
I-- I JUST MISSED YOU, I GUESS.
YOU GETTING SENTIMENTAL IN YOUR OLD AGE, LOGAN?
NAH.
I'M RIGHT HERE, LOGAN. I'M NOT GOING ANYWHERE.

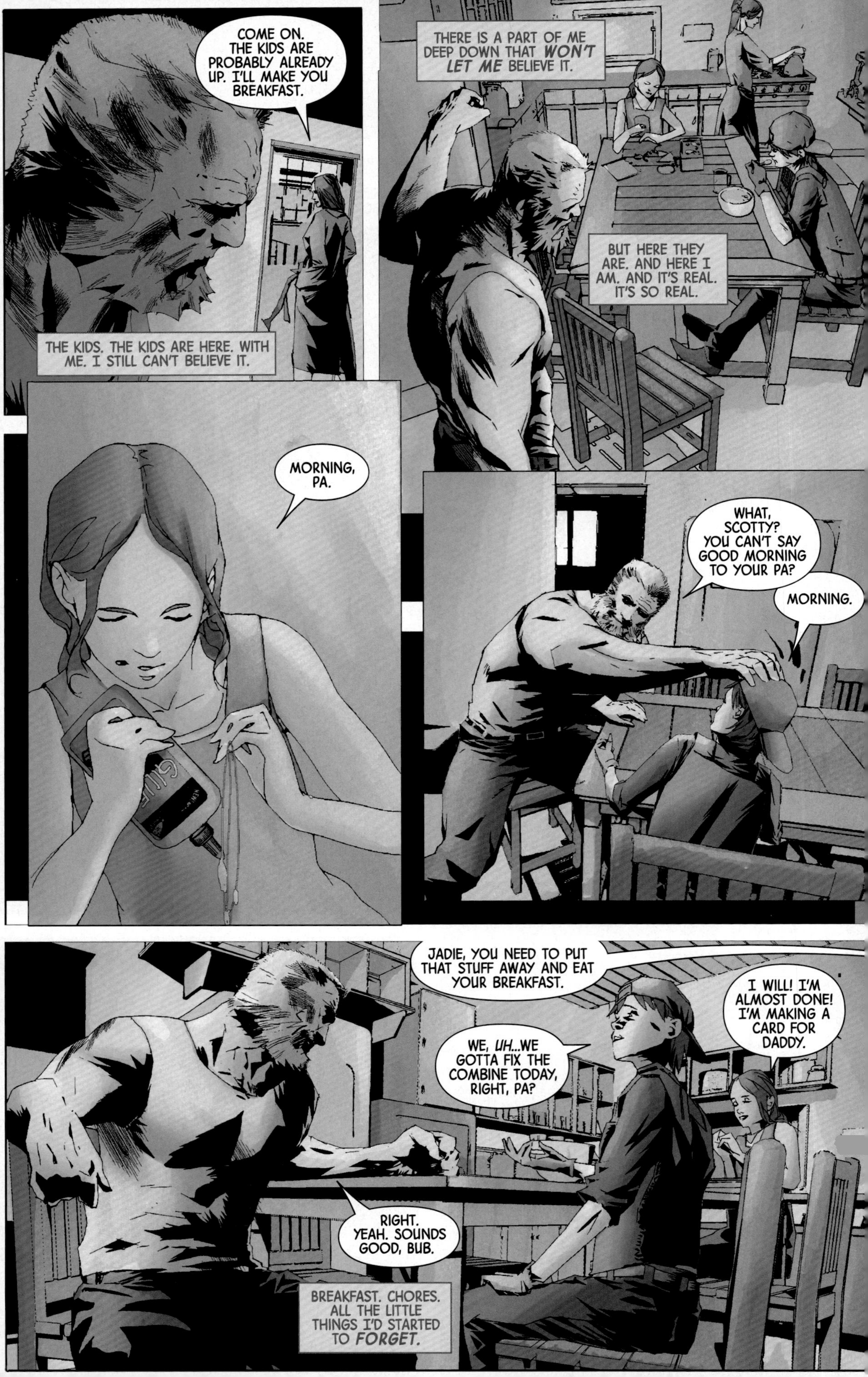
COME ON. THE KIDS ARE PROBABLY ALREADY UP. I'LL MAKE YOU BREAKFAST.
THE KIDS. THE KIDS ARE HERE. WITH ME. I STILL CAN'T BELIEVE IT.
THERE IS A PART OF ME DEEP DOWN THAT WON'T LET ME BELIEVE IT.
BUT HERE THEY ARE. AND HERE I AM. AND IT'S REAL. IT'S SO REAL.
MORNING, PA.
WHAT, SCOTTY? YOU CAN'T SAY GOOD MORNING TO YOUR PA?
MORNING.
JADIE, YOU NEED TO PUT THAT STUFF AWAY AND EAT YOUR BREAKFAST.
I WILL! I'M ALMOST DONE! I'M MAKING A CARD FOR DADDY.
WE, UH...WE GOTTA FIX THE COMBINE TODAY, RIGHT, PA?
RIGHT. YEAH. SOUNDS GOOD, BUB.
BREAKFAST. CHORES. ALL THE LITTLE THINGS I'D STARTED TO FORGET.

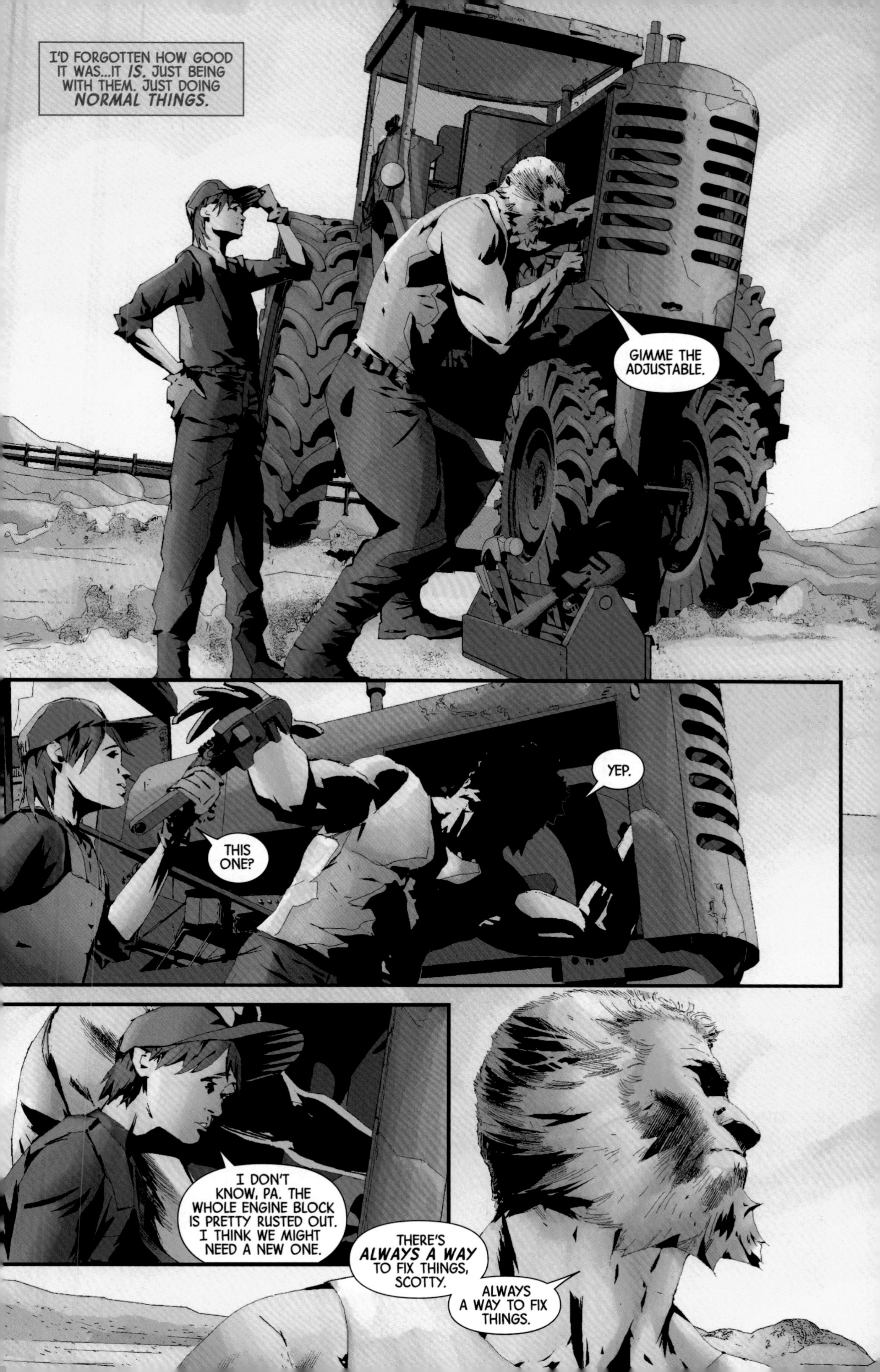
I'D FORGOTTEN HOW GOOD IT WAS...IT IS. JUST BEING WITH THEM. JUST DOING NORMAL THINGS.
GIMME THE ADJUSTABLE.
THIS ONE?
YEP.
I DON'T KNOW, PA. THE WHOLE ENGINE BLOCK IS PRETTY RUSTED OUT. I THINK WE MIGHT NEED A NEW ONE.
THERE'S ALWAYS A WAY TO FIX THINGS, SCOTTY.
ALWAYS A WAY TO FIX THINGS.

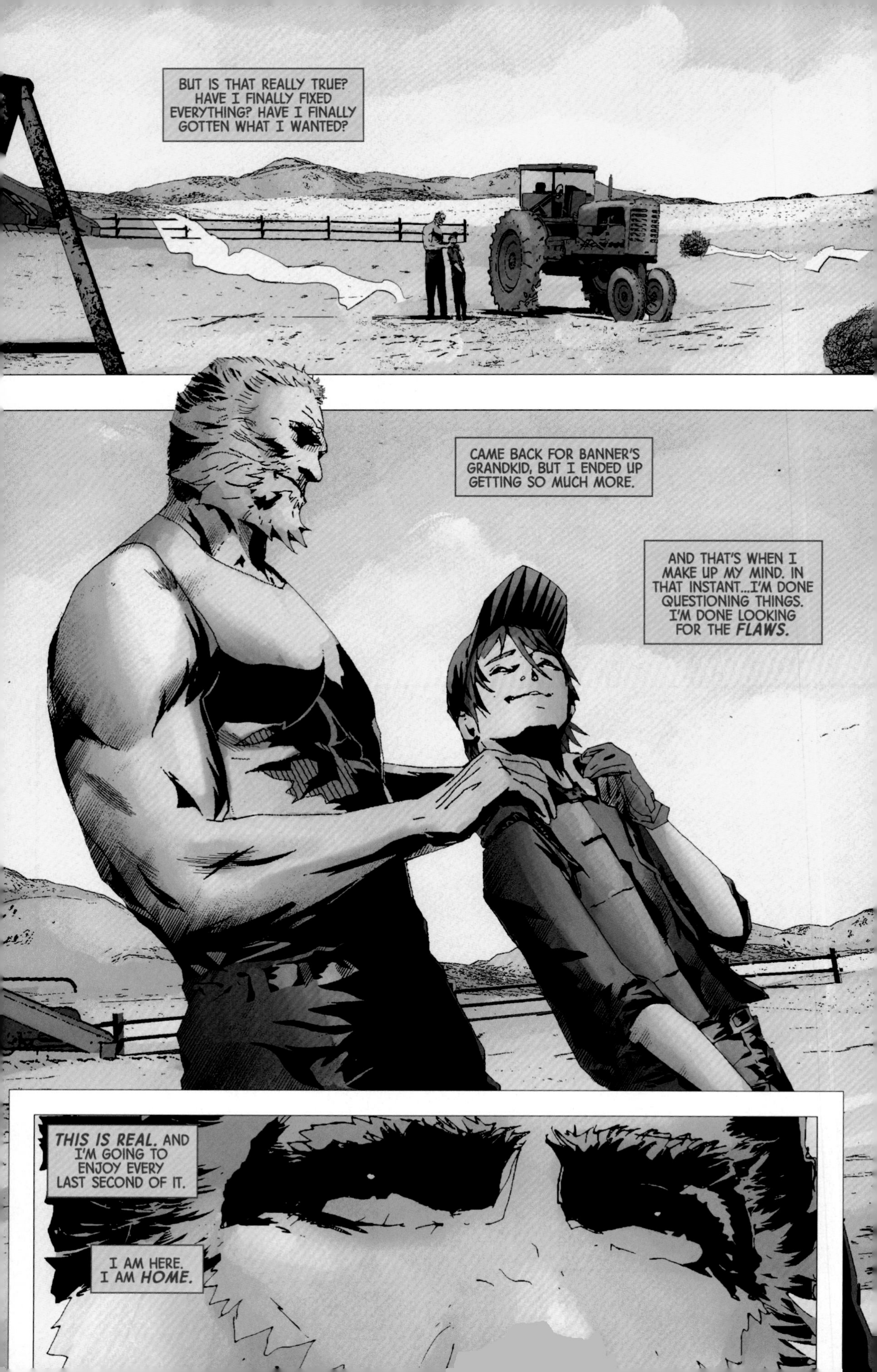
BUT IS THAT REALLY TRUE? HAVE I FINALLY FIXED EVERYTHING? HAVE I FINALLY GOTTEN WHAT I WANTED?
CAME BACK FOR BANNER'S GRANDKID, BUT I ENDED UP GETTING SO MUCH MORE.
AND THAT'S WHEN I MAKE UP MY MIND. IN THAT INSTANT...I'M DONE QUESTIONING THINGS. I'M DONE LOOKING FOR THE FLAWS.
THIS IS REAL. AND I'M GOING TO ENJOY EVERY LAST SECOND OF IT.
I AM HERE. I AM HOME.

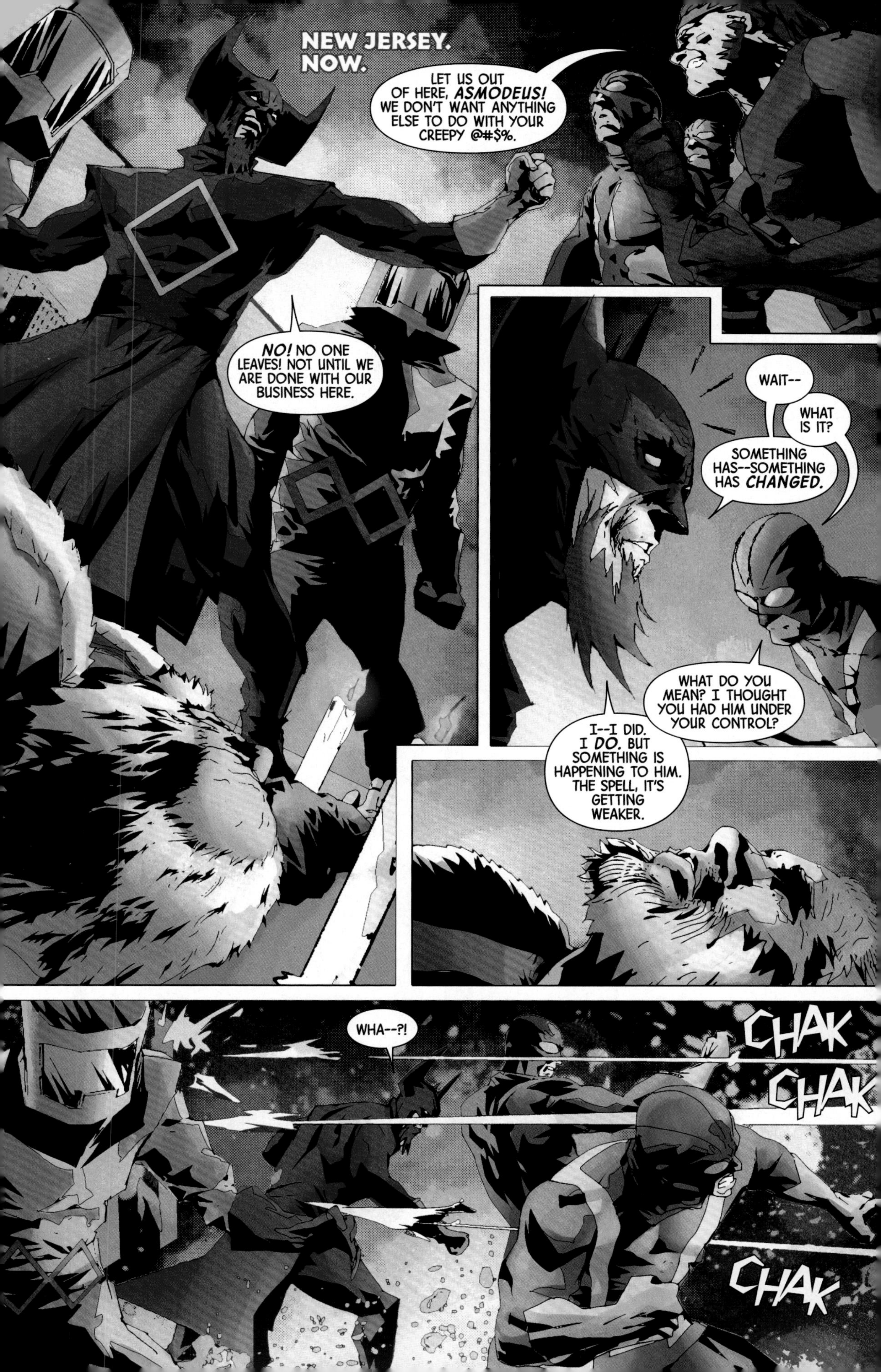

NEW JERSEY. NOW.
LET US OUT OF HERE, ASMODEUS! WE DON'T WANT ANYTHING ELSE TO DO WITH YOUR CREEPY @#$%.
NO! NO ONE LEAVES! NOT UNTIL WE ARE DONE WITH OUR BUSINESS HERE.
WAIT--
WHAT IS IT?
SOMETHING HAS--SOMETHING HAS CHANGED.
WHAT DO YOU MEAN? I THOUGHT YOU HAD HIM UNDER YOUR CONTROL?
I--I DID. I DO. BUT SOMETHING IS HAPPENING TO HIM. THE SPELL, IT'S GETTING WEAKER.
WHA--?!
CHAK
CHAK
CHAK

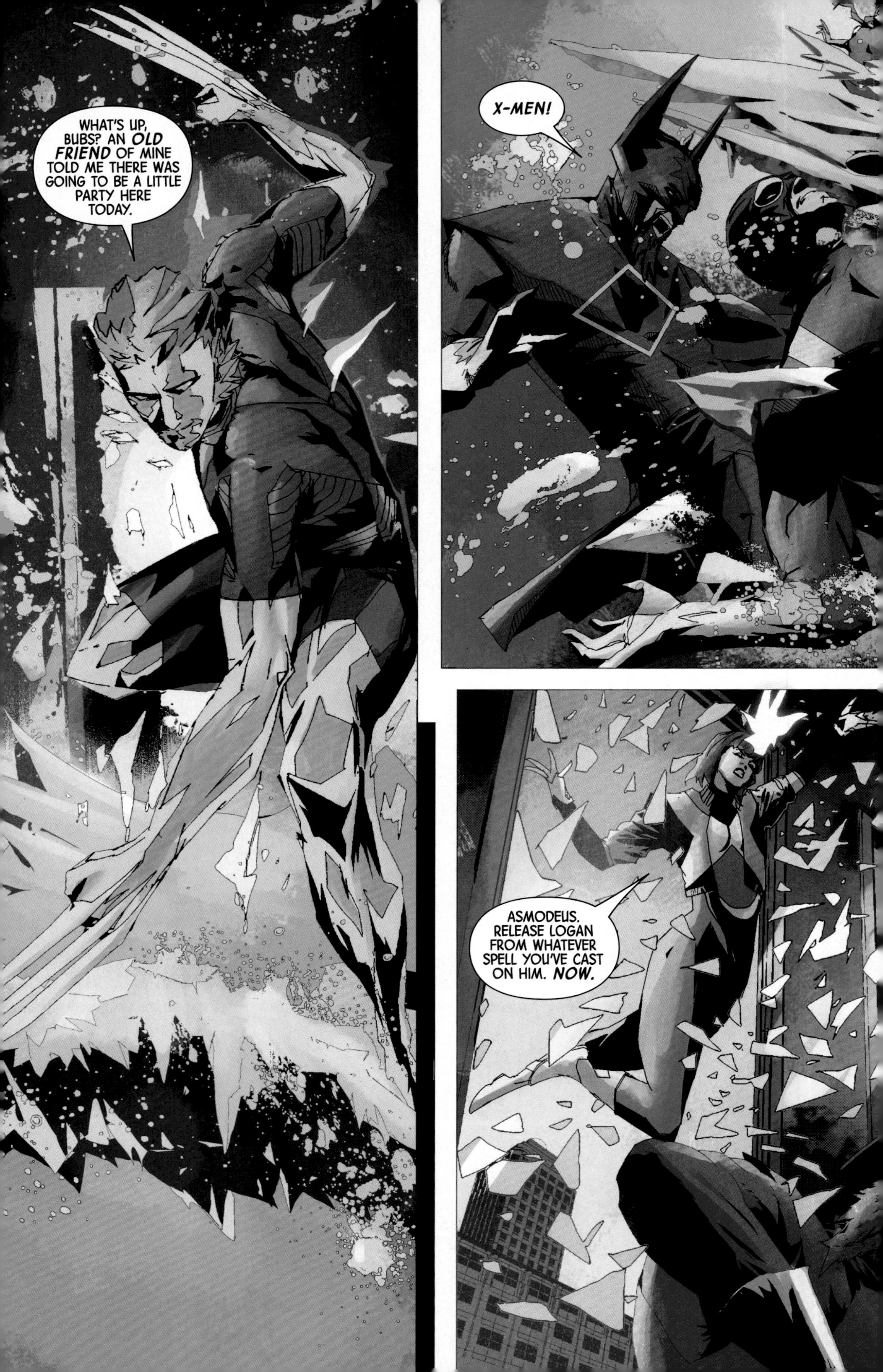
WHAT'S UP, BUBS? AN OLD FRIEND OF MINE TOLD ME THERE WAS GOING TO BE A LITTLE PARTY HERE TODAY.
X-MEN!
ASMODEUS. RELEASE LOGAN FROM WHATEVER SPELL YOU'VE CAST ON HIM. NOW.

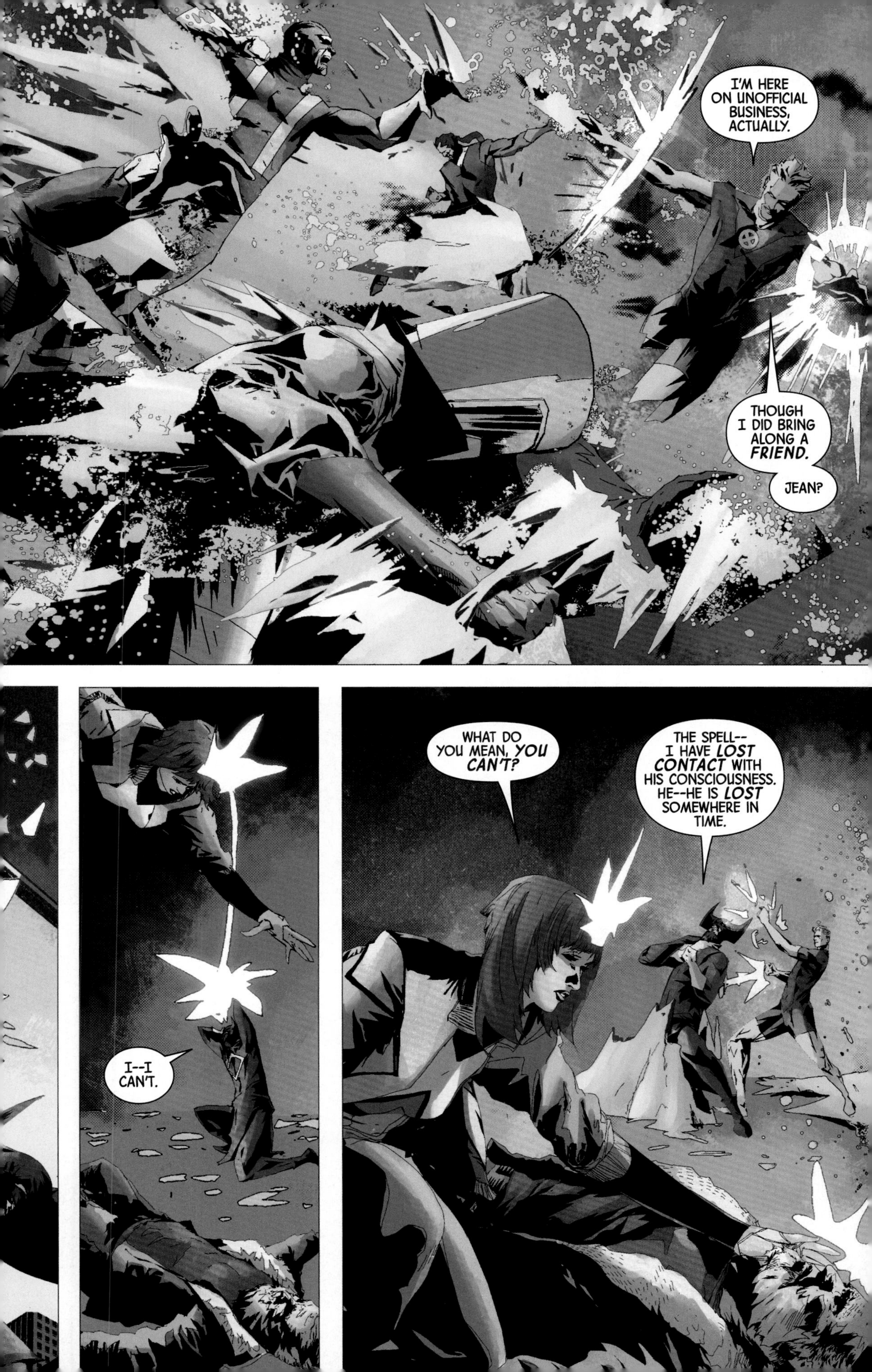
I'M HERE ON UNOFFICIAL BUSINESS, ACTUALLY.
THOUGH I DID BRING ALONG A FRIEND.
JEAN?
I--I CAN'T.
WHAT DO YOU MEAN, YOU CAN'T?
THE SPELL-- I HAVE LOST CONTACT WITH HIS CONSCIOUSNESS. HE--HE IS LOST SOMEWHERE IN TIME.

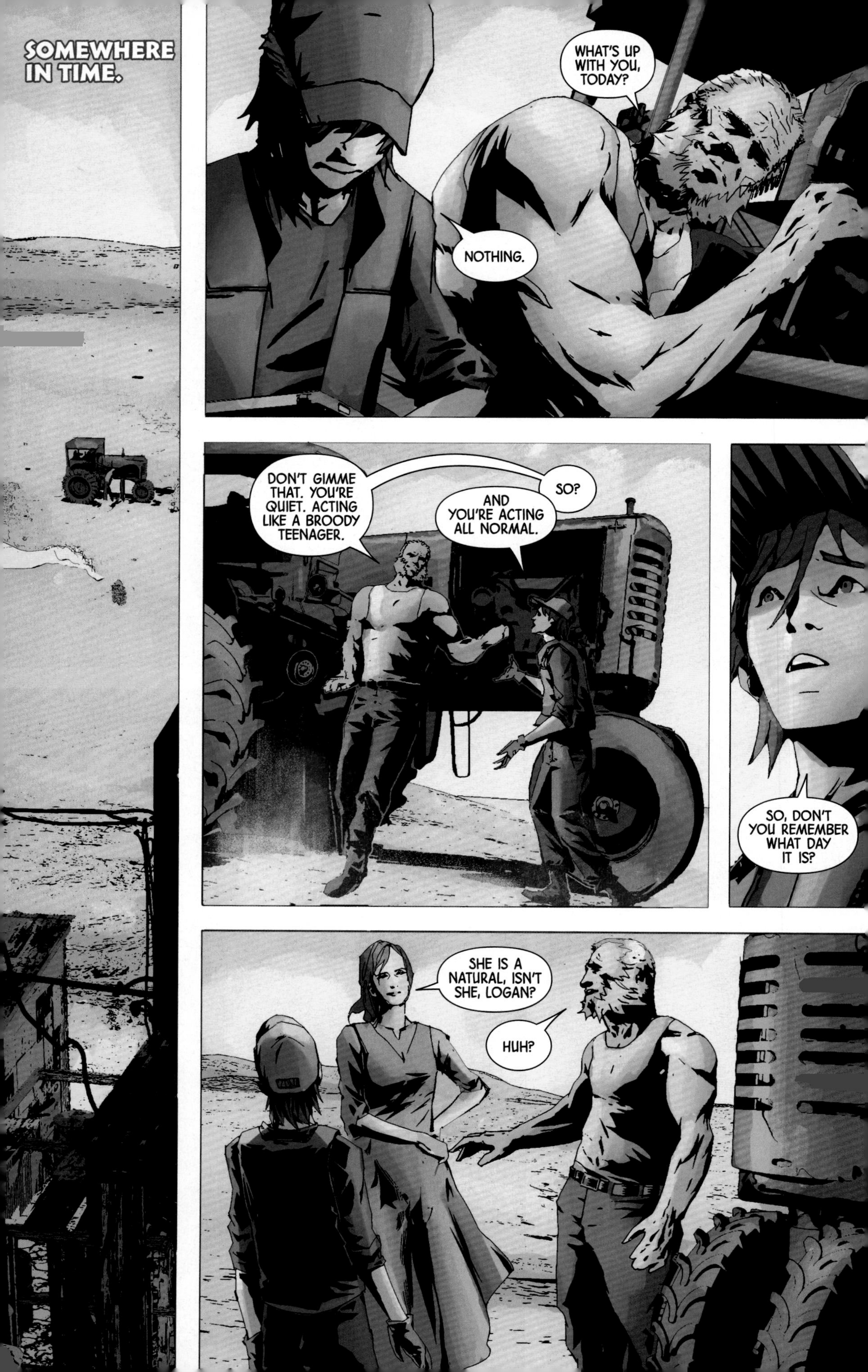
SOMEWHERE IN TIME.
WHAT'S UP WITH YOU, TODAY?
NOTHING.
DON'T GIMME THAT. YOU'RE QUIET. ACTING LIKE A BROODY TEENAGER.
SO?
AND YOU'RE ACTING ALL NORMAL.
SO, DON'T YOU REMEMBER WHAT DAY IT IS?
SHE IS A NATURAL, ISN'T SHE, LOGAN?
HUH?

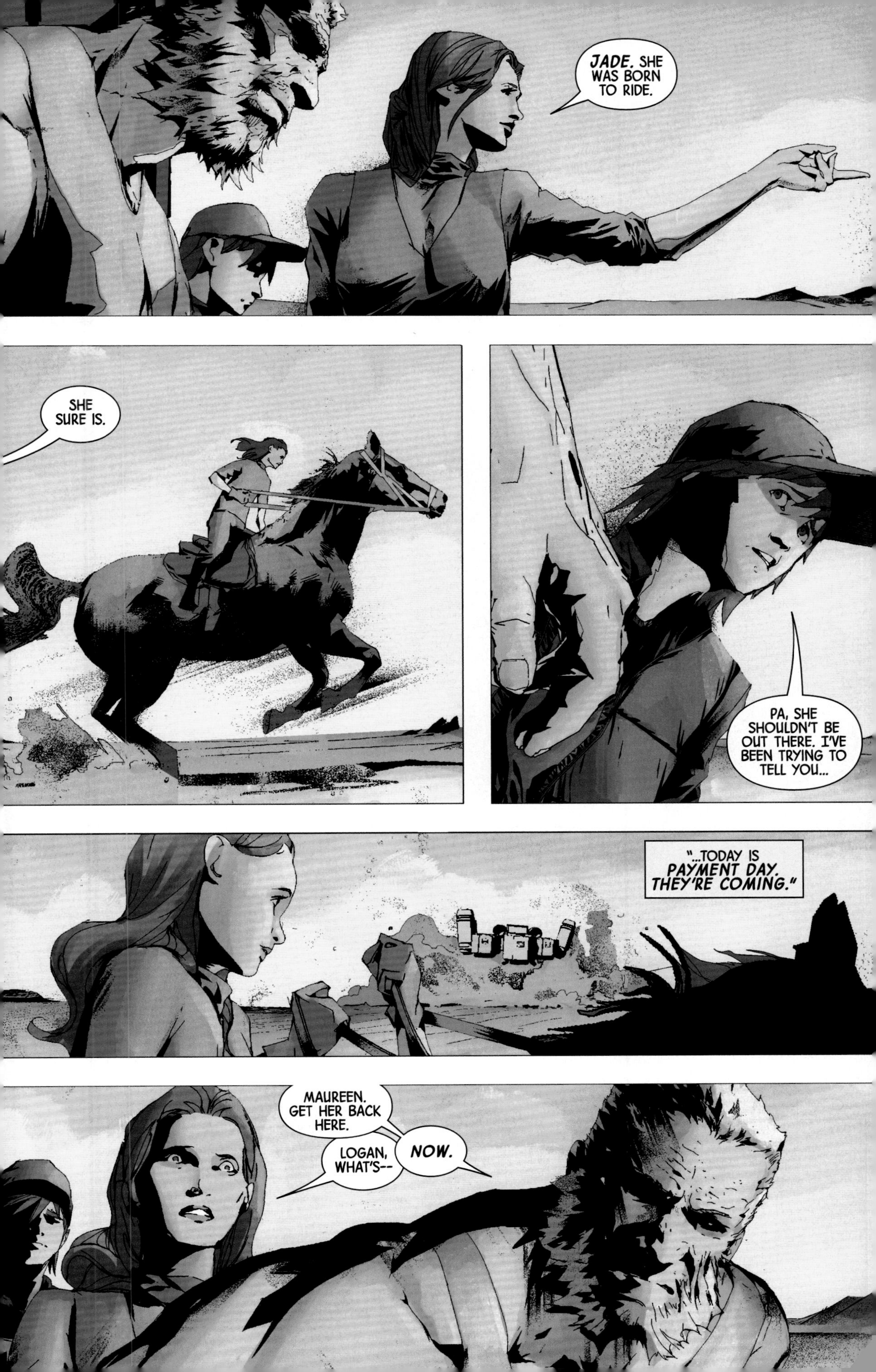
JADE. SHE WAS BORN TO RIDE.
SHE SURE IS.
PA, SHE SHOULDN'T BE OUT THERE. I'VE BEEN TRYING TO TELL YOU...
"...TODAY IS PAYMENT DAY. THEY'RE COMING."
MAUREEN. GET HER BACK HERE.
LOGAN, WHAT'S--
NOW.

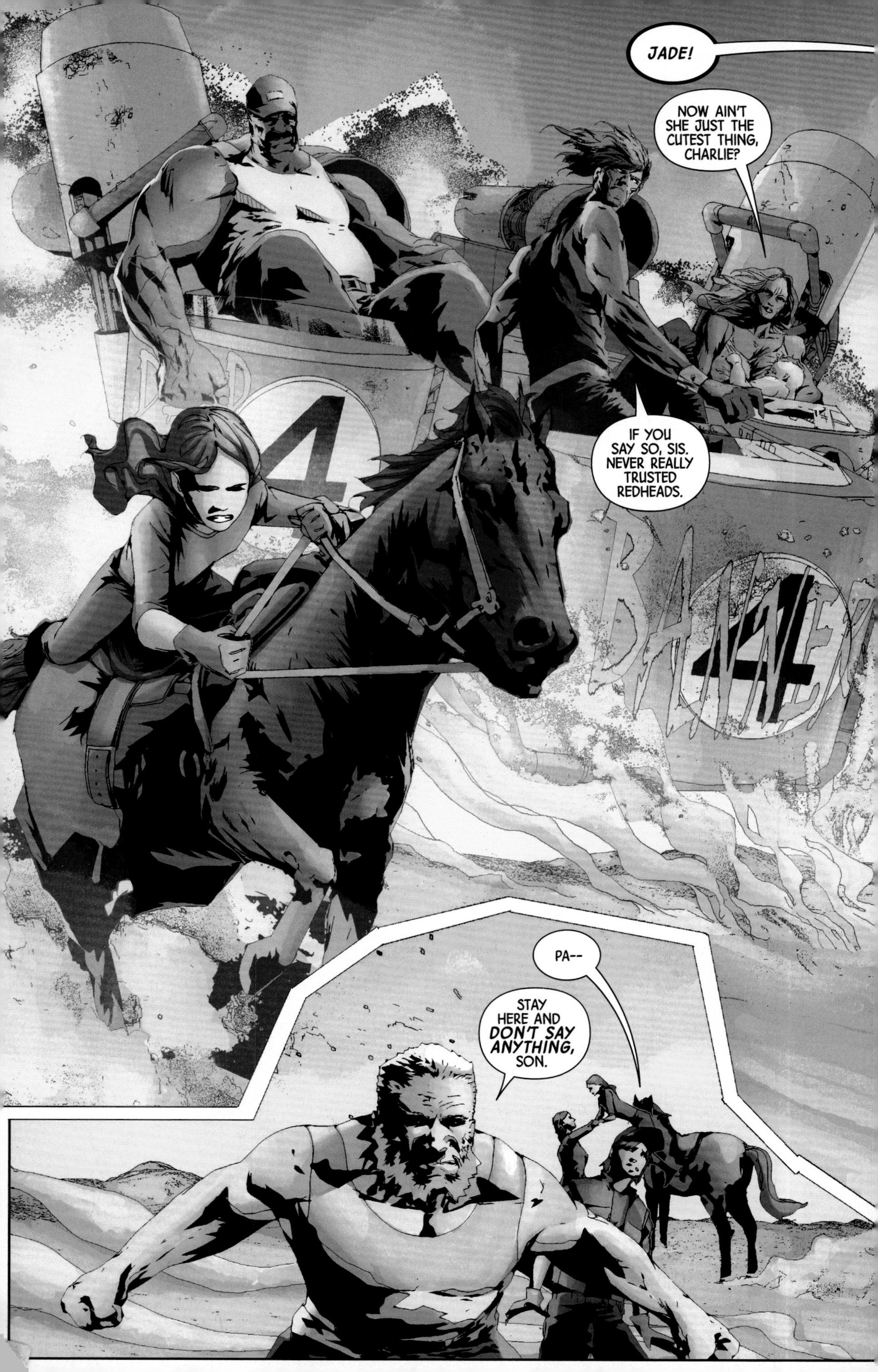
JADE!
NOW AIN'T SHE JUST THE CUTEST THING, CHARLIE?
IF YOU SAY SO, SIS. NEVER REALLY TRUSTED REDHEADS.
PA--
STAY HERE AND DON'T SAY ANYTHING, SON.

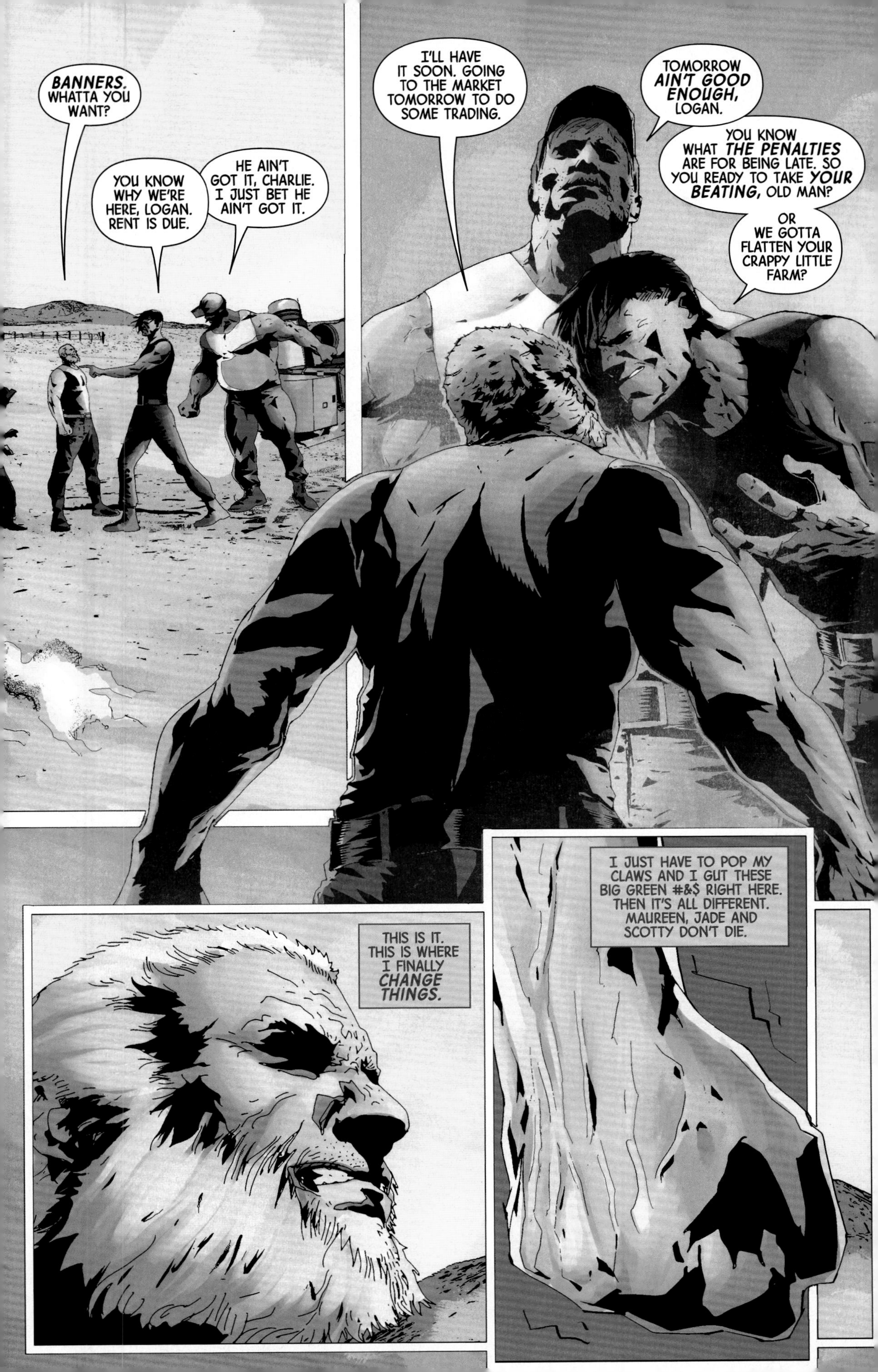
BANNERS. WHATTA YOU WANT?
YOU KNOW WHY WE'RE HERE, LOGAN. RENT IS DUE.
HE AIN'T GOT IT, CHARLIE. I JUST BET HE AIN'T GOT IT.
I'LL HAVE IT SOON. GOING TO THE MARKET TOMORROW TO DO SOME TRADING.
TOMORROW AIN'T GOOD ENOUGH, LOGAN.
YOU KNOW WHAT THE PENALTIES ARE FOR BEING LATE. SO YOU READY TO TAKE YOUR BEATING, OLD MAN?
OR WE GOTTA FLATTEN YOUR CRAPPY LITTLE FARM?
THIS IS IT. THIS IS WHERE I FINALLY CHANGE THINGS.
I JUST HAVE TO POP MY CLAWS AND I GUT THESE BIG GREEN #&$ RIGHT HERE. THEN IT'S ALL DIFFERENT. MAUREEN, JADE AND SCOTTY DON'T DIE.

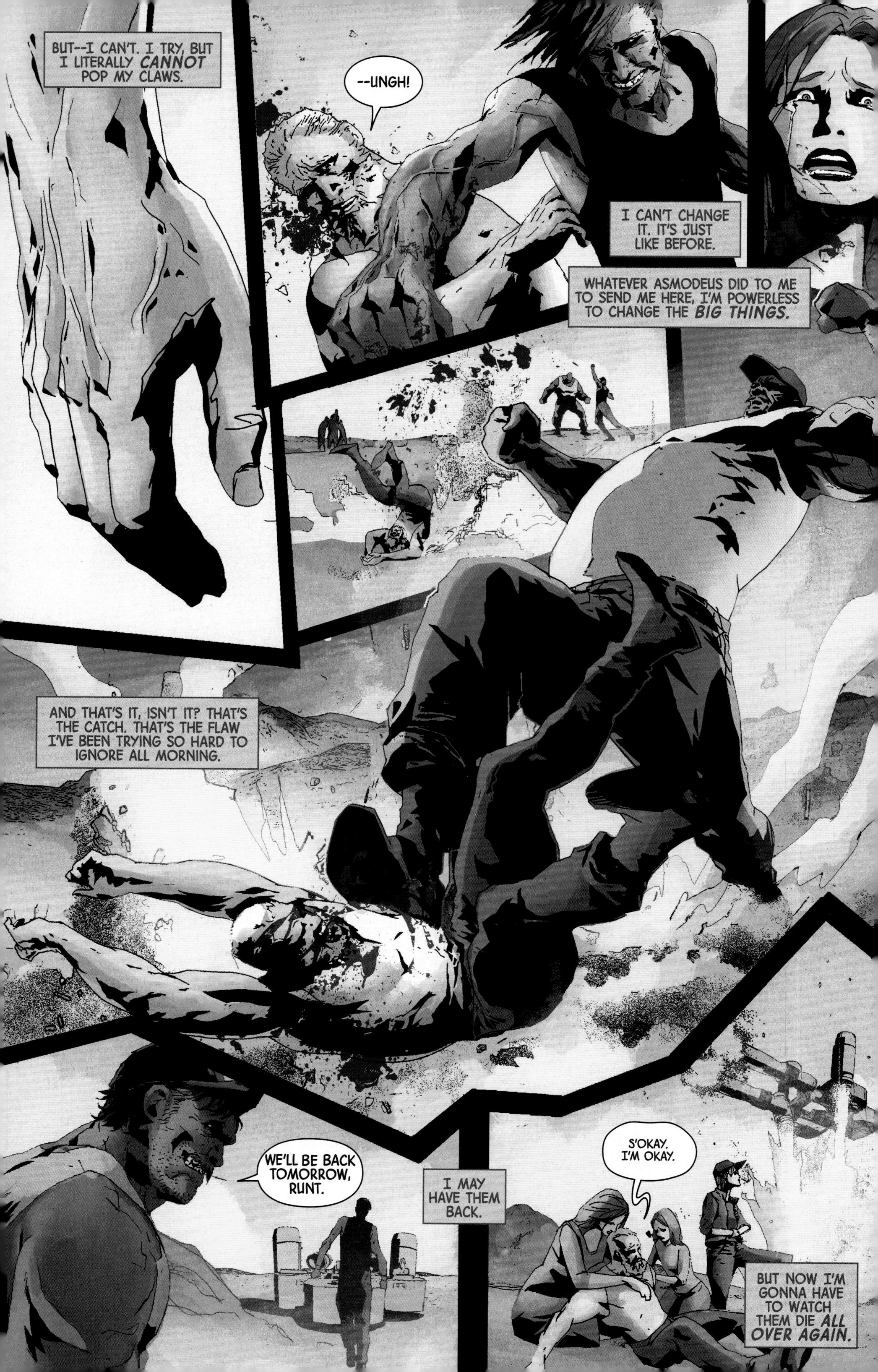
BUT--I CAN'T. I TRY, BUT I LITERALLY CANNOT POP MY CLAWS.
--UNGH!
I CAN'T CHANGE IT. IT'S JUST LIKE BEFORE.
WHATEVER ASMODEUS DID TO ME TO SEND ME HERE, I'M POWERLESS TO CHANGE THE BIG THINGS.
AND THAT'S IT, ISN'T IT? THAT'S THE CATCH. THAT'S THE FLAW I'VE BEEN TRYING SO HARD TO IGNORE ALL MORNING.
WE'LL BE BACK TOMORROW, RUNT.
I MAY HAVE THEM BACK.
S'OKAY. I'M OKAY.
BUT NOW I'M GONNA HAVE TO WATCH THEM DIE ALL OVER AGAIN.

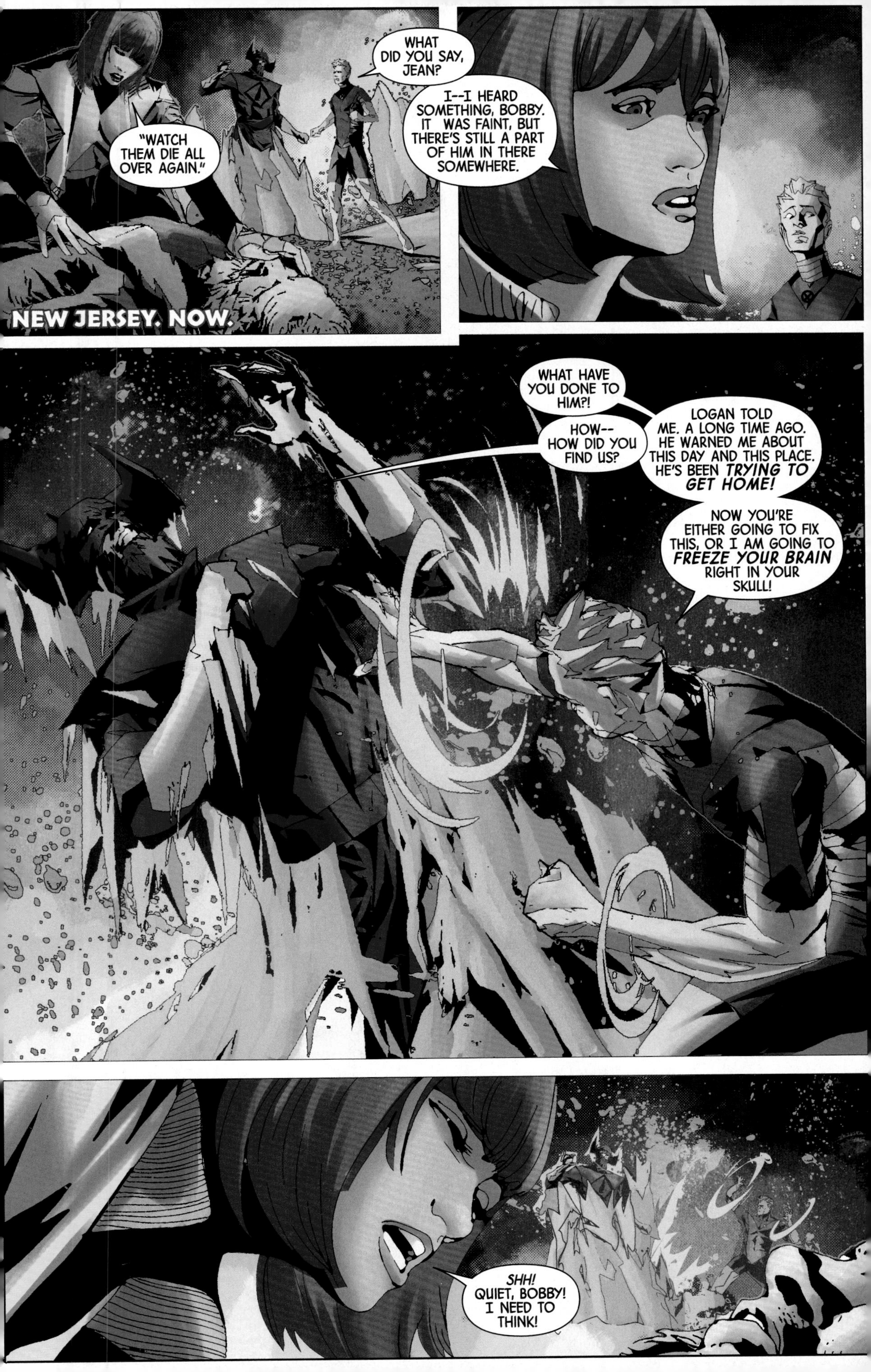
"WATCH THEM DIE ALL OVER AGAIN."
NEW JERSEY. NOW.
WHAT DID YOU SAY, JEAN?
I--I HEARD SOMETHING, BOBBY. IT WAS FAINT, BUT THERE'S STILL A PART OF HIM IN THERE SOMEWHERE.
WHAT HAVE YOU DONE TO HIM?!
HOW--HOW DID YOU FIND US?
LOGAN TOLD ME. A LONG TIME AGO. HE WARNED ME ABOUT THIS DAY AND THIS PLACE. HE'S BEEN TRYING TO GET HOME!
NOW YOU'RE EITHER GOING TO FIX THIS, OR I AM GOING TO FREEZE YOUR BRAIN RIGHT IN YOUR SKULL!
SHH! QUIET, BOBBY! I NEED TO THINK!

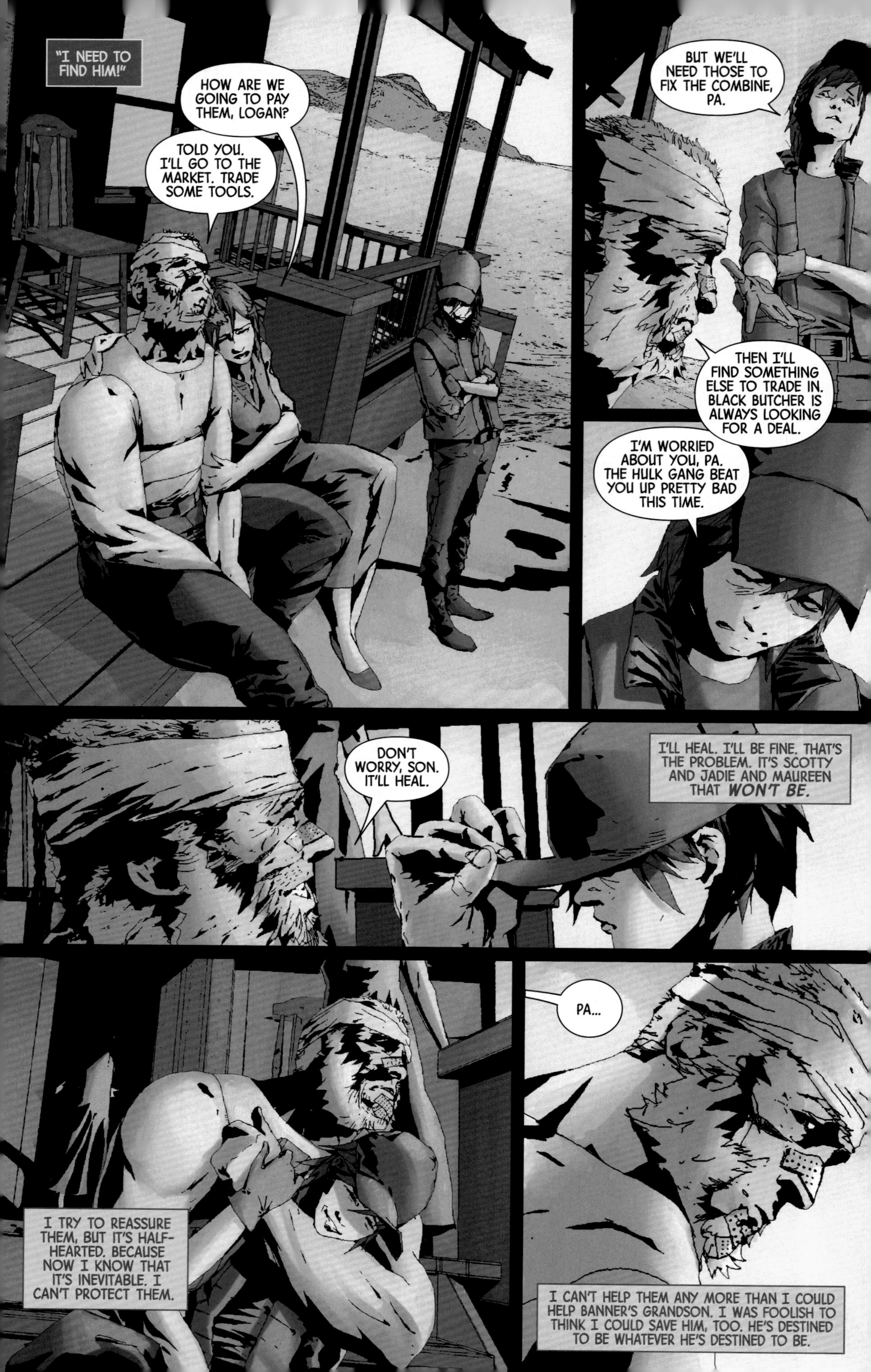
"I NEED TO FIND HIM!"
HOW ARE WE GOING TO PAY THEM, LOGAN?
TOLD YOU. I'LL GO TO THE MARKET. TRADE SOME TOOLS.
BUT WE'LL NEED THOSE TO FIX THE COMBINE, PA.
THEN I'LL FIND SOMETHING ELSE TO TRADE IN. BLACK BUTCHER IS ALWAYS LOOKING FOR A DEAL.
I'M WORRIED ABOUT YOU, PA. THE HULK GANG BEAT YOU UP PRETTY BAD THIS TIME.
DON'T WORRY, SON. IT'LL HEAL.
I'LL HEAL. I'LL BE FINE. THAT'S THE PROBLEM. IT'S SCOTTY AND JADIE AND MAUREEN THAT WON'T BE.
I TRY TO REASSURE THEM, BUT IT'S HALF-HEARTED. BECAUSE NOW I KNOW THAT IT'S INEVITABLE. I CAN'T PROTECT THEM.
PA...
I CAN'T HELP THEM ANY MORE THAN I COULD HELP BANNER'S GRANDSON. I WAS FOOLISH TO THINK I COULD SAVE HIM, TOO. HE'S DESTINED TO BE WHATEVER HE'S DESTINED TO BE.

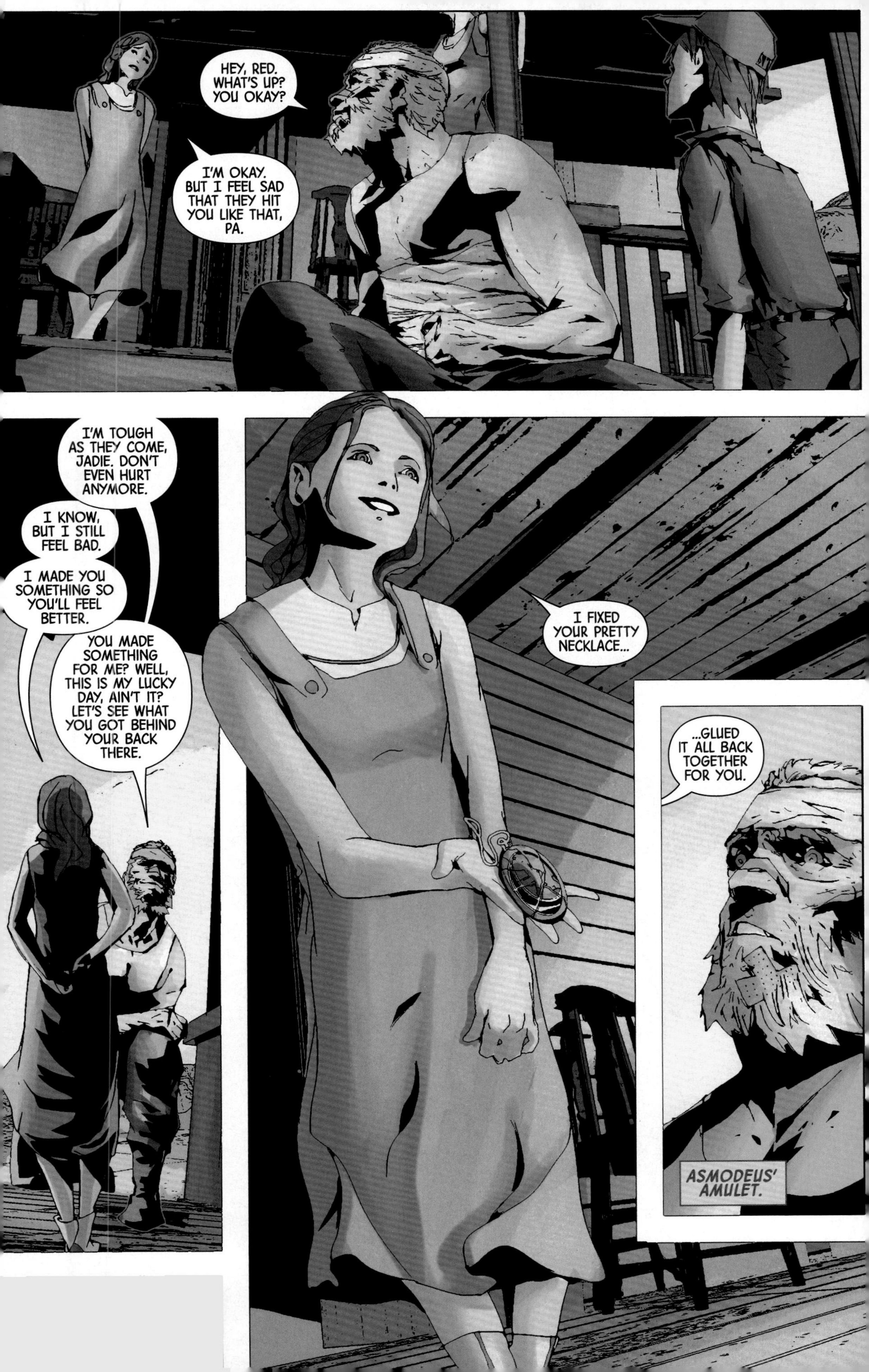
HEY, RED. WHAT'S UP? YOU OKAY?
I'M OKAY. BUT I FEEL SAD THAT THEY HIT YOU LIKE THAT, PA.
I'M TOUGH AS THEY COME, JADIE. DON'T EVEN HURT ANYMORE.
I KNOW, BUT I STILL FEEL BAD.
I MADE YOU SOMETHING SO YOU'LL FEEL BETTER.
YOU MADE SOMETHING FOR ME? WELL, THIS IS MY LUCKY DAY, AIN'T IT? LET'S SEE WHAT YOU GOT BEHIND YOUR BACK THERE.
I FIXED YOUR PRETTY NECKLACE...
...GLUED IT ALL BACK TOGETHER FOR YOU.
ASMODEUS' AMULET.

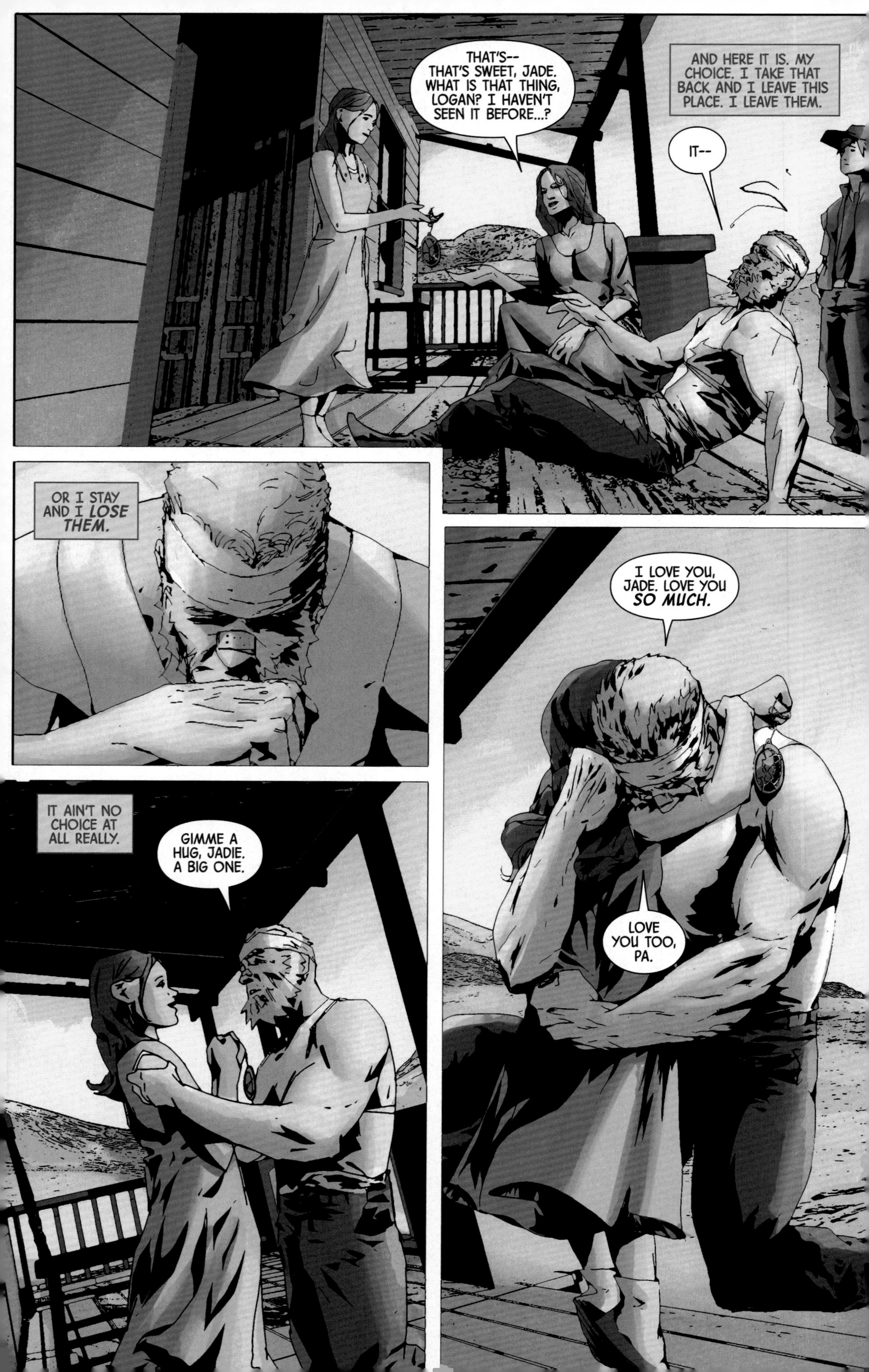
THAT'S-- THAT'S SWEET, JADE. WHAT IS THAT THING, LOGAN? I HAVEN'T SEEN IT BEFORE...?
AND HERE IT IS. MY CHOICE. I TAKE THAT BACK AND I LEAVE THIS PLACE. I LEAVE THEM.
IT--
OR I STAY AND I *LOSE THEM.*
IT AIN'T NO CHOICE AT ALL REALLY.
GIMME A HUG, JADIE. A BIG ONE.
I LOVE YOU, JADE. LOVE YOU *SO MUCH.*
LOVE YOU TOO, PA.

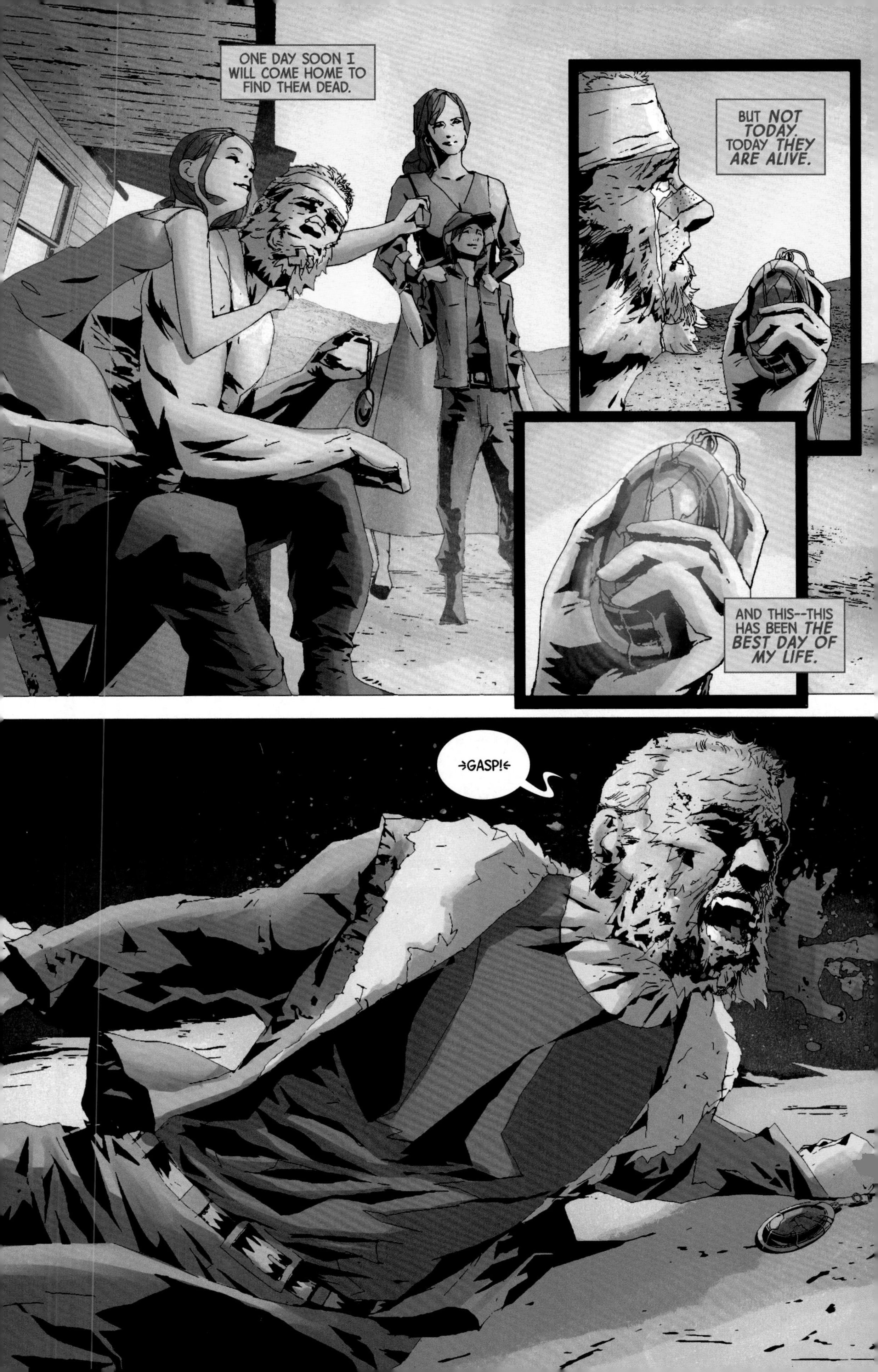

ONE DAY SOON I WILL COME HOME TO FIND THEM DEAD.
BUT NOT TODAY. TODAY THEY ARE ALIVE.
AND THIS--THIS HAS BEEN THE BEST DAY OF MY LIFE.
GASP!

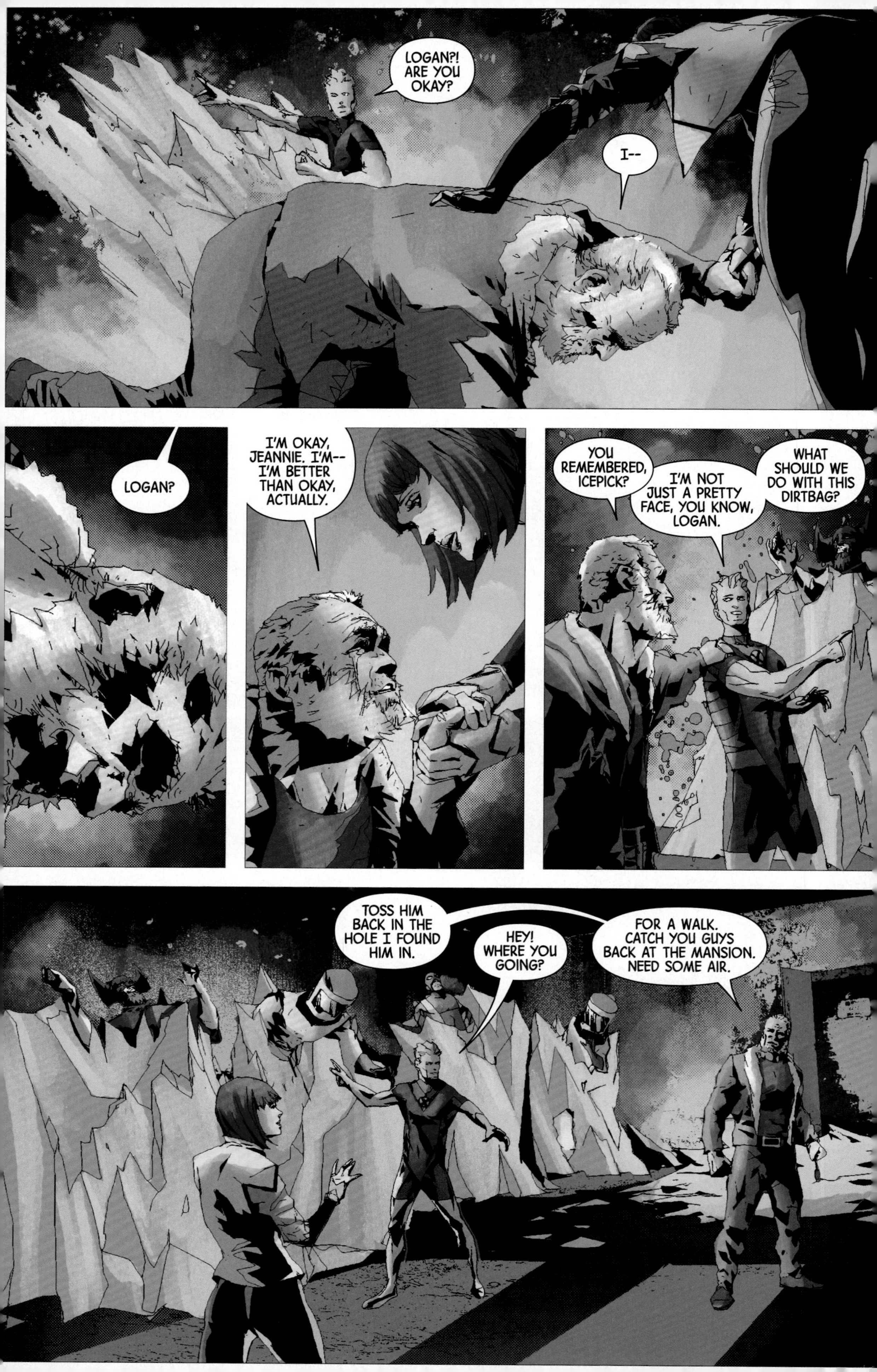
LOGAN?! ARE YOU OKAY?
I--
LOGAN?
I'M OKAY, JEANNIE. I'M-- I'M BETTER THAN OKAY, ACTUALLY.
YOU REMEMBERED, ICEPICK?
I'M NOT JUST A PRETTY FACE, YOU KNOW, LOGAN.
WHAT SHOULD WE DO WITH THIS DIRTBAG?
TOSS HIM BACK IN THE HOLE I FOUND HIM IN.
HEY! WHERE YOU GOING?
FOR A WALK. CATCH YOU GUYS BACK AT THE MANSION. NEED SOME AIR.

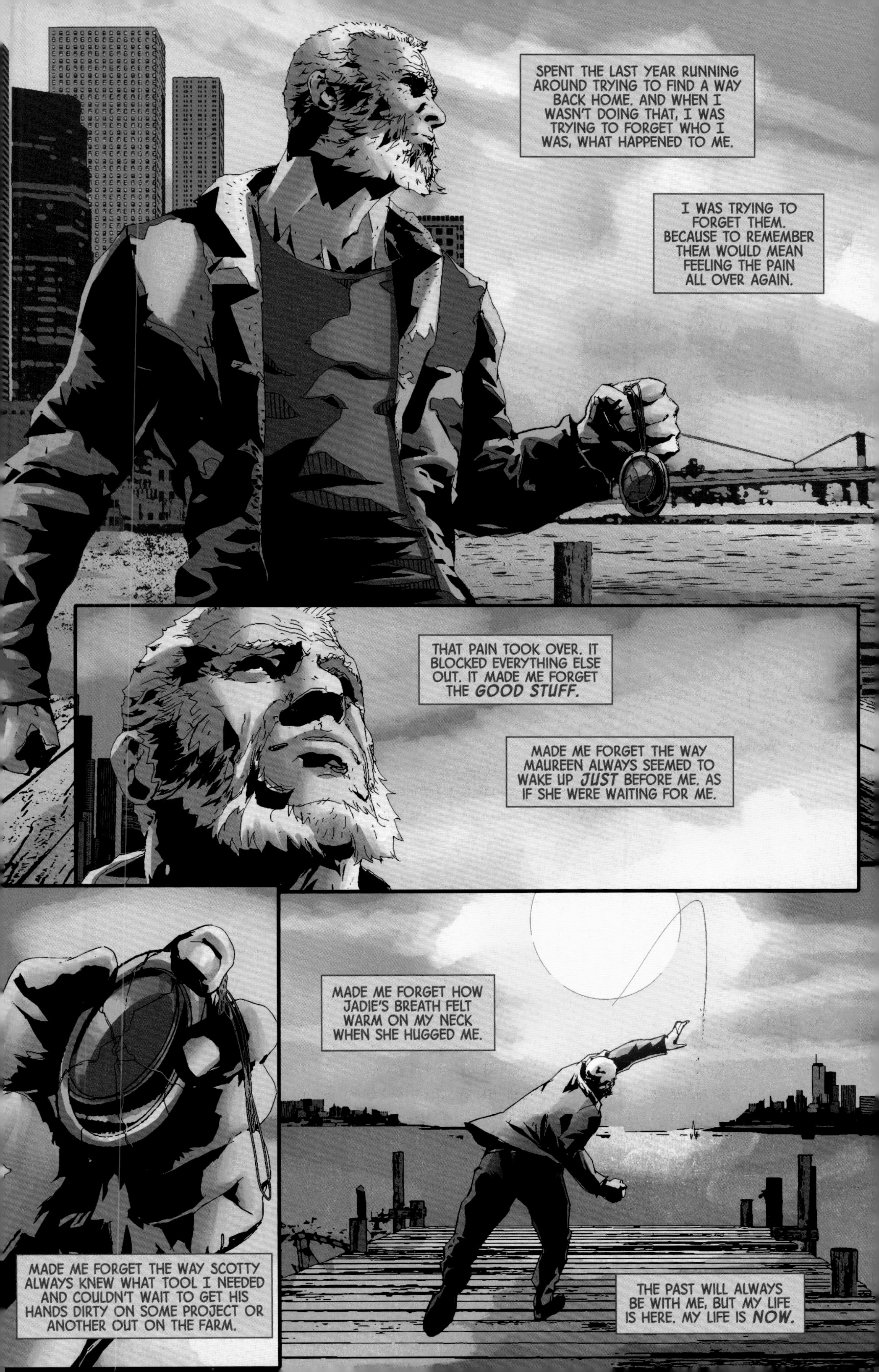
SPENT THE LAST YEAR RUNNING AROUND TRYING TO FIND A WAY BACK HOME. AND WHEN I WASN'T DOING THAT, I WAS TRYING TO FORGET WHO I WAS, WHAT HAPPENED TO ME.
I WAS TRYING TO FORGET THEM. BECAUSE TO REMEMBER THEM WOULD MEAN FEELING THE PAIN ALL OVER AGAIN.
THAT PAIN TOOK OVER. IT BLOCKED EVERYTHING ELSE OUT. IT MADE ME FORGET THE GOOD STUFF.
MADE ME FORGET THE WAY MAUREEN ALWAYS SEEMED TO WAKE UP JUST BEFORE ME. AS IF SHE WERE WAITING FOR ME.
MADE ME FORGET THE WAY SCOTTY ALWAYS KNEW WHAT TOOL I NEEDED AND COULDN'T WAIT TO GET HIS HANDS DIRTY ON SOME PROJECT OR ANOTHER OUT ON THE FARM.
MADE ME FORGET HOW JADIE'S BREATH FELT WARM ON MY NECK WHEN SHE HUGGED ME.
THE PAST WILL ALWAYS BE WITH ME, BUT MY LIFE IS HERE. MY LIFE IS NOW.

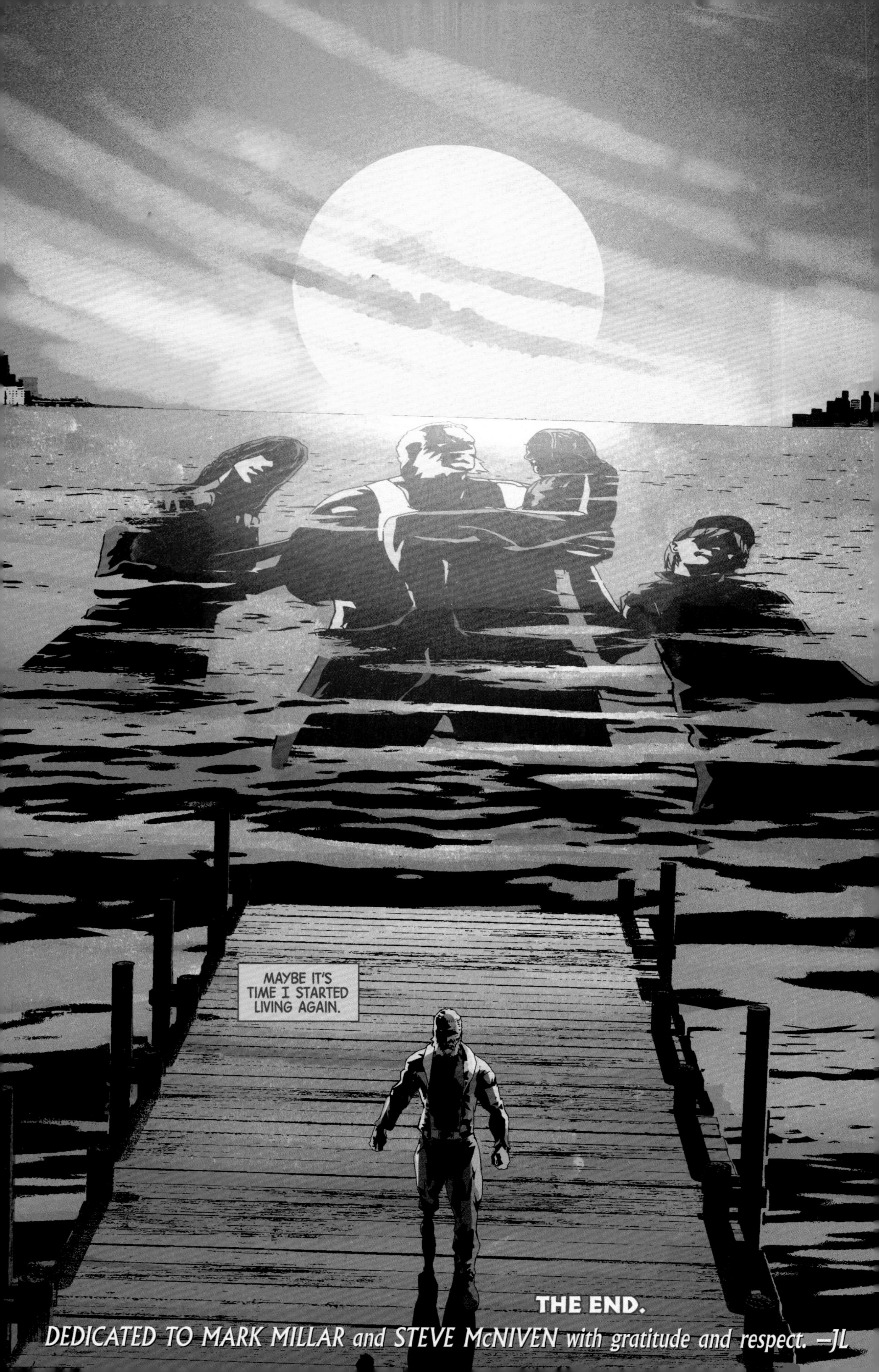
MAYBE IT'S TIME I STARTED LIVING AGAIN.
THE END.
DEDICATED TO MARK MILLAR and STEVE McNIVEN with gratitude and respect. —JL